GET RICH SLOWLY

GET RICH SLOWLY

BUILDING YOUR FINANCIAL FUTURE
THROUGH COMMON SENSE

❯❯❯ ❮❮❮

William T. Spitz

Treasurer, Vanderbilt University

Macmillan Publishing Company New York

Maxwell Macmillan Canada Toronto

Maxwell Macmillan International

New York   Oxford   Singapore   Sydney

Macmillan Publishing Company
866 Third Avenue
New York, NY 10022

Maxwell Macmillan Canada, Inc.
1200 Eglinton Avenue East
Suite 200
Don Mills, Ontario M3C 3N1

Macmillan Publishing Company is part of the Maxwell Communication
Group of Companies.

Library of Congress Cataloging-in-Publication Data

Spitz, William T.
    Get rich slowly : building your financial future through common
sense / William T. Spitz.
        p.   cm.
    Includes index.
    ISBN 0-02-613211-7
    1. Finance, Personal.   2. Investments.   3. Portfolio management.
I. Title.
HG179.S5556   1992   91-28979
332.024—dc20   CIP

Macmillan books are available at special discounts for bulk purchases for sales
promotions, premiums, fund-raising, or educational use. For details, contact:

Special Sales Director
Macmillan Publishing Company
866 Third Avenue
New York, NY 10022

10 9 8 7 6 5 4 3 2 1

Book design by M 'N O Production Services, Inc.

Printed in the United States of America

Acknowledgments

Get Rich Slowly is ostensibly a treatise on investments. But, in reality, this is a book about the application to the financial markets of good old common sense. Some of my friends would have argued that any book that I could write on common sense would necessarily be of limited duration. Despite their doubts, I managed to complete a work of standard length, although you can be the judge of how much wisdom it actually contains. However, there can be no doubt that I have demonstrated at least a modicum of good sense by virtue of having called on a number of talented individuals to help bring this project to fruition. The final result benefited significantly from their hard work, insights, and enthusiasm.

First, I owe a great debt to Sue Lockmiller, who converted my handwritten scrawl to the printed word. She was a model of patience and composure throughout countless revisions and rewrites.

Tom Burish, Steve Cates, David Dreman, Tom Fitzgerald, and Jerry Smith were all kind enough to read the initial draft and each made a number of useful suggestions regarding both form and content.

I would like to offer special thanks to Norman Moore, who edited and polished this work. In addition to his technical skill with the English language, Norman has a gift for identifying points that require amplification or clarification. My editor at Macmillan, Rick Wolff, took over where Norman left off. Rick helped me understand my reader and his suggestions greatly improved the flow of the book and made it infinitely more "user friendly." I am particularly grateful to both Rick and Macmillan for recognizing the potential value in the book that I proposed to them and for their willingness to take the risk of working with an unproven author.

Dan Sulkin of Vanderbilt's Owen School of Management is responsible for the book's graphics. In addition to Dan, a number of my colleagues at the Owen School provided encouragement and support.

Throughout this project, Lee Giovanetti and Peter Miller have been my primary cheerleaders. Lee convinced me to persevere during each of the several periods during which I seemed to lose momentum, and Peter was able to persuade the world that it needed yet another book on investments.

Charlie Ellis of Greenwich Associates and Hunter Lewis of Cambridge Associates are largely unaware of their contributions to this work. But their imprints are unmistakable. Both are known as innovative thinkers, and their rational approach to investing has greatly influenced my own view of the financial world.

Finally, I owe a particular note of thanks to my family. During the year I devoted to completing this book, they tolerated a preoccupied and part-time husband and father. I hope they will accept the dedication of this book to them as partial compensation for their sacrifice.

To my family

Contents

CHAPTER 1

TAKING CHARGE

I have thought that a man of tolerable abilities may
work great changes if he first forms a good plan and
makes the execution of that same plan his whole study
and business.

—Benjamin Franklin

》》 《《

Psychologists have identified a condition known as sensory overload in which human beings have trouble functioning as a result
of too many stimuli to their senses. This condition can be brought
on by excessive amounts of noise, activity, and information—
even information claiming to be helpful. If you have tried to stay
on top of the financial world, you undoubtedly have had a brush
with this syndrome.

Investors are deluged with "timely" information on the stock
market, the outlook for the economy, and which securities to
buy and sell. Not only is there a great deal of information,
but much of it is contradictory. Consider the following typical
headline from the May 7, 1990, edition of the *Wall Street Journal*:

> One long time Bull believes rally is about to burst from the
> gloom. . . . While other analysts see rough times ahead for the
> Dow Jones Industrial Average.

Consider also the contradictory advice of the professionals. At
any given time, economists seem to be equally divided between

1

growth and recession scenarios, and every market guru recommends a different group of stocks. To make matters even worse, Wall Street regularly creates new products and trading vehicles that expand the universe of investment opportunities. I don't know about you, but I feel a case of sensory overload coming on!

Perhaps even worse than the sheer volume of conflicting information is the fact that much of it is focused on "making a quick buck." You probably get calls from brokers offering to let you in on the next big winner. Newsletters and business publications tell you which mutual funds will be "hot" this year. Many strategists tout their ability to call every major turn in the market. And, of course, you get hot tips at cocktail parties from people who brag about the killing they just made from stock in Universal Widget Technologies. This kind of hype creates an atmosphere in which many investors think they are only one trade away from instant wealth. After all, everyone else is getting rich, why shouldn't I?

The fact is that everyone else is *not* getting rich. Quite the contrary, the world is full of frustrated, disappointed investors. More often than not, the quest for instant wealth leads investors to fad investments, to an emotional roller coaster, and, perhaps, to financial ruin.

But there is another way. You can become a successful investor through a proven means that requires only modest effort on your part. Knowledgeable investors know that there is only one dependable way to get rich, and that way is *slowly*, through consistent, steady progress. *The key to getting rich slowly is an organized investment program that is designed to meet the specific needs of the investor.* As Benjamin Franklin said, "a man of tolerable abilities" can accomplish a great deal by carefully formulating and implementing a plan. The method detailed in this book will guide you in creating a plan that is right for you, and that plan will work whether you have $5,000, $50,000, or $500,000 to invest. A side benefit of your plan will be your ability to ignore all the noise, activity, and information that cause sensory overload. Instead, you will be able to focus on the truly important issues of controlling risk and creating a portfolio that will meet your return objectives. Most important, an organized investment program will put you in control of your own financial destiny.

»   Why Is an Investment Plan Important?   «

Would you attempt to run a major corporation without a strategic plan? How comfortable would you be if your doctor began a surgical procedure without a specific objective? Does it make sense to attempt to build a house without a set of blueprints? Undoubtedly, you think each of these questions so nonsensical that it seems silly to even ask the question.

Virtually every aspect of our daily lives is governed by some form of strategy, plan, budget, or schedule. Unfortunately, this businesslike approach has never completely permeated the investment world. Very few individuals approach the management of their assets in an orderly fashion. And to my continued amazement, even large, "professionally" managed pools of capital are sometimes run by the seat of someone's pants.

The desirability of an organized approach to investing is hardly a new idea. In his 1950 book, *Our Investment Philosophy*, noted investor T. Rowe Price said: "An investment philosophy is a system of general beliefs about how investment funds should be managed. Unfortunately, most people have no clear thought-out investment philosophy and do not follow any plan." But let's get more specific about why an investment plan is important.

First off, each individual's needs are different. Different portfolios, therefore, are right for different individuals. How will you know which is appropriate for you unless you first establish some objectives and guidelines? In other words, you must create a framework to govern your investment decisions.

Second, controlling risk is the key to becoming a successful investor. It isn't really that difficult. But you must include the right kinds of investments in your portfolio and in the correct proportions. Making these decisions requires some education and planning.

A third reason for some structure is the necessity to keep score. How are you going to measure the success of your program if you don't have some goals and objectives to serve as benchmarks? It is important for you to know if you are not meeting your goals and to change your plans accordingly.

The final reason for an organized program is the most important: *to protect your assets from your emotions.* Don't take it personally. Everyone is subject to swings in emotion, fads, manias, and the herd mentality. Human beings are social animals who naturally seek approval and acceptance from their fellow men. Conformity is the path of least resistance. When Wall Street is surging ahead and the financial press is full of rosy predictions, it is easy and comfortable to jump on board. Similarly, gloom and uncertainty make it awfully tempting to sell at the bottom of a market downturn.

I can think of only two ways for you to avoid the temptation to join the herd. First, you can secret yourself on an island in the Caribbean and shun any contact with the financial world. (It is no accident that well-known investor John Templeton lives in the Bahamas.) If this option isn't feasible, you will have to settle for the second choice: to create a structured investment plan. Why does this work? If you do a good job setting up your program, you will know exactly what might happen to your portfolio over *any* given period of time. For example, you will know that your portfolio might decline 15% in one out of every twenty-five years or so. If you can't live with that sort of decline, of course, you should design a different portfolio.

Here's the important point: If and when the bad year actually comes along and your portfolio declines by 15%, you won't be surprised. You won't panic and make what will turn out to be a bad decision to sell. Lest you think that this is not a real danger, I need only remind you of the stock market crash of 1987. Many individual investors and some large pension funds panicked and sold all of their stocks on October 19 or 20. Those sellers who did not later reinvest in the stock market missed a nice recovery in the remainder of 1987 and exceptional returns in 1988 and 1989 of 16.6% and 31.6%, respectively. Similarly, an investment plan that removes impulse decisions will prevent you from being taken in by slick salesmen offering "surefire" investments.

By now, you should accept the need for a framework that can bring order, confidence, and control to your investments. How do you create such a framework? This book details a five-step process through which you can develop a sophisticated investment program and enjoy successful results. At this point, let's preview the five steps that you will use to accumulate wealth slowly and consistently.

»»_____ Five Steps to an Investment Program _____«««

Step 1 Establish your investment objectives.

Step 2 Decide which types of investments to include in your portfolio (stocks, bonds, money market funds, etc.).

Step 3 Decide how to allocate your funds between these investment categories.

Step 4 Select individual investments within each category.

Step 5 Review and update your program once a year.

The first step in organizing your program is to establish its objectives. What are you trying to accomplish with your investments? Are you saving for a college education, preparing for retirement, or trying to amass an estate for your heirs? What rate of return do you need in order to achieve your specific objectives and is it realistic and achievable? Will the pursuit of this return require you to accept a level of risk that is inappropriate given your financial status and emotional makeup? You will have to deal with each of these questions, and the result will be a specific statement of your goals.

Once you establish your goals, the second step is to decide what types of investments should be included in your portfolio. The list of potential investments is endless and utterly confusing.

Major full-service brokerage firms deal in stocks, bonds, real estate, money market instruments, foreign securities, futures, options, commodities, precious metals, and dozens of other categories. Obviously, you can't own them all. Most investors should hold U.S. stocks, foreign stocks, small company stocks, bonds, and real estate. In addition, investors with short time horizons should allocate a portion of their dollars to money market funds. By combining these asset types, you will create a portfolio that should yield attractive rates of return while minimizing risk.

Having settled on the types of investments you want to consider, the next step is to decide what percentage of your portfolio should be devoted to investments in each category. In order to make this step as easy as possible, Chapter 7 includes a table of asset mixes recommended for different kinds of investors at each stage in their lives. Once you select *your* mix, it should remain basically unchanged unless you change your objectives.

The decisions you make in completing the first three steps create the framework of your portfolio. Step four, then, is to decide how you actually invest your funds to constitute that portfolio. Will you purchase mutual funds, hire an adviser, or do you have the time and know-how to select your own investments? Selecting your own investments demands a major commitment of time and effort. Most people, therefore, should either purchase mutual funds or hire a manager to handle a separate account. Mutual funds are preferable for most investors. I recommend that you select one mutual fund for each of the asset types in your portfolio—in other words, between three and five funds. Most of the information you will need to select your funds is readily available. While you should not take this selection process lightly, neither should you lose any sleep over it because spreading your money among a number of different funds dampens the effect of a shortfall in any single one.

The final step in the process involves monitoring and control. Are you meeting your goals? Are your investments performing as expected? Has anything changed in your personal circumstances that would call for a change in your investment strategy? Should you add an additional investment category to your lineup? You need to ask each of these questions at least annually and reevaluate your program to make sure that everything is on track. Periodically, you may have good, sound reasons to modify your program. But one thing you should never do is change your plan in response to a sudden shift in the stock market. This is the very type of irrational behavior that your program is designed to eliminate because such behavior is financially destructive.

>> **The Tortoise and the Hare** <<

Now that you have enjoyed a glimpse of an organized approach to investing, its merits may be seen quickly by contrasting it with the more traditional method used by most investors. The typical investor limits his or her investments to domestic stocks, bonds, and perhaps money market funds. The percentage allocated to each is frequently the result of a random decision taken without much thought and with little attention paid to the needs of that particular investor. This investor's stock portfolio frequently consists of only a few holdings that are rarely selected according to disciplined criteria. More often than not, the stocks were purchased as a result of a "story" told by a persuasive salesman. This typical investor doesn't really know where his portfolio is headed or how much risk he's taking. If he's lucky, his approach to investing may generate a satisfactory rate of return. But it is more likely that he will have good years and bad and a disaster is not out of the question.

In contrast, if you follow the recommendations in this book, you should enjoy a satisfactory return, and your portfolio will be relatively stable. This may sound a little like motherhood and apple pie, but it is much more than that. A stable portfolio will let you sleep better at night, *and* it will provide you with more money over the long run.

To make this point, consider the following variation on the old fable of the tortoise and the hare. The tortoise earns 10% *every* year for ten years. Never more than 10%, never less. At the end of the ten years, his $100 investment is worth $259.37. In contrast, the hare's portfolio fluctuates a great deal from year to year. Specifically, his $100 investment earns the following returns:

Year 1	20%	Year 6	5%
Year 2	0	Year 7	40%
Year 3	30%	Year 8	−20%
Year 4	−10%	Year 9	20%
Year 5	15%	Year 10	0

If you add up the hare's returns and divide by ten, you will find that his average annual return is 10%, the same as the tortoise's. But the hare ends up with only $227.85, which is 12% *less* than the tortoise accumulated. This fable demonstrates the basic rule of finance that says that a stable portfolio will achieve greater wealth than a volatile one with the same average return. So, in structuring your investment program, we will concentrate on assembling a portfolio that generates an attractive rate of return *and* is as stable as possible.

» Compound Interest Makes It Happen «

The tortoise beats the hare through the "miracle" of compound interest, which Albert Einstein suggested was the greatest invention of modern times. Compound interest is actually a simple concept. At the end of one year, a $100 portfolio earning 10% will be valued at $110. Assuming the $10 in earnings is reinvested in the portfolio rather than spent, the second year's earnings will be 10% of $110, or $11. In year three, the portfolio will earn $12.10, and so on. Compound interest is a powerful force because your earnings are increasing every year, and at an accelerating rate.

Because of this acceleration, a portfolio earning 9% annually will double every eight years; a 12% return will achieve a doubling in only six years. A thirty-year-old investor who contributes $2,000 annually to an IRA will have $542,000 available at retirement if he earns an annual return of 10%. The key is to *consistently* earn the 10% return. If you earn reasonable rates of return and avoid serious losses, compound interest will work for you—and you *will* get rich slowly.

» **Ready, Set, Go** «

We are now ready to move to a detailed discussion of the first step in your program: setting investment objectives. In addition to absorbing this material, you will have to analyze your own psyche. Are you a risk taker? Do you need to sleep soundly every night? No investment program is "better" or "worse" than any other. Different programs are right for different individuals. The final decision is yours! After all, this book is about taking control of your own financial destiny.

One word of caution: There are no secret formulas, guarantees, free rides, black boxes, or gurus who can provide a sure path to riches. This book will, however, provide you with all the know-how necessary to become a successful investor. Two things are not included: time and patience. They are your responsibility.

» _____ **Key Points to Remember** _____ «

- The key to successful investing is a good plan.
- Even moderate rates of return can lead to significant wealth due to the power of compound interest.

CHAPTER 2

INVESTMENT OBJECTIVES

There are two times in a man's life when he should
not speculate: when he can't afford it and when he
can.

—Mark Twain

»» ««

Deep in his heart, every investor has the same objective: a high
rate of return with little or no risk. Wouldn't it be wonderful if
it were that easy! In an ideal world, each of us would load up
our portfolios with high-powered investments that would allow
us to "get rich quick," and this book would not be necessary.
Unfortunately, the laws of economics took over when we left the
Garden of Eden. In the real world, these laws force us to make
some difficult choices when we invest.

» **Risk and Return** «

Investment choices result from the immutable fact that there is
a tradeoff between risk and return. In order to accept more risk,
any rational person should expect and demand a higher rate of
return. Similarly, any investment that promises a high potential
return carries with it a great deal of risk.

While this most fundamental of financial principles is both

logical and well documented by dozens of academic studies, Wall Street likes to pretend that it does not exist. You have probably seen advertisements for investments that promise both high returns and low risk. Professional money managers are fond of showing charts that demonstrate how they have earned a higher return than their peers while assuming less risk. In other words, their great skill allowed them to defy the laws of finance. *Don't believe it!* A high-risk investment that has worked out will *seem* to have involved relatively little risk. But that is *after* the fact! Before the fact, you should expect the inherent relationship between risk and return to hold, and your plan should be built accordingly.

Determining your investment objectives is, therefore, a balancing act. If you want to earn a high rate of return, you will have to accept a high level of risk. If you can't live with a lot of risk, you will have to accept less return. You can't have it both ways!

Perhaps the best way to visualize the relationship between risk and return is through Chart 2.1 (see page 12), which is a simple graph that is found in every basic investment textbook. Each of the points on the line represents a different combination of risk and return. For example, Point B provides a higher rate of return than Point A, but at the expense of more risk. Similarly, Point C entails both greater risk and greater return than either of the other two combinations. While there are an infinite number of points on the line, we will consider only risk:return combinations between Point A and Point C, because that spectrum should cover the needs of most investors. In essence, setting your investment objectives is just the process of finding the location between these points that best reflects your financial needs and personality.

In this chapter, you will identify your broad financial goals and determine how much return will be necessary to achieve them. Chapter 3 provides historical perspective on rates of return as well as guidance on what rates to expect in the future. This information will allow you to determine whether your return goals are realistic. Thereafter, Chapters 4 and 5 deal with risk.

Up to this point, I have referred to risk as if everyone knows what it is. In fact, most people know only that they don't want "too much" risk; they have no clear understanding of how to measure and control it. By the time you finish Chapter 5, you will understand risk and will have chosen levels of risk and return that are consistent with one another and right for you. Returning to the risk:return chart, you will identify yourself as an A, B, or C.

To bring these abstract ideas closer to home, let's briefly evaluate two very different investors. The first is a sixty-five-year-old retiree who is interested only in preserving his capital and receiving a secure stream of income. In all likelihood, his needs would best be served at Point A—that is, low risk and low return. The second investor is a single, thirty-five-year-old attorney who seeks maximum return with little concern for earning current income or for avoiding risk. He or she sounds like a C to me. Obviously, the needs of these two individuals differ significantly, their goals are radically different, and their attitudes regarding risk and return are widely divergent. Once we place each of them

Chart 2.1   The Relationship Between Risk and Return

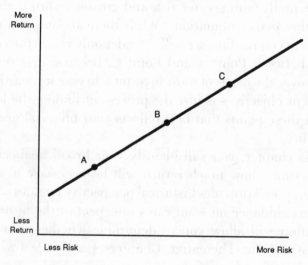

in the proper risk:return category, an investment program can be tailored to their specific needs. And as you might expect, their portfolios will be very different.

Most investors couch their goals in simple terms, such as "growth," "income," "balanced," or "capital preservation." Unfortunately, these terms mean different things to different investors, and they provide little information regarding the actual risk and return involved. In contrast, we will focus carefully on *your* needs and place you in the right risk:return category.

»   Your Financial Goals   «

Spending money today is certainly more fun than saving it for tomorrow. So why then do we save? The answer is simple: We save in order to meet future needs. Some of these needs are fairly predictable with respect to both timing and amount, good examples of which are your children's college education and income for your retirement years. Other future needs, such as money for an emergency or an inheritance for your children, are less well defined; you don't really know how much you will require or when you will need it. But, in either case, you are saving and investing to meet a goal that is important to you. While everyone has these goals in the back of their mind, few actually sit down and identify them. If you are not among the few, this chapter is for you!

Since this book is designed to help you accomplish *your* goals, why don't you start out on the right foot by actually spelling them out in plain English. A good example might be, "I would like to save enough money to send my child through both college and graduate school." To help you along, this list covers many of the broad financial goals that investors have:

- Provide for educational costs
- Save for retirement living expenses
- Build an estate for heirs
- Keep assets one already has intact

- Protect one's assets from inflation
- Protect against disability or death
- Provide resources for a needy relative
- Save to purchase a first or second home
- Improve one's standard of living
- Make one's assets "grow"
- Make a bundle

Obviously, you may have other goals that are equally or more important to your circumstances. In addition, most individuals find that their financial plans include a mixture of several specific goals and some general ones. Do your best to list all of your objectives, both general and specific. I would not be surprised if you are having a tough time developing your list—it isn't easy. After digesting the next couple of chapters and the specific examples included in them, you may want to modify your initial list. But ultimately, you need to finalize your goals because the investment strategy you select will be based on them.

Once you have decided upon your broad financial goals, the next step is to translate them into a risk:return combination that meets your needs. Depending upon the nature of your goals, you will need to attack this problem either from the "risk" side or from the "return" side. Remember, risk and return always travel together, so once one is determined, the other falls automatically into place. If, on the one hand, your goals are fairly specific, we can calculate the rate of return necessary to achieve them, and you can then decide whether the associated level of risk is one that you find comfortable. If not, you will have to change your goals to lower your risk and, consequently, your return. In other words, we will focus on *return* and let risk fall into place. On the other hand, if your financial goals are fuzzy, we will approach the tradeoff from the risk side. In this case, when you decide how much risk you can live with, the corresponding rate of return will be dictated to you. In either instance, therefore, you will end up with a specific risk:return combination that is right for you. You are then ready to move on to the remaining four steps in creating your investment program.

To make all of this clear, why don't we work through some examples? We will begin with a specific, well-defined goal that obliges us to approach the tradeoff from the "return" side.

Saving for College

We will assume that you have a five-year-old son and want to begin saving money for his college education. You hope that Junior will attend your alma mater, where costs currently run about $15,000 per year including tuition, room, and board. Education costs have risen at a rapid rate in recent years, and it seems safe to assume that they will continue to increase at a healthy clip in the future. The Consumer Price Index (CPI), is a measure of inflation that takes into account increases in prices for a variety of goods and services purchased by the average consumer. Many economists believe that this index will show price increases of about 5% a year for the foreseeable future. To be conservative, we will assume that college costs will increase at a rate 2% faster than the CPI—in other words, at a 7% annual rate. Finally, after carefully analyzing your budget, you determine you can put aside $325 per month for this savings program. Let's recap the key assumptions:

»	**College Savings Program**	«

	Key Assumptions
Child's age	5, with 13 years until college
Today's college cost	$15,000 per year
College costs increase	7% per year
Monthly savings	$325, until first college year

Given these assumptions, we can calculate the amount of money that must be available at the beginning of Junior's freshman year to fund his four-year education. Then we will estimate the rate of return you must earn on your $325 monthly investment to accumulate this sum.

An increase in college costs of 7% per year means that next year's cost will be $16,050 (7% more than $15,000), and that the following year's tab will rise to $17,173.50 (7% more than $16,050). If you continue to do this calculation for thirteen years, you will arrive at the annual cost of attending college when Junior begins his freshman year. A much easier way to get this answer is to use a compound interest table or calculator. The table provided in Appendix 1 tells you that the future value of $1.00 growing at 7% annually for thirteen years is $2.41. Therefore, the annual cost of college in Junior's freshman year will be $15,000 multiplied by $2.41 or $36,150. Scary isn't it! In Chapter 1, I referred to the miracle of compound interest that allows one to amass a significant portfolio while earning only moderate returns. Unfortunately, compound interest also affects future costs; thus, as seen in this instance, even moderate infla-tion produces frightening educational expenses after thirteen years. So if Junior finishes college in four years, the total tab will be $36,147 times four, or $144,600, which is the sum you need to amass by the time Junior enters college. (This assumes that interest earned on the remaining balance during college will take care of cost increases during the sophomore through senior years.) You are now in a position to state a specific goal for your investment program, which is, "Over the next thirteen years, I need to accumulate $144,600 in order to meet college expenses."

What will it take to reach this goal? Remember, you decided earlier to put aside $325 per month toward this savings program. The question that must be answered is: What rate of return will you have to earn on your portfolio to make sure that $144,600 is available at the end of thirteen years? Determining this rate requires a long calculation that is almost impossible to do by hand. Moreover, compound interest tables will not help because this problem has too many periods (i.e., 13 years times 12 months per year equals 156 periods). To work this problem, I recommend that you purchase or borrow a calculator with a compound interest function. Each calculator is a little different, but the sequence is normally as follows:

Step 1   Enter the number of monthly periods, which is 156
Step 2   Enter the monthly savings amount, which is $325
Step 3   Enter the required future value, which is $144,600
Step 4   Solve for the required return, which will be a monthly rate

The answer will have to be multiplied by twelve in order to calculate an annual rate. If you have done these steps correctly, you will have determined a required return of 14.2% per year. This is the return necessary to ensure that 156 monthly payments of $325 each will be equal to $144,600 after thirteen years. This must be an after-tax return; if it is not, you will need to pay taxes due on annual earnings from another source of cash. Once again, this example demonstrates the power of compound interest, because you end up with a portfolio valued at $144,600 despite having contributed only $50,700 (156 × $325).

You have just learned how to convert a broad financial goal into a specific investment objective that will serve as the foundation of your investment program and against which you can easily measure your progress over time. To round out your knowledge, let's look at another example of a common financial goal that can be translated into a specific return objective. While the details of this example are very different, the process of solving it is exactly the same as that employed in the college savings example. You should be able to use this process to solve any similar problem once you get this next exercise under your belt.

Saving for Retirement

We will assume that you are forty years old and expect to work for twenty-five more years until the normal retirement age of sixty-five. Your current salary is $25,000, and you assume it will increase yearly at about the national inflation rate of 5%. While doing research, you find that financial planners often use a rule-of-thumb that calls for retirement income equal to 75–90% of your salary immediately prior to retirement. In other

words, if your salary should grow from its current level of
$25,000 to $100,000 at age sixty-five, you would need income
of $75,000 to $90,000 a year during retirement in order to
maintain your life-style. Why do your income needs decrease
during retirement? In all likelihood, your large expenditures
for college expenses and mortgage obligations will have been
completed by this point, and you need no longer spend money
on work-related items such as clothing and commuting. On the
other hand, you would like to have the financial wherewithal to
travel during retirement, and unforeseen medical costs always
represent a potential threat that you want to guard against. You
will probably think of a few other factors of this kind that will
affect your particular situation upon retirement. After taking all
of these factors into consideration, you conclude that your annual retirement income should be 90% of your final salary.

Next, you arrange a meeting with the company's personnel
officer and learn that the combination of payments from Social
Security and the company's pension plan can be expected to
provide roughly half of your desired retirement income. Therefore, your financial goal is to save enough money during your
remaining working years to provide the other half of the income
desired for your retirement needs. To keep this example simple,
we will assume that your children will win athletic scholarships
to college and that you feel no particular responsibility to build
an estate on their behalf.

To accomplish your objective, we will assume you can save
$350 per month, or $4,200 annually from your salary. This
amount is actually unrealistic because $4,200 represents almost
17% of your current salary, whereas the average American saves
less than 5% of his or her income. More likely, you would commit
to a percentage about double the average, say 10%, which would
result in your saving $2,500 in the first year and annually in-
creasing amounts thereafter because of rises in your salary. However, this version makes the calculations required much more
difficult so why don't we stay with the simpler example. Once
again, the key assumptions for computing the rate of return
required are as follows:

»	Retirement Savings Example	«

Key Assumptions

Current age	40, with 25 years remaining in working career
Current salary	$25,000, with 5% annual growth expected
Desired retirement income	90% of final year's salary
Source of retirement income	50% from Social Security and pension; 50% from savings program
	$4,200 annual savings (contributed once a year)

The first step in working this problem is to determine what your salary will most likely be during the final year of your working career. Referring to Appendix 1, we find that the future value of $1.00 growing at 5% for twenty-five years is $3.39. Therefore, your salary at age sixty-five will be $3.39 multiplied by $25,000, or $84,750. Recall that your desired retirement income is 90% of that amount, or $76,275. Half of this sum, or $38,137.50, will be provided by Social Security and your company's pension plan. Hence, your investment program must generate an equal amount.

You would like to spend your retirement enjoying yourself rather than worrying about your finances. This suggests that you should consider purchasing an annuity from a highly rated insurance company to meet the balance of your income needs. Let's assume further that when you retire, both you and your spouse will be sixty-five. It is reasonable to assume that good-quality annuities will yield about 9% per year. Based on these inputs, your insurance salesman informs you that $358,000 will be necessary to purchase an annuity that will generate $38,096 annually for both of your lives beginning on your retirement date.

The final step is to calculate the rate of return that will be required to ensure that twenty-five payments of $4,200 each will be valued at \$358,000 upon your retirement. Once again, the calculator sequence is as follows:

Step 1   Enter the number of periods, which is 25
Step 2   Enter the *annual* savings, which is \$4,200
Step 3   Enter the future value, which is \$358,000
Step 4   Solve for the required annual return

The answer should be a rate of 9.05%. As was the case in the college savings example, this rate must be an after-tax return or you will have to pay taxes from another source of cash. In a retirement savings program, however, you might be able to use tax deferred investments such as Individual Retirement Accounts (IRAs) or deferred annuities that reduce your actual tax burden.

At this point, you should recognize that you followed the same process in both examples. In this example, you began with the general goal of providing for your retirement; you then gathered the information required to calculate a specific investment objective: to earn 9.05% annually on your savings. In the other example, you began with the objective of educating your son and found that you would have to earn 14.2% a year on your investments to achieve this goal. Another familiar example might be the accumulation of funds for the down payment on a house. From what you have learned so far, you know that the rate of return required for this would be calculated in the same manner.

While this book is primarily oriented toward individual investors, some of you also serve as trustees of retirement funds or in other fiduciary capacities. The information you are learning will also be relevant to these roles. For example, the framework of the college savings example can be applied to a fund-raising drive to build a new addition on your church. Also, the typical corporate pension plan, which promises the employee a certain amount of income during retirement, is conceptually the same as the retirement income example. In fact, every pension plan employs an actuary to do a more sophisticated version of the calculations we just completed.

All of these examples have a critical ingredient in common:

they call for you to have a specific amount of money available at a specific time. Each, therefore, resulted in a specific target rate of return that was necessary to achieve a broad financial objective. If you develop your goals in this fashion, you will embark on your investment program with an important advantage: a good indication at the outset that your goals are reasonable. This advantage can be clearly illustrated with the college savings example. You need to know first, as will be explained in Chapter 3, that you can expect to earn yearly returns of 8–12% on a range of diversified portfolios. While not out of the realm of possibility, the 14.2% required return in the college savings example is beyond the high end of my return range. Since risk and return are related, you can be sure that the risk associated with a 14.2% annual rate of return is substantial.

Given the difficulty (and perhaps improbability) of achieving a 14.2% return, as well as the risk involved, you might decide to adjust the goals and assumptions underlying your program. First, you might consider a less expensive college. Rather than attending your alma mater, Junior could go to the state university, where current costs run about $10,000 per year as compared with the $15,000 figure used in the example. If you keep all of the other assumptions constant, this change decreases the required return on your portfolio to 9.1%—a rate that is certainly more realistic and entails a good deal less risk.

A second alternative, if your budget could handle it, would be to put aside more than $325 every month. For example, an increase to $400 lowers the return target to 11.6%. While this target rate is still at the high end of the range, it is considerably more manageable than a return target of 14.2%. As a third option, you could choose a moderate-risk investment program that you know will provide less than the 14.2% target return, and either make up the shortfall through borrowing or ask Junior to get a part-time job.

By going through this exercise, you can make an informed decision about the realism of your goals and the risk necessary to achieve them. You end up with a risk:return combination that you understand and are comfortable with. Moreover, once your

portfolio is in place, your target rate of return allows you to
measure your progress and revise your plans as necessary. For
example, failure to meet your return target for a long period of
time might lead you to change your college plans, to increase
your monthly savings, or to plan for a shortfall—just as you
might do when setting up your investment program.

»   **The Dragon**   «

J. R. R. Tolkien said, "It doesn't do to leave a dragon out of your
calculations if you live near him." In the investment world,
inflation is the primary dragon, and we *all* live near him. In
setting your investment objectives and monitoring your progress,
it is critical to keep inflation in the forefront of your thinking.
One simple calculation will help you keep the inflation factor in
sight. When you subtract your assumed inflation rate from your
target rate of return, the remainder is your target *real* or after-
inflation return. In the college savings example, we assumed
annual increases in college costs of 7% and calculated a required
return of 14.2%. The target *real* return, then, is 14.2% less 7%,
or 7.2%. Similarly, the retirement income example was based
on a 5% annual salary increase and a target *real* return of 9.05%
less 5% or 4.05%.

Why is the real target of any value to you? Suppose that five
years have passed and the actual return on your college savings
portfolio has been 13.2% per year instead of 14.2%. Your initial
response might be that you have failed to meet your target, and
therefore it is necessary to change your plans. However, if the
actual increases in college costs have been 6% rather than the
7% assumed, you have still earned a real return of 7.2% (13.2%
less 6%) during the five-year period. Thankfully, everything is
still on track! The final step in the five-part program outlined
in this book involves an annual review of the progress of your
portfolio. To do this correctly, you must review your initial financial goals, the key assumptions underlying your calculations,
and the actual return on your portfolio. Therefore, make sure

that you write down all of this information and keep it with your other important financial papers.

<h2>»   A Word on Current Income   «</h2>

Our two examples resulted in specific *total* return objectives. The total return includes current income such as dividends and interest, as well as any appreciation. If your primary investment objective is to generate income, you may think that none of this risk:return business applies to you. Well, you're wrong! Retired individuals, foundations, endowments, and some trust funds have in common the necessity to rely on their portfolios for current support. In fact, many such investors state their goals in terms of the amount of annual income that must be generated by the portfolio. Unfortunately, investment policies designed to maximize dividends and interest may be destructive to a long-term investment program.

Many individuals who have significant income requirements choose to invest most or all of their money in long-term bonds. Among the primary investment categories, these bonds provide the highest annual current income. This approach is based on the fact that the interest payment on the bond provides a secure income stream. Moreover, the relative certainty that your principal will be repaid upon maturity provides a false sense of security. After all, since you will get both interest payments and a guaranteed return of principal, how could you be taking any risk?

Remember that dragon! As you will discover, the risk of losing money in most types of investments is slight for investors with time horizons of ten years or more. The risk of a loss in purchasing power, however, is significant; inflation is the investor's primary enemy. To make this point, suppose you had invested all of your money in U.S. government bonds in 1972. Assuming that you purchased bonds with a face value of $25,000, their coupon or interest rate of 6% would have paid you $1,500 in annual income. During the next ten years, inflation averaged

8.6% per year. At the end of this period, your annual income of $1,500 had the purchasing power of $657, which means that your living standard declined by almost 60%. Had you sold the bonds during this period, you probably would have suffered a substantial loss of principal because high rates of inflation usually lead to rising interest rates that in turn cause bond prices to decline. However, even if you held on to them and they were redeemed at their face value of $25,000, ten years of inflation would have significantly reduced the amount of goods and services that could be purchased with this sum. Although bonds may be a satisfactory means of supplying current income over a short period of time, they also subject you to a serious decline in your life-style over the long haul. Obviously, this is not a satisfactory strategy.

Because inflation has been more moderate in recent years, the effect of employing a current income strategy has been less severe, although still present. But another troubling strategy has taken its place. Reaching for that extra dollar of income led many investors in the 1980s to purchase low-quality, or "junk," bonds. Junk bonds were issued by tax-exempt entities, such as the Washington Public Power System, as well as a variety of corporations involved in leveraged buyouts, mergers, and recapitalizations. At the time these bonds were issued, their proponents cheered their high return while downplaying the risk involved. Investors thought they had finally discovered the proverbial "free lunch." Unfortunately, a wave of defaults and the decimation of the junk-bond market have taught a new generation of investors that risk and return are inextricably coupled.

While some investors concentrate all their assets in bonds to produce income, others follow an equally dangerous approach in which they rely primarily on capital appreciation to meet their spending needs. In this case, they sell off a few shares of appreciated stock here and there and spend the proceeds after putting aside funds to meet any tax liability. This strategy works well as long as the stock market is rising, but a substantial bear market can be devastating. To make this point, we will focus on an extreme example. Suppose your portfolio consists solely of emerging growth stocks that pay no dividends but are expected to appreciate 12% annually. Further, we will assume you need to draw $2,000 annually from your portfolio, which is initially valued at $25,000. If the stocks appreciate as expected, you are in great shape! You sell enough stock to generate the $2,000 necessary to live on. The other $1,000 in return remains in the portfolio, which means that it will be valued at year end at $26,000. Next year, you will earn 12% of $26,000, or $3,120, and you will reinvest $1,120 after withdrawing $2,000 for income needs. And this process continues forever. This is compound interest at its best.

But now, assume the stock market falls 10% per year over a five-year period. (Although rare, this could indeed happen.) As a result of the market decline and your annual withdrawals, the value of the $25,000 portfolio at the end of five years would be only $6,572. If the market does not snap back quickly, your annual spending requirement of $2,000 will deplete your assets in just over three additional years. Once again, this was a very unsatisfactory way to meet your needs.

But there is a better way! If your primary investment objective is to meet income needs, the best strategy is to choose a portfolio that provides enough current income, such as dividends and interest, to meet a healthy portion of your annual needs and, at the same time, generates a total return sufficient to protect you from inflation. As an example, consider a balanced portfolio that consists of various types of stocks, government bonds, and real estate. Without getting into all of the details just yet, a reasonable mix of these investments might be expected to earn a total return of 10–11% per annum. Investments could be selected so that this return would consist of approximately 5% from dividends and interest and 5–6% from capital appreciation. Now, if your annual spending needs are $2,000 and your beginning portfolio value is $25,000, this balanced fund would provide $1,250 in current income that you could supplement with $750 in appreciation. If the portfolio provides a total return of 10–11% as expected, you would still be able to reinvest $500 to $750 per year as a hedge against inflation. And in a truly dismal market, the 5% current yield would prevent the kind of principal encroachment that so devastated the portfolio in the example above.

The moral of this story is that the process of selecting an investment strategy is really no different for income-oriented investors than for those who seek total return. It is a process that balances risk and return while seeking stability and consistency.

» The Back Door to Objectives «

All of the financial goals we have considered so far have been specific ones that permit you to calculate a target rate of return that can be balanced with risk to determine the optimum combination. However, in the real world, few individuals are able to focus on their goals with such precision and most investors' plans consist of some specific objectives as well as a number of general ideas about the shape of their financial futures. These investors must follow the "back door" approach to selecting a risk:return combination—that is, focus on risk and allow return to fall into place.

For example, consider a corporate executive whose children are already educated and who expects his company's pension plan to provide adequately for his retirement. In all likelihood, his mortgage has been paid off, he has acquired all the worldly goods he will ever need, and he has accumulated plenty of cash to meet any emergency needs. Yet he continues to save and invest. He wishes to leave his children a modest nest egg but has no strong feelings regarding how large his estate should be. In this instance, his program is not directed toward a specific goal, but he is hopeful that his investments will "grow." Without a specific goal in mind, he can approach the risk:return issue only from the risk perspective.

Other examples of "back door" investors are those who are only interested in preserving their capital—in other words, keeping the dollars they already have accumulated. Still others define capital preservation in terms of offsetting the ravages of inflation.

And many investors are simply putting aside money for a rainy day. In all of these cases, both the amount of money desired and the date when it must be available are unclear.

Perhaps the most important example of all is the objective of providing retirement income through profit sharing, 401(k), and the other types of defined-contribution retirement plans that are widely in use today. Under traditional, defined-benefit plans, the employee is promised a certain amount of income during retirement, and the company's responsibility is to make sure that sufficient funds are available to meet that promise. In contrast, defined-contribution plans call for the company to make a periodic contribution to a fund on the employee's behalf, and it then becomes the employee's responsibility to designate how the money is invested. Moreover, the employee assumes *all* of the investment risk. To make matters even worse, few employers are willing to give much investment advice because of their concerns about potential liability. The result: More than 35 million Americans are left to fend for themselves, and only a small proportion of them are equipped to make investment decisions in a truly informed manner.

Let's assume you are a participant in your company's profit-sharing plan. First, you have little or no control over the amount of money that is contributed to the plan on your behalf, and the amount and timing of withdrawals after retirement are largely dictated by Internal Revenue Service (IRS) regulations. Your broad financial goal, therefore, must be general rather than specific, namely: to accumulate as much money as possible in this plan to ensure a comfortable retirement. Given the nature of these plans, the only element you really control is the division of your assets among stocks, bonds, and other types of investments. Typically, the personnel officer of your company tells you that you can divide your money among up to ten different mutual funds that the company has selected. How in the world can you make this decision? As it turns out, most participants in these plans allocate the bulk of their assets to bonds or other rather conservative investments, because they view these investments as "safe." While some make this decision because they are truly averse to risk, most really don't understand the tradeoff between risk and return. The bottom line is that many such employees are taking far too little risk and, consequently, are realizing far too little return from those investments. The inevitable result for these individuals will be a lower standard of living during retirement. In general, I estimate that the typical participant in a defined-contribution plan could raise his retirement income by as much as 20% simply by doing a better job of making choices among the plan's options.

I don't want you to make this mistake. As you learned earlier, when your goal lacks a specific return objective, you must approach the risk:return tradeoff from the risk side. Remember Chart 2.1, which portrayed the basic relationship between risk and return? I indicated that you must ultimately decide whether your needs are best met by points A, B, or C. In reality, these three risk:return combinations are not enough to satisfy the objectives of a broad array of individuals. Therefore, Chapter 5 provides detailed information about *seven* levels of risk. A more appropriate depiction of the risk:return relationship is, therefore, illustrated in Chart 2.2. Combinations one through seven cover a broad spectrum of risk and return. For that reason, most investors will be able to identify with one of these risk levels.

Let's return to the profit-sharing plan example. As a participant, you must decide on an appropriate investment strategy based only on the general goal of maximizing your retirement income. How do you make this decision? Once you have studied the information in Chapter 5 regarding the actual risk associated with each of the seven levels, you will choose the maximum level of risk you are comfortable with. Key factors in your decision will include your age and time horizon, the availability of other assets to meet your needs, your job prospects, and most important, your emotional capacity to handle a market decline. Let's say you opt for the risk level at point four on the curve, this book will help you construct the best possible investment strategy for this risk level. As it turns out, you can expect your portfolio to earn about 10.5% per year. If this isn't enough return, you will have to rethink your position on risk. Do you

Chart 2.2   Risk and Return

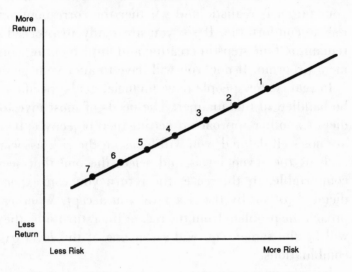

really need to be that cautious? Couldn't you afford to stretch just a little? The decisions about higher or lower risk and return will always be yours. But remember, you can't have it both ways.

»   Only *You* Can Set Your Objectives   «

From this chapter you should have learned several key points. This book is designed to help you assemble an investment program that will meet your needs. The result of your effort will be a specifically tailored, customized portfolio. To do this correctly, the starting point must be the risk and return combination that is best attuned to your personality and financial situation. Finding that combination is a process of distilling all of your financial goals and objectives.

The best way to begin this process is to list all of your financial goals in plain English. If these goals call for having a specific amount of money available at a specific time, you can calculate a required target rate of return. You can then determine whether your target is realistic and whether the corresponding level of risk is comfortable. If so, you are ready to proceed with the remaining four steps in creating and implementing your investment program. If not, you will have to alter your goals.

In reality, few people have financial goals specific enough to be handled in this manner. The needs of most investors, then, dictate another approach to setting their objectives. If your goals are not well defined, you will focus on the risk associated with each of the seven levels and select the one that seems most comfortable. In this case, the return you can expect will be dictated to you by the risk level you accept. Whether you approach the problem from the risk or the return side, the outcome will be the same: You will select one of the seven risk:return combinations.

It is important to remind you that determining your risk exposure is a subjective, personal exercise. There is no right or wrong answer. Moreover, your financial goals as well as your feelings about risk will change over the course of your lifetime; thus, this process must be repeated regularly.

Many investors are disappointed with the return on their investments because of their exaggerated, unrealistic expectations. Investment books that promise 20% a year with no risk and cocktail party braggarts simply compound the problem. The next chapter provides you with historical data on rates of return as well as educated guesses regarding those rates in the future. You may think that you or your hired guns will do better than these forecasts, but I wouldn't bet my financial future on it.

>>> _____ **Key Points to Remember** _____ <<<

- Risk and return are related—you can't have one without the other.
- The most satisfied investors are those who establish specific and realistic objectives.

CHAPTER 3

INVESTMENT RETURNS
Past, Present, and Future

Only robbers and gypsies say that one must never return where one has been.

—Søren Kierkegaard

»» ««

The ultimate goal of this book is to help you construct an investment portfolio that is likely to achieve your return objectives at a risk level you understand and are comfortable with. The best way to select your portfolio is to evaluate a number of alternatives. For you to determine how different portfolios might behave in the future, it is necessary to make some assumptions regarding the returns you can expect on the various investments the portfolios include. Moreover, it is critical that you find out if your investment objectives are unrealistic so as to revise your plans. For both of these reasons, we must venture into the muddy waters of forecasting returns on stocks, bonds, and other types of investments. While it is dirty, dangerous work, someone has to do it!

The investment world is characterized by hype, exaggeration, and blatant self-promotion. Wall Street would have you believe that market gurus and fund managers consistently earn extraordinary returns. Every brokerage firm boasts of the superior performance of its list of recommended stocks. And we have already discussed the fact that all of your friends brag about the large

31

portfolios they are amassing. In this frothy environment, investors can easily lose their perspective on what they realistically should expect to earn on their investments.

An additional hazard is the tendency of investment professionals to focus primarily on short-term results. This focus is the result of sophisticated performance analysis that places great pressure on money managers since their returns are examined in excruciating detail. Perhaps even more dangerous is the propensity of many investors to extrapolate recent returns (both good and bad) into the future. This practice is risky because returns fluctuate significantly over time.

You are probably aware that yearly returns on U.S. stocks fluctuate a great deal. But Table 3.1 shows that even annual returns averaged over ten-year periods vary considerably. Had you extrapolated the 1.8% annual return from 1931 to 1940 over the ensuing fifty years, or the 16.2% return from 1951 to 1960 over the ensuing thirty years, you would have clearly been way off the mark. An investment plan should be based on rates of return that will be sustainable over the duration of your program. In other words, you should structure your portfolio on the basis of returns that are most likely to occur over the long term, say a twenty- to fifty-year period. How in the world does one go about predicting returns over a fifty-year period?

»»   Table 3.1   Annual Returns on Stocks by Decade   ««

1901–10	7.2%
1911–20	3.2%
1921–30	13.8%
1931–40	1.8%
1941–50	13.4%
1951–60	16.2%
1961–70	8.1%
1971–80	8.4%
1981–90	13.9%

Source: Cambridge Associates, Inc.

» Linkages Between Markets «

Some investors argue that they are hard pressed to forecast what will happen in the financial markets over the next year much less to predict a fifty-year return. They suggest that it is impossible to make long-range forecasts so one shouldn't even try. In fact, the opposite is true. It is indeed difficult, if not impossible, to guess what markets will do over the short term, but we can make longer term forecasts with a little more confidence. This added confidence stems from the fact that returns on different types of investments are governed by fundamental economic forces that cause markets to move back in line when they temporarily get out of kilter. When markets do stray from the norm, it frequently lasts longer than expected, and the extent of the deviation is often surprising. But ultimately, given enough time, they return to normal. This tendency to return to normal occurs because markets are linked together and the return on one type of investment influences the return on others.

In order to understand these linkages, let's consider an example in which you inherit $50,000 from a long-lost relative. In simple terms, you have two choices: spend it or save it. As was pointed out in Chapter 2, spending is certainly more fun than saving, so you will select the thriftier alternative only if you expect to gain something. What you hope to gain is a return on your savings that will allow you to buy, at a future date, more goods and services than the $50,000 will purchase currently. Suppose you are considering buying a $50,000 sports car with your inheritance. Instead, you decide to invest these funds, and they grow to $60,000 at the end of five years. If the price of the car also rises to $60,000, you gained nothing by virtue of your investment. You are no better off than you were five years ago; your car dealer got it all anyway. Therefore, the most basic investment objective of any rational person is to earn a return greater than inflation—in other words, to improve one's purchasing power. This explains why the return on very short term, safe investments such as U.S. Treasury Bills should be modestly above the rate of inflation. Stated another way, short-term interest rates are directly linked to inflation.

To take this example a step further, suppose instead that your $50,000 is safely invested in ninety-day U.S. Treasury Bills, and your broker advises you to switch to *thirty-year* U.S. Treasury Bonds. To tie up your money for such a long period, you would clearly demand a premium return on the bonds as compared to the yield on the bills. While the amount of this premium will fluctuate over time—and may even be negative for brief periods—you can be confident that you will earn a higher return on the longer-term investment. Therefore, the return on Treasury Bonds is linked to the return on Treasury Bills, which, in turn, is linked to the rate of inflation.

After taking your broker's advice, a friend suggests that you liquidate your thirty-year government bonds and move the proceeds to thirty-year bonds issued by a corporation, maybe Philip Morris or General Motors. Since the maturity of the corporate bonds is the same as that of the government bonds you own, no additional time commitment is involved. But the Treasury Bonds are fully guaranteed by the U.S. government, whereas the corporate bonds are subject to the risk of default. In other words, a corporation might not be able to pay interest or principal upon the bonds' maturity. While this risk is minuscule for bonds issued by strong companies such as those in this example, there is still a chance. Therefore, you should demand a higher rate of return on corporate issues to compensate for this added risk. However, if this risk premium becomes too large, investors will sell their government bonds and purchase corporate issues, which will force the relationship between them back to normal. So the return on corporate bonds is largely a function of government bond returns and, in practice, is another link in the chain that reaches all the way back to inflation.

The final link is the relationship between corporate bonds and the stock of their issuers. The interest on a bond is paid before shareholders receive dividends, and in the event of the liquidation of the company, the bondholders have first claim on the assets. Owning the stock of a company, therefore, is less secure than owning its bonds, and any reasonable person would demand a higher rate of return. But there must be a linkage between the returns on stocks and bonds issued by the same company. As you will see in a moment, market forces will take over if this relationship is seriously violated.

I have shown that the returns on stocks, corporate bonds, U.S. government bonds, and Treasury Bills are related, and all are tied to the rate of inflation. If the return on any of these investment categories gets out of line, certain forces will return it to the proper relationship. For example, suppose corporate bonds offer an unusually high rate of return as compared to stocks—that is, bonds are very "cheap" and stocks "expensive." Sophisticated investors will quickly become aware of this discrepancy and respond by selling their stocks and buying bonds. At the same time, corporations will issue stock and use the proceeds to retire their outstanding bonds. Both of these forces will cause stock prices to fall and bond prices to rise. And as stock prices fall, their prospective returns will increase until the balance is restored.

These linkages go much further than the examples cited. In a global economy increasingly connected by electronics, the returns on different stock markets around the world are becoming ever more interdependent. As an example, should European stock markets seem to offer better returns than their American counterparts, money will flow out of the United States until the proper relationship is restored.

Does it seem reasonable to think that the returns on real estate investments are related to those on stocks? You probably are hard pressed to see any connection, but there is one. Almost all real estate is financed with borrowed money, and interest rates determine the cost of that borrowing. Interest expense affects directly the profitability of the property and, ultimately, your return as the owner. At the same time, the return on stocks is influenced by interest rates, as was demonstrated by the chain described above. While the relationship is distant, it is clear that the same market forces affect returns on both of these investment types because those forces impact interest rates.

By now you probably want to know where all of this talk about linkages is headed. First, we will examine historical returns on different types of investments to quantify these linkages. We may then adjust some of them to reflect changes in the financial markets. Finally, we will use these relationships to make educated guesses regarding the course of future returns. Our forecasts can never be perfect, but these linkages allow our predictions of returns from different types of investments to be consistent with one another and to be within the ballpark. Since we are neither robbers nor gypsies, let's return to where we have been so that we may better understand where we will be in the future.

>> **Historical Returns** <<

A discussion of the returns on stocks or bonds always raises the question of which stocks or bonds were measured. To deal with this issue, most analysts use a market index that includes a large number of securities and, thereby, is representative of the market as a whole. While the Dow Jones average is probably best known among several market indices, most professional investors actually use the Standard & Poor's 500 Index as a proxy for the U.S. stock market. This index consists of the stocks of five hundred of America's largest companies, and in total, they represent about 75% of the collective value of all stocks traded in the United States. Similar indices are available for bonds, real estate, and foreign securities. As we consider past and future returns, we will always focus on an index that is representative of all securities in the investment category being discussed.

It is also important to note that return studies always consider *total* returns, which include current income, such as dividends and interest, as well as any appreciation. For example, the long-term return on common stocks of 10.1% per annum consists of dividends equal to 4.7%, on average, and appreciation of 5.3%.

One word of caution: Historical returns are dependent upon the actual period studied. A thirty-year period beginning at the bottom of the depression in the 1930s will show a substantially larger return than a thirty-year period beginning prior to the crash in 1929. Therefore, it is important to look at a very long period to make fair judgments, and it is useful to focus on different periods to ensure that the results are consistent. With all of this background in mind, let's examine the annual average of total returns for different investment types during the period from 1926 to 1990. These rates are shown in Table 3.2.

These long-run returns portray the linkages between investments that were discussed earlier in this chapter. First, U.S. Treasury Bills provided a return that exceeded the rate of inflation by .6% per year (3.7% less 3.1%)—in other words, investors gained a little purchasing power every year. Long-term government bonds yielded an extra .8% every year compared to Treasury Bills as a reward for committing to their longer maturity. Corporate bonds provided still another .7% as compensation for the risk of default. Common stocks provided a return almost double that of corporate bonds as a reward for their higher risk. Finally, the return on small stocks was another 1.5% higher than common stocks. Small companies frequently grow at much faster rates than their larger counterparts. In addition, they tend to be less seasoned, more prone to failure, and certainly more volatile. For all of these reasons, you would expect to earn a higher return on their stocks as compared to the blue chips.

One simplistic approach to forecasting future returns is to assume that the long-run averages presented in Table 3.2 con-

»»   Table 3.2   Annual Returns 1926–90   «««

Common stocks	10.1%
Small-company stocks	11.6%
Long-term corporate bonds	5.2%
Long-term government bonds	4.5%
Intermediate-term government bonds	5.0%
U.S. Treasury Bills	3.7%
Inflation	3.1%

Source: Ibbotson Associates

tinue ad infinitum. Indeed, some advisers argue that past returns are as good a guess as any other regarding the outlook for the future. I think we can do better than that. Some of the information in Table 3.2 may no longer be very relevant, which suggests that we ought to look at more recent data as a basis for comparison. For example, inflation has averaged about 6% per year over the past fifteen years; that rate is almost twice the long-term average of 3.1%. Perhaps inflation will soon return to its long-run level, but I would not bet on it. In addition, government bonds currently yield about 8%, significantly above the 4.5% average for the long-term period. Finally, capital market relationships do change over time and our forecasts of future returns should take those changes into account. So let's take a look at return data for the last ten years, 1981–90, and then later compare this period with the longer-term perspective.

In general, the linkages and patterns that we have come to expect held true for the 1980s. There were, however, a few surprises. First, you will note that small stocks substantially *underperformed* their larger counterparts, a fact that seems to defy logic and be contrary to historical trends. But this aberration can be explained. While small stocks do indeed tend to outperform larger stocks over time, their superior return usually comes in spurts. Their return greatly exceeds the return on stocks of larger companies for a time, but they then lag for a few years until the cycle begins again. From 1974 through mid-1983, small companies provided annual returns that averaged 28.4%, strikingly above the 10.6% return on the Standard & Poor's 500. The trend then reversed: small-company stocks earned 2.2% per year from mid-1983 through 1990 as compared to 13.6% for the S&P 500. Therefore, the bulk of the period from 1981 to 1990 represented a portion of the cycle in which small companies underperformed. This cyclical performance does not in any way detract from the long-run attraction of small stocks; in fact, one could make a case that the cycle is about to reverse.

Second, this decade was a wonderful period for savers. Whereas the return on Treasury Bills exceeded inflation by .6%

»Table 3.3   Investment Returns 1981–90 (Annual Rates)«

Common stocks	13.9%
Small-company stocks	9.3%
Long-term corporate bonds	14.1%
Long-term government bonds	13.8%
Intermediate-term bonds	12.5%
U.S. Treasury Bills	8.6%
Inflation	4.5%

Source: Ibbotson Associates

per year over the 1926–90 time frame, the spread during the past decade was 4.1% (8.6% less 4.5%). In other words, even the most cautious investor was able to enhance his purchasing power simply by investing in short-term government securities. In fact, were this relationship to hold for about seventeen years, the investor would double his purchasing power by owning this essentially risk-free security.

Third, the most striking thing about the 1980s was the high rate of return provided by both stocks and bonds. Stocks exceeded their long-range average by 3.8% per year and the return on government bonds was over three times the historical level. Moreover, stocks provided positive returns in eight out of the ten years and the worst year (1981) recorded a modest loss of 5%. Bonds provided a negative return in only one of the ten years (1987) and that loss was limited to only 2.8%. One interesting characteristic of this period was the fact that bonds provided essentially the same return as stocks. I will argue shortly that it is reasonable to expect bond returns in the future to exceed historical levels, but I cannot justify returns equal to those on stocks. Just as it did not seem sensible to blindly extrapolate the long-run average returns into the future, it would be dangerous to assume that the wonderful returns experienced during the last decade could continue indefinitely. The right targets, therefore, probably lie somewhere in the middle.

Real Returns

The most reasonable way to forecast rates of return is to subtract inflation from historical results in order to calculate a real or after-inflation return. This real return provides the investor with the gain in purchasing power that is necessary to induce him to save rather than to spend. Unless there is a major change in the capital markets, there is no reason for an investor to change the amount of real return he demands. This real return can, therefore, be added to an inflation forecast to estimate future returns. One advantage of this approach is that it is based on the historical linkages between different types of investments. At the same time, predictions of future returns are tied to forecasts of *future* inflation rather than to a historical average that may no longer be relevant. To make this concept clear, recall that stocks have provided a long-term return of 10.1% per annum while inflation averaged 3.1%. Real or after-inflation returns, therefore, averaged 7% (10.1% less 3.1%). If we expect inflation to average 5% in the future, then a reasonable forecast of the return on stocks is 12% (7% plus 5%).

The average annual rates of *real* return for the past ten years and the longer time frame of 1926–90 are provided in Table 3.4. These real returns were calculated by subtracting the actual rate of inflation from the returns presented in Tables 3.2 and 3.3.

The real returns in Table 3.4 essentially mirror the absolute returns displayed in Tables 3.2 and 3.3—that is, recent results for all types of investments substantially exceed the long-term averages. So we are again left with the question of whether recent or long-term averages are to be heeded. My approach is to analyze the environment for each investment category to determine whether something important has changed and, if so, should be considered a permanent change. If not, it is probably best to stick with the long-run averages for that particular category. If something has changed permanently, I adjust my forecast accordingly.

Every investment professional will tell you that the return on

» **Table 3.4   Real or After-Inflation Returns** «

	1926–90	1981–90
Common stocks	7.0%	9.4%
Small-company stocks	8.5%	4.8%
Long-term corporate bonds	2.1%	9.6%
Long-term government bonds	1.4%	9.3%
Intermediate-term government bonds	1.9%	8.0%
U.S. Treasury Bills	.6%	4.1%

Source: Ibbotson Associates

a stock must be related to the growth in the underlying company. Similarly, the return on the entire stock market must be tied closely to the growth in our overall economy. Therefore, one explanation for the comparatively higher returns on U.S. stocks during the 1980s could be faster growth in the U.S. economy. Unfortunately, there is no evidence that we experienced an acceleration in growth; in fact, many would argue that our economy lost momentum in comparison to other industrial powers throughout the world. Another explanation for higher returns could be an increase in volatility, or fluctuations in securities. Since investors don't like this, it is reasonable that they would demand a higher return on a stock that fluctuates a great deal as compared with the more stable variety. Despite public perception to the contrary, stocks in the aggregate were no more volatile during the decade than they have been historically; actually, stocks were a bit more stable than in some prior periods. Therefore, volatility doesn't explain the past decade's higher returns either. After considering these and other factors, I conclude that there were *no* fundamental changes in the stock market during the 1980s and, thus, that recent real returns were abnormally high. In this instance, it makes sense to revert to the long-term averages that call for 6–7% real returns on common stocks and 8–9% on small-company stocks.

However, things have changed in the bond market and I believe it is fair to assume that the historical relationships are no longer relevant. Whereas the volatility of stocks has not changed significantly, long-term U.S. government bonds have been about one and a half times more volatile during the past ten years than their long-term history. Bonds were traditionally viewed as rock-solid, stable investments. It is now perfectly normal for interest rates to fluctuate by as much as 1% or 2% during a given year. That range of fluctuation causes the prices of bonds to increase or decrease by up to 20% or so. Why this increase in volatility?

The most logical explanation would be greater fluctuations in the rate of inflation. Remember that inflation basically determines the yield on both Treasury Bills and Treasury Bonds, and fluctuations in inflation should therefore translate into volatility in bond prices. Unfortunately, this is not the answer. Inflation has been a bit more volatile in recent years than in the late 1950s and early 1960s, but it has been less volatile than in some other periods. Something else must be going on.

I believe there are three factors that explain this phenomenon. The first is the deregulation of the banking system, which allowed interest rates on deposits to change with supply and demand. While the yields on savings accounts used to be fixed, banks must now set their rates competitively to attract deposits, and this competition causes fluctuations in interest rates in general. Second, institutional investors now dominate most capital markets. In the past, individual investors purchased bonds for their steady income stream and locked them in the safe-deposit box until maturity. Today, pension funds and other tax-free investors trade freely between stocks, bonds, and other investments depending upon the outlook for each category. This increase in bond trading activity also increases volatility. Finally, the globalization of financial markets has increased the flow of capital across borders. The ever-changing flow of capital causes changes in interest rates at home and abroad. In other words, U.S. interest rates are influenced by what is going on in Germany, Japan, and other key economies.

All of these changes seem to be permanent, which suggests that volatility in bond prices should remain fairly high, and that historical real returns on both Treasury Bills and Treasury Bonds are too low for forecasting purposes. On the other hand, their returns during the 1980s seem unusually high. For example, I cannot think of a good reason for U.S. Treasury Bills to provide a 4.1% return after inflation. After all, these are safe, short-term, and highly liquid securities. My best guess is that Treasury Bills will provide real returns of 1–2% and long-term Treasury Bonds will yield 3–4% after inflation.

»   Returns on Real Estate and Foreign Stocks   «

As you will soon discover, diversified portfolios should hold investments beyond the traditional categories of stocks, bonds, and money market securities. Two of the most important are real estate and foreign stocks.

Data on real estate returns are much less reliable than data on marketable security returns. First, real estate market indices have been available for only twenty years or so, which is not enough time to establish a high level of confidence. Since stocks and bonds trade daily, it is easy to measure the changes in their prices used to calculate rates of return. In contrast, properties do not change hands often, and perforce, return calculations must be based on appraised values that may or may not be valid. Finally, because each property is different, any given portfolio of real estate might behave very differently from a market index. Despite all of these problems, a number of studies have concluded that real estate has provided a real return of about 6%, which is fairly competitive with common stocks. Recent returns on real estate have been quite disappointing, however, and a number of forecasters believe it will take as long as a decade to work through the oversupply problems created by the building boom in the 1980s. But since an investment program should be based on long-range return estimates, I am willing to stick with the historical level of real return of about 6% on real estate investment.

Many U.S. investors now own shares of stock in corporations based outside the United States. Since currencies were fixed prior to 1973, foreign stock returns over the past ten to fifteen years are relevant for forecasting purposes. For the ten years ending in 1990, a widely used index of foreign stocks indicated a 16.4% total annual return versus 13.9% for the Standard & Poor's 500 Index. This strong return on foreign stocks was heavily influenced by the decline of the U.S. dollar in world markets. But that plunge appears to be over, and it seems unlikely that the dollar will drop appreciably from current levels. Moreover, the increasing linkages between global financial markets should bring foreign returns more closely in line with those of U.S. stocks. However, since many countries' economies are growing faster than our own, it is reasonable to expect a slightly higher return from non-U.S. equities. Therefore, I will assume real returns on foreign stocks of 7–8% as compared to my expectations of 6–7% on domestic stocks.

» Forecasts «

Now that we have forecasted real rates of return on investments of different types, we must convert them to total returns, because the latter rates determine how much wealth you actually accumulate. You will remember that the total return is found by adding the real rate to an inflation forecast. We must, therefore, make an inflation assumption. Since my crystal ball is no clearer than anybody else's, I will rely primarily on historical experience. You will recall that the long-term average rate of inflation has been about 3.1%, whereas the past ten years were characterized by inflation averaging 4.5%. Since most democracies have a bias toward inflation—and in the interest of conservatism—I opt for the more recent experience and assume a 5% annual rate for future inflation. Now we can bring all of our estimates together to make specific forecasts, which is exactly what the figures in Table 3.5 do for us.

The right-hand column, which contains my "best guesses," shows that you can reasonably expect to earn a return between 6% and 14% per year if you chose to put all of your eggs in only

»   Table 3.5   Projected Long-Range Annual Returns   «

Category	Inflation	Real Return %	Absolute Return %	Best Guess %
U.S. stocks	5%	6–7	11–12	11
Foreign stocks	5%	7–8	12–13	12
Small-company stocks	5%	8–9	13–14	14
U.S. government bonds	5%	3–4	8–9	8
Real estate	5%	5–6	10–11	10
U.S. Treasury Bills	5%	1–2	6–7	6

one of these baskets. At one extreme, the cautious investor who opts for U.S. Treasury Bills can expect to earn about 6%. At the other extreme, an adventurous investor can expect to earn as much as 14% from small-company stocks. As you will discover later, diversification is the key to controlling risk, and that key dictates that your portfolio contain investments in several of these categories. In Chapter 7, I will suggest that virtually every investor should hold assets in at least three categories, and most should hold assets in as many as five. The inclusion of three to five different categories in your portfolio should negate the effect of a poor prediction in any one investment type. Various combinations of the investments types listed in Table 3.5 can be expected to earn a total return that averages between 8% and 12% per year over a long period.

Some might argue that these return estimates are too low, while others may quibble with my assumptions regrading one particular category or another, but I don't believe anyone will find either my estimates or my assumptions unreasonable. And it is preferable to build your investment program on the basis of conservative, rather than aggressive, estimates and hope for a positive surprise. These estimates represent my best guesses as to the returns that will be earned on a particular *market*. In fact, the returns you actually earn could be very different. If the person managing your portfolio has unusual skill at selecting securities or timing markets, it is possible that you will greatly

exceed my market estimates. Needless to say, the converse could
also be true.

In Chapter 2, you learned how to determine your target rate
of return; this chapter forecasted returns with which you can
judge whether your target is both realistic and achievable. You
will recall that the college savings example required a 14.2%
rate of total return, while the retirement income example called
for a return of 9.05%. Clearly, the latter return is quite achievable, but the former represents a considerable stretch given the
forecasted range of 8–12%. Having dealt with the "return" side
of risk:return tradeoffs, it is now time to consider risk. Chapter
4 is devoted to helping you understand what risk is and how you
control it. Chapter 5 then helps you decide how much risk you
can tolerate.

»»—————— **Key Points to Remember** —————— **«««**

- An investment program should be based on long-term relationships between risk and return.
- Since markets are governed by powerful economic forces, one
  can make educated guesses regarding future rates of return.
- Diversified portfolios should provide future returns of 8–12%,
  depending upon the risk assumed.

CHAPTER 4

INVESTMENT RISK
What Is It and How Do You Control It?

Never was anything great achieved without danger.
—Machiavelli

》》 《《

The most difficult part of investing is understanding and evaluating risk. To begin with, no single definition of risk is uniformly accepted throughout the investment world. Historically, investors looked at risk primarily from a credit point of view—that is, a "risky" stock or bond was one associated with a company in poor financial condition or one characterized by untested management, fierce competition, or a variety of other qualitative attributes. Many investors define risk in terms of losing money; as long as they don't suffer a loss, everything is okay. Professional investors and academics view risk in terms of volatility; a security that fluctuates a great deal is considered "risky."

Unfortunately, even if there was universal agreement on how to define and measure it, investment risk would still be a difficult topic. The problem is that risk taking is a very personal thing. Two people with identical financial circumstances and objectives might have quite different portfolios because of their emotional makeups. No one can tell you how much risk you should take, that has to be your decision.

Finally, risk can be a touchy subject because it involves a great deal of emotion and, consequently, frequently causes otherwise sensible individuals to act irrationally. It has been my experience that most people *overestimate* the risk of investing, and this misperception causes them to construct unnecessarily conservative portfolios. After all, markets do go up on average, and while negative years occur regularly, it is rare for a diversified portfolio to experience a severe decline over a long period. Unusually cautious investors are giving up significant amounts of return in pursuit of a security blanket they probably do not need. For example, a $25,000 portfolio will grow to $436,235 over thirty years assuming a 10% return. (This ignores taxes and assumes reinvestment of all income.) A more cautious investment approach that reduces the return to 9% will decrease the ultimate value of the portfolio to $331,692, which represents a lost opportunity of $104,543, or 24%, by comparison. If you truly cannot tolerate the risk inherent in a higher-return portfolio, then you must be content to accept a lower rate of return. But you should make that decision only after carefully weighing both your circumstances and the actual risk involved.

So, we are dealing with a difficult topic. But if you take the time to understand investment risk and your own psyche, you will be able to structure a portfolio that will withstand a tough environment without causing you to panic and make a foolish decision. This is not to say that your portfolio will never decline in value. It will! But when the inevitable bear market does come along, you will be mentally prepared for the decline because you understand exactly how much risk you have assumed. In this chapter, you will learn what risk is and how to control it.

» **Various Definitions of Risk** «

Let's begin by looking at various definitions of risk that have been used over the years. When I entered the investment business during the early 1970s, most practitioners looked at risk from a credit-quality point of view. This approach was largely subjective or qualitative in nature and was based on perceptions of a given company's strengths and weaknesses. Analysts began by evaluating the financial strength of the company. A "risky" company was characterized by a large amount of debt, a lack of liquidity, or poor cash flow. In addition, good researchers looked at a wide array of factors that might influence the future performance of the company—factors such as the competitive environment, changes in technology, the economic outlook, regulatory issues, and perhaps most important, an assessment of the company's management. The result of all this was a subjective rating of the company's "quality" for investment purposes. A low-rated company was considered risky while a high-rated one was considered safe. In essence, this process is identical to the analysis that Moodys and Standard & Poor's use to rate bond issues today. While this measure is an excellent means of evaluating the ability of a company to repay its debts, it falls short as a measure of the risk in a company's stock.

This "credit quality" concept of risk has two problems. First, it is largely subjective and does not result in information that can be used to compare different investment types. For example, it would be nice if we could somehow compare the risk in stocks to that in real estate. The second problem with this measure is more serious. It ignores the important factor of the price of various companies' stocks. Even though companies A and B might have identical quality ratings, the fact that A's stock price had doubled while B's remained unchanged has serious implications for the amount of risk inherent in the two stocks.

If you have a long memory, you might recall the "Nifty Fifty" era of the early 1970s in which a small group of stocks sold at exceptionally high prices compared with the rest of the stock market. Included in this group were such wonderful companies as International Business Machines (IBM), Xerox, and Coca-Cola. In the 1974 bear market, the prices of many of the "Nifty Fifty" stocks declined from 50% to 75% or, in some cases, even more. Yet these were high-quality, financially strong companies that continued to grow at above-average rates; thus, they were *not* risky from the traditional standpoint. Obviously, this qualitative measure of risk does not capture everything that an investor needs to know.

Investors have always had a fixation on losing money. I can't tell you how many times investors have told me that they are holding on to a stock until the price recovers to their cost. It doesn't occur to them that another stock might offer greater potential than the one they are holding, and that by switching and realizing the loss, they will enhance the ultimate value of their portfolio. In any case, too many individuals perceive risk as the chance of losing money. This is a poor way of thinking about risk!

To make this point, we can use the retirement savings example from Chapter 2. Recall that we calculated that a 9.05% annual return was necessary to ensure the availability of the desired amount of income after age sixty-five. Let's assume that you invested your annual contributions in U.S. Treasury Bills and earned a return of 7% per year over the twenty-five years remaining in your working career. By investing in Treasury Bills, you never suffered a loss, which means that you never took any risk. Right? Wrong! If you needed to earn 9.05% to meet your retirement needs, and you actually earned 7%, you failed. Despite a lot of years of hard work and diligent saving, your living standard during retirement will be lower than hoped for. In my view, *that* is risk! Whether or not you lose money in any given period really has nothing to do with the accomplishment of your objectives. Once again, this measure of risk does not capture everything you need to know.

Another definition of risk that became popular in the high-inflation era of the 1970s was the risk of a loss in purchasing power. This risk stems from the fact that a given investment provided a rate of return that appeared enticing but, in the final analysis, was not sufficient to offset inflation. While 6% government bond yields appeared attractive in 1972, they turned out to be poor investments because inflation averaged better than 8% over the next ten years. In other words, bond-holders steadily lost purchasing power. This risk has diminished somewhat since the early 1980s due to lower rates of inflation, but it nevertheless remains a factor that should be considered in your plan. But again, this definition of risk is not broad enough

Chart 4.1   Range of Stock Prices Over a One Year Period

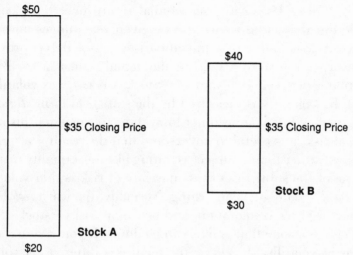

to take into account all of the factors that should be considered. In our example, the saver earned 7% every year on his investments versus a target return of 9.05%. Since this example assumed a 5% inflation rate, this saver actually gained purchasing power every year. So while he suffered no purchasing power risk, he still failed to meet his objectives. Back to the drawing board.

The measure of risk used today by both academics and practitioners is volatility. A stock or bond whose price fluctuates a great deal is considered "risky" because it creates uncertainty regarding the value of the investment at any given point in the future. Consider Chart 4.1. While stock A and stock B both close on December 31 at $35 per share, stock A trades in a $20 to $50 range while B fluctuates only between $30 and $40. On any given date, therefore, you would be less certain of A's value than you would be of B's value. This uncertainty implies greater risk because you cannot predict how much you will realize from your investment should you be forced to liquidate.

To be a little more precise, volatility is measured by analyzing how much the return on an investment fluctuates around its average return. This takes into account current income, such as dividends and interest, as well as any change in its price. Suppose stock A provides an average annual return over ten years of 10%, but the actual return in any given year ranges normally between 28% and −8%. In comparison, stock B also provides an average return of 10%, but the actual return in each year fluctuates between 19% and 1%. Stock A is twice as volatile as stock B. Volatility is measured by the statistical term *standard deviation*. While you need not know how to calculate this measure of risk, it is useful to understand that the result is a specific number rather than a subjective rating like most quality ratings.

One of the subtleties of this measure of risk is that volatility can be a "good" or "bad" thing. Normally, the word *risk* has a purely negative connotation, and hence, a "risky" stock would be defined as one that is likely to go down. If you define risk in terms of volatility, however, the picture is different. A volatile or risky stock can go up or down by an equal amount, which means that "risk" entails both danger and opportunity. In either case, though, volatility does create uncertainty, and investors dislike that condition above all others.

The underlying rationale for the use of volatility as a measure of risk is that it captures everything known about a given investment. In today's highly competitive markets, investors are constantly analyzing each company's financial information as well as the competitive environment, new products, management, and a variety of other factors. All of this information is somehow distilled into a decision to buy or sell, and the price of the investment moves accordingly. If the outlook for a company is highly uncertain, some investors will buy while others sell, and the result will be substantial fluctuations in the stock's price. Measuring the fluctuation in the return on a security, therefore, captures the opinions of all investors regarding the risk and opportunity inherent in it.

This measure of risk has a number of advantages and several drawbacks not found in the traditional alternatives. First, it is specific and quantifiable. By measuring the volatility of return on an investment, you gain the ability to compare it to other investments on an apples-to-apples basis. Therefore, we can compare the volatility of stocks to that of bonds, real estate, or any other category of investment. More important, this measure allows us to analyze the combined risk in a portfolio that consists of stocks, bonds, and other investment classes. The second advantage of this measure of risk is that it takes into account everything that is known about a given investment, including its current price.

One drawback of using this statistical measure is that volatility changes over time. As was pointed out in Chapter 3, bonds were more volatile during the 1980s than they had been in most periods. In this case, simple extrapolation of past risk would have underestimated the amount of volatility that you would have actually experienced in bond returns. In order to estimate future returns, we examined historical relationships and then modified them to reflect changes in the environment. Similarly, estimates of future volatility must be based on past data with a "fudge factor" that is heavily influenced by more recent experience.

The more important drawback of this measure of risk is that most individuals are uncomfortable with mathematics and statistics, and that renders the concept of standard deviation difficult for them to identify with. For example, if the standard deviation of investment A is 18% while that of investment B is 9%, you probably understand that A is twice as volatile as B, but you still have no idea what any of this means to you and your investment program. To make your life easier, I'll use statistical information to develop some tables that show how different investments ought to behave in the future. Using this approach, I will tell you what the return on a variety of portfolios should be as well as how often each will suffer a decline. I will even estimate how bad a drubbing each might take in a bad market. Obviously, these estimates can never be exactly correct, but they do provide a fair representation of what will happen to various portfolios over time. Making these estimates involves some number crunching that I don't want to bore you with. But the result is a way of thinking about risk that incorporates the best features of the traditional measures while avoiding their drawbacks.

»»   **My Own Definition of Risk**   ««

An ideal measure of risk would be one that is easy to understand and is tied directly to your investment objectives. My approach to evaluating risk, though based on the statistical analysis discussed earlier, can be presented in a way that is familiar and personal. Specifically, I think about risk from two points of view. First, what are the odds that I will achieve my long-term rate of return target. Stated negatively, what is the risk that I will *not* achieve my target? Second, how much of a loss could I experience without going into a state of panic and making a decision that I will later regret. Let's look at these individually.

In Chapters 2 and 3, you learned how to identify the target rate of return necessary to achieve your financial objectives. This was not an academic exercise. The return you earn will impact your ability to educate your children, provide for a comfortable retirement, or pass on an estate to your heirs. Failure to achieve your target will force you to change your plans and could materially affect your quality of life. Your investment program, therefore, should offer high odds of achieving your target. Obviously, nothing is guaranteed in the investment business. But by using statistical analysis, we can estimate the odds that a given portfolio will achieve a specified rate of return. Suppose your target return is 10% per year over a five-year time period. Portfolio A offers better than a 60% chance of achieving that return while portfolio B only provides a 25% chance of success. Without any other information, you would certainly choose portfolio A, because it offers better than even odds of meeting your goals. Unfortunately, the process is not that easy, because portfolio A also provides a greater risk of short-term loss. This is the point at which my second measure of risk comes in.

In an ideal world, every investor would focus on a long time horizon and would create an investment plan strictly on the basis of what was best over the long run. No one would worry about what happened to his portfolio as a result of short-term swings in the market. For better or worse, we do not live in an ideal world, and few investors have the discipline to ignore short-term trends completely. If you discovered that your portfolio had declined 20% during the market crash on October 19, 1987, did you panic? If so, you had taken too much risk in your portfolio. Almost any decision that you make during a panic is likely to turn out to have been ill advised. Therefore, we want to structure your portfolio in such a way that the worst possible short-term loss we can imagine will not cause you to panic and make a radical change in your investments.

Returning to our example, portfolio A provides a higher probability of achieving the 10% target than portfolio B, because it offers a higher long-term average return. Over the years, A will earn on average about 12%, while B will average only about 8%. Unfortunately, in a weak stock market, portfolio A could lose as much as 25% of its value, while the loss on B might be limited to only 7%. So we are back to tradeoffs. Once again, given some forecasts and a bit of fancy mathematics, we can calculate the odds of losing money in any given year as well as the magnitude of the loss you might expect in a "bad" stock or bond market. These estimates will never be perfect, but they provide you with a good sense of the exposure of your portfolio to short-term swings.

The next chapter will bring together these two measures when they are applied to the seven different levels of risk. No rule-of-thumb or simple formula, however, can provide an easy answer as to which level is appropriate for you. Instead, you will have to analyze the tradeoffs involved and determine what seems most comfortable. Your ideal portfolio will offer good odds of achieving your target but with a "worst case" loss that will not unnerve you.

»»   Controlling Risk Through Diversification   ««

Now that you know what risk is, how do you control it? The first and most basic way of dampening risk is through diversification—that is, by the inclusion in your portfolio of a variety of different investments. Capital markets and individual securities

Chart 4.2   Movement of Stock Prices Over Time

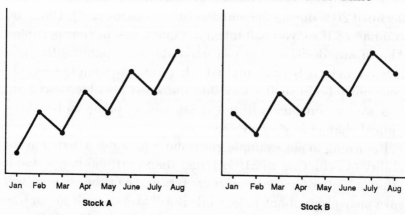

Stock A

Stock B

do not always move in tandem. When some securities are decreasing in value, others are moving in the opposite direction. By combining several different investments in a portfolio, you can smooth out the effect of a violent movement in any one security.

When you hear of an investor who has been wiped out, you can usually be certain that he was "betting the ranch" on one particular investment. In contrast, truly diversified portfolios are rarely devastated irrespective of what is going on in any particular market. If all you learn from this book is to be sure that your portfolio is diversified, I will have served you well.

Almost everyone has seen charts in the _Wall Street Journal_ showing movements in the price of a given stock. Consider the hypothetical stock price patterns in Chart 4.2. As you can see, the prices of both stock A and stock B fluctuate a great deal over time, but when one is in a period of decline, the other tends to rise by an equal amount. A portfolio consisting solely of either one of these stocks would be very volatile. But a portfolio consisting of equal amounts of stock A and stock B would be quite stable. In Chart 4.3, the price patterns of the two stocks are superimposed on one another. The straight line represents the value of the portfolio, which increases at a steady rate.

A portfolio should be diversified at each of two levels. First,

Chart 4.3 A Stable Portfolio

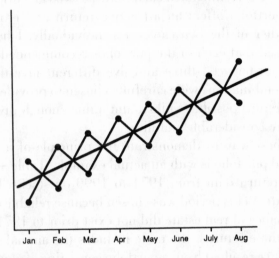

every portfolio should have several *types* of investments—stocks, bonds, gold, or money market securities. Second, within each of these asset categories, the portfolio should hold a number of specific securities. It is critical for an investor to understand diversification, so let's go into detail on each of these levels.

The key to portfolio diversification is to choose investments whose prices do not move in tandem with one another and to add new categories only if they behave differently from those you already hold. Ideally, you would need to choose only two investments that move in exact opposition to one another such as stocks A and B in Chart 4.2. In an imperfect world, however, you must select a number of different categories that move together to a greater or lesser extent. To make this concept clear, suppose your portfolio consists entirely of long-term U.S. government bonds. A surge in inflation almost always causes a rise in interest rates, which in turn causes the price of bonds to fall. Rising inflation, therefore, could have a very negative impact on the value of your portfolio. In contrast, real estate tends to benefit from inflation, because the landlord is able to increase rents. Moreover, inflation causes the replacement cost of real estate to increase, making existing properties more valuable. So, in a period of poor bond returns, real estate is normally in its heyday.

By owning investments in each of these two categories, the combined portfolio offers an attractive return and is more stable than either of the two categories individually. I have already mentioned that each of the portfolios recommended in Chapter 7 includes between three and five different investment types. These combinations were carefully chosen to provide the highest rate of return possible while maintaining enough diversification to ensure considerable stability.

The best way to demonstrate the principle of a diversified, balanced portfolio is with an actual example. Table 4.1 provides annual return data from 1971 to 1990 on stocks, bonds, and real estate. (This period was chosen because reliable data on the performance of real estate did not exist prior to 1971.) In addition to these returns, the table includes the annual return that would have resulted from a portfolio consisting of equal amounts of stocks, bonds, and real estate. Over the entire twenty-year period, the annual return on stocks, as measured by the Standard & Poor's 500, averaged 11.1%. During this period, the stock market provided negative returns in five years. In two of these years, 1973 and 1974, it suffered fairly severe losses of 14.8% and 26.4%, respectively. Thus, if all of your money had been invested in stocks during this period, you would have earned a satisfactory return, albeit with a bumpy ride. On the other hand, suppose you had invested one-third of your money in each category and, once each year, made any changes required to begin the next year with exactly one-third of your funds allocated to each. Over the entire period, your return would have averaged 10.3% per year, which is only .8% less than the return on the pure stock portfolio. But rather than five negative years, you would have experienced only two, and the worst year would have yielded a loss of only 7.4%. The portfolio of three investment categories would have been about 50% less volatile than the Standard & Poor's 500 stock index.

It almost seems too good to be true! By investing in three different categories, you were able to substantially lower the volatility of your portfolio without a large sacrifice of your return. If there is any "free lunch" in investing, this is it! There is no

» **Table 4.1   A Balanced Investment Program** «
(Annual % Returns)

Year	Stocks	Bonds	Real Estate	Equally Weighted Portfolio
1971	14.6%	11.0%	9.2%	11.6%
1972	18.9	7.3	7.5	11.2
1973	(14.8)	1.2	7.5	(2.0)
1974	(26.4)	(3.1)	7.2	(7.4)
1975	37.2	14.6	5.7	19.2
1976	23.6	18.7	9.3	17.2
1977	(7.4)	1.7	10.5	1.6
1978	6.4	(.1)	16.0	7.4
1979	18.2	(4.2)	20.8	11.6
1980	32.3	(2.8)	18.1	15.9
1981	(5.0)	(1.3)	16.9	3.5
1982	21.5	42.5	9.4	24.5
1983	22.4	6.3	13.2	14.0
1984	6.1	16.9	13.1	12.0
1985	31.6	30.1	9.8	23.8
1986	18.6	19.9	6.4	15.0
1987	5.1	(.3)	5.3	3.4
1988	16.6	10.7	7.1	11.5
1989	31.7	14.2	6.0	17.3
1990	(3.1)	6.8	1.2	1.6
Annual Return (compounded)	11.1%	8.9%	9.9%	10.3%
Standard Dev.	17.0%	12.1%	4.9%	8.4%

Source: Cambridge Associates; Frank Russell Company; Calculations by William T. Spitz.

magic involved. The key is to select categories that offer attractive returns but do not move in concert with other investment vehicles.

The second key to diversifying your portfolio is to diversify the investments owned within each category. Let's consider

Chart 4.4   The Relationship Between the Number of Stocks in a Portfolio and Risk

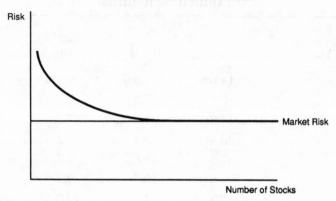

stocks first. To a greater or lesser extent, all stocks are affected by what is happening to the market as a whole. When the market is rising, most stocks will rise with it. But each stock's price is also affected by factors that are unique to its company. For example, a change in upper management will impact one company without having any wider influence on the market. These kinds of occurrences are often quite negative for a company's stockholders. If your stock portfolio consists of only a few holdings, a negative event that impacts the price of one of them could have a major effect on the performance of the entire portfolio. There is always risk in owning stocks. But a portfolio of only a few issues substantially increases that risk without any offsetting increase in return.

Every investor, therefore, should own a number of securities to ensure that his risk is minimized. Chart 4.4 makes this point graphically. As the number of separate stock holdings is increased, the risk declines to that of the overall market, which is both manageable and fairly predictable. A portfolio with as few as twenty different stocks could eliminate all unnecessary risk. But these stocks would have to be carefully chosen to encompass a variety of different industries as well as other financial characteristics. For most investors, a portfolio of at least fifty holdings provides a comfortable level of stock diversification. Similarly, the bond portion of most investors' portfolios should contain a number of issues to reduce the impact of a default. And real estate investments must be diversified by property type and geography.

This principle of diversification is the most important single concept in finance. Large, professionally managed funds frequently hold as many as three hundred different stocks, between thirty and fifty bond issues, and dozens of properties. While you may think it is impossible to achieve this level of diversification in your portfolio, you can, in fact, come close, and this is discussed in later chapters.

»   Controlling Risk Through Asset Allocation   «

The second means of controlling risk is through asset allocation, or the division of your money among different types of investments. Studies show that as much as 90% of the risk and return on your portfolio is related to how much of your money is invested in stocks versus bonds versus other categories. In other words, the individual stocks and bonds you pick are considerably less important than the percentage of your portfolio that is allocated to each category. If you allocate a greater proportion of your portfolio to higher risk investments, the risk and return on the overall portfolio will increase. Similarly, you can decrease risk for your overall portfolio by emphasizing more conservative investments. Once again, let's look at an example.

Historically, stocks have been considered riskier than bonds. Therefore, a portfolio heavily weighted with stocks should have produced a higher return and more risk than one tilted toward bonds, and that is exactly what happened. Table 4.2 summarizes the results of two portfolios for the period from 1901 to 1990. The first consisted of 75% stocks and 25% bonds while the other was structured with these weightings reversed. Both portfolios were rebalanced once a year to keep those weightings constant. As you might have expected, the portfolio that emphasized stocks provided a 2.2% higher rate of return but at the expense of more

Table 4.2   Portfolio Performance 1901–90

	75% Stocks/ 25% Bonds	25% Stocks/ 75% bonds
Average return	8.70%	6.50%
Number of loss years	24	18
Years with losses greater than 10%	9	1
Years with losses greater than 20%	4	0
Worst annual loss	32.9%	12.2%

Source: Cambridge Associates, Inc.; calculations by William T. Spitz

risk. It experienced losses in twenty-four out of ninety years, and it was not all that unusual to experience losses of 10% or even 20%. In contrast, the more conservative portfolio experienced six fewer losses and, more important, was basically insulated from severe declines. This last point is graphically illustrated by the fact that the "worst case" loss on the higher-risk portfolio of almost 33% was more than two and a half times the 12.2% decline on the more conservative fund.

»»   **Risk in Perspective**   «««

To recap, there are two important dimensions of risk. Over the long haul, your investment program should offer the highest possible odds of meeting your return objective. Stated differently, you want to minimize the chance of coming up short. While all investors should focus only on the long term, no one is immune from short-term swings in emotion. Therefore, you must design your portfolio to prevent a short-term loss that might cause you to panic and jeopardize the ultimate success of your program.

Risk is controllable through diversification and asset mix. By diversifying your fund, you can eliminate a great deal of the risk inherent in investing. It is also possible to fine-tune the remaining risk by emphasizing higher- or lower-risk investment categories.

While you can never totally divorce yourself from risk, these techniques will put you in the driver's seat and you will control the risk you assume.

Employing these techniques, however, is not an exact science. The process of picking an appropriate risk level is very subjective, and risk-control techniques cannot guarantee that you will never experience an unpleasant surprise. But building your program on these principles will place you way ahead of most people in controlling your financial destiny.

»» _____ **Key Points to Remember** _____ ««

- A "risky" portfolio is one that does not provide a high enough return to accomplish your objectives or is likely to suffer a temporary loss that would cause you to panic.
- Happily, risk is controllable through diversification and by carefully dividing your funds among different types of investments.

CHAPTER 5

HOW MUCH RISK SHOULD YOU TAKE?

You shouldn't own common stocks if a decrease in
their value by 50% would cause you to feel stress.
—Warren Buffet

》》 《《

The time has come for you to make the tough decisions! The
choices you are about to make will set the tone for your investment program and will ultimately determine how rich you get
and whether it happens sooner or later. If the goals you developed in Chapters 2 and 3 were both specific and achievable, you
are now ready to determine how much risk is associated with
them. If you took the "back door" approach to setting your
objectives, you must now select the maximum level of risk you
can tolerate. But in either case, you will not be able to proceed
any further in creating and implementing your program until
you have chosen one of the seven risk levels that are explained
in this chapter. While I provide information and guidance to
help you, the final decision about risk must be yours.

As has been briefly mentioned, two individuals with identical
financial circumstances might have widely different investment
portfolios because of their personal attitudes toward risk. The
amount of risk that is appropriate for you to assume is a function
of *both* your financial circumstances and your emotional
makeup. Evaluating your financial status is fairly easy. The

tough part is assessing your emotional status: How much of a risk taker are you?

We begin this step in the process by considering the concept of the investor life cycle that describes the needs of the "typical" investor at each stage in life. You should have no difficulty placing yourself in the appropriate stage. At each, I recommend a specific risk level for "aggressive," "moderate-risk," and "low-risk" investors. Some individuals can quickly identify with one of these categories and are ready to move on. In case you're not sure where you fit, I have provided considerable background information on assessing your financial and emotional capacity to take risk. With this added information, you should be able to review the recommended risk levels for each stage in the investor life cycle and make your own decision. Finally, we will examine actual risk-and-return data for each of the seven levels to ensure that you are comfortable with your choice.

» The Investor Life Cycle «

The investor life cycle is based on the notion that the financial needs of most individuals change over the course of their lives, and those changes follow a pattern that is fairly consistent. None of us like to think that we exactly fit a given pattern or mold, but the investor life cycle does accurately portray the financial seasons we all live through. Different financial experts divide this cycle into different phases and label them differently. I use four stages that cover your life from early adulthood through retirement.

I call the first stage the *household formation* period. Normally, this phase covers individuals from age twenty to about thirty, but the span has lengthened somewhat in recent years due to the tendency of young adults to marry later and defer having children until after their careers are well established.

Unfortunately, most of us enter this stage with essentially no financial assets, and in fact, many have substantial debts that were accumulated during college and graduate school. Moreover, most couples begin this stage with relatively few worldly goods. The household formation period, therefore, is usually characterized by consumption rather than by saving. During this period, most couples begin to buy household possessions, acquire their first homes, and spend a never-ending stream of money on the many needs of children.

Since very few persons have any assets at this point, the primary financial goal during this stage is to acquire sufficient life, health, and disability income insurance to ensure that the family has a secure source of income. Any saving you are able to do thereafter should first be directed toward accumulating an emergency reserve. Most financial planners suggest that you should have between three and six months of normal income available in a bank or money market fund to meet any emergency needs. Once you accumulate this reserve, any additional savings are generally directed toward acquiring sufficient funds to make a down payment on a house.

The risk tolerance of most investors is very low during most of this stage. Emergency reserves and your "down payment" fund should normally be invested in certificates of deposit, Treasury Bills, or a high-quality money market fund. However, if you are lucky enough to have any extra funds to invest for long-term growth, you should be willing to take quite a bit of risk, because your time horizon may be as long as forty years. For example, any contributions made on your behalf to a retirement plan should certainly be invested in one of the higher-risk options. (This will be considered later on.)

I have labeled the next stage in life the *early accumulation* phase. This period normally covers ages ranging from about thirty to forty-five or so. At this point in life, many persons are firmly established in their careers and have enjoyed promotions and a resultant growth in their income. Moreover, most couples will have purchased a residence by this time, and most of the costs of filling it with furniture are in the past. During this stage, therefore, many young adults have their first ability to do some serious saving. In fact, it becomes critical for them to begin putting away money because college education is just around the corner. The example in Chapter 2 showed just how difficult a task providing funds for college expenses can be. It is also important to begin saving for retirement because any funds put aside during this period will benefit from twenty to thirty-five years of compound interest, which makes the task much easier.

The early-accumulation stage is usually the period in which you can and should take maximum risk in your portfolio. If you are successful at investing, the benefit will be tremendous because of your long time horizon. Also, you still have plenty of years to recover from a poor investment. The bulk of your portfolio should be invested in stocks and a large percentage of your stocks should consist of smaller companies that offer high potential returns. While this book will not deal with options, futures, and other similarly aggressive investments, this is the stage in life at which those asset types make the most sense. Similarly, for investors who are inclined to use borrowed money or "margin," now's the time.

The next stage in life is the *maximum accumulation* phase, which usually spans the period from age forty-five to about sixty. Since many individuals choose to extend their careers beyond age sixty-five, however, this stage is frequently extended. Most workers reach the peak of their careers during this phase of life and enjoy the highest level of income that they are likely to obtain. In addition, many of the major financial obligations in life, such as education and mortgages, are history by the middle years of this stage. Therefore, the combination of peak earnings and diminished obligations should allow one to maintain a high living standard and to put aside significant amounts of money. It is during this period that you are most likely to accumulate sufficient funds to meet your retirement needs and, if you are lucky, to build a sizable estate to pass on to your heirs.

Most investors still have the ability to assume a high level of risk during this phase because of peak earnings and a time horizon that is still quite long. However, the natural tendency to become more conservative with age begins to cause many investors to become more concerned about "keeping what they have" as opposed to "making a bundle." Therefore, it is not unusual for investors to tone down their risk level a little bit as compared to the previous stage. At this point, your portfolio should remain diversified and balanced with a heavy emphasis on equities. To dampen your risk just a bit, it may make sense to decrease the emphasis on small stocks in favor of the larger blue-chip variety. If you have been engaging in high-risk strategies of one kind or another, you probably want to eliminate them and adopt more passive strategies.

The final stage in life encompasses the years immediately prior to *retirement* as well as the retirement years themselves. While this stage traditionally began at about age sixty, the recent tendency toward longer working careers may postpone its onset in many instances. During this period, the financial strategy of most investors reverses. Rather than accumulating funds, retirees usually draw upon their savings. Rather than seeking to increase their net worth, most retirees are concerned primarily with avoiding serious losses. Finally, the primary investment objective of most retirees is the generation of maximum income.

Conventional wisdom suggests that retired individuals should structure their portfolios in a highly cautious manner and should be unwilling to accept any significant risk. Actually, a great deal of logic supports this view. The time horizon of retirees is certainly shorter than that of younger investors, and their natural tendency toward conservatism is an important emotional factor. Moreover, the fact that retirees are no longer earning a salary places additional demands on their portfolio as the principal, sometimes sole, source of income. For all of these reasons, investors should exercise great care during this stage. Still, there is great danger in adopting too cautious an approach!

The dragon is always lurking in the distance. Inflation can have a dramatic effect on the quality of life during retirement unless you are prepared for it. As was mentioned in Chapter 2, the combined life expectancy of a husband and wife, upon reaching age sixty-five, is almost twenty-five years. If annual inflation averages 5%, a pension of $50,000 per year will buy goods and services worth only $14,765 at the end of a twenty-five-year time horizon. In other words, the retirees' living standard would decline by almost 70% during their senior years. Therefore, you must invest your funds in a way that will offset the ravages of inflation. The portfolios recommended later for risk levels five and six answer this need. These portfolios, while designed to provide relative stability and a high degree of current income, still contain enough exposure to stocks and real estate to provide an effective inflation hedge.

» **Recommended Risk Levels** «

The investor life cycle concept is relatively simple and straight-forward, and I doubt that you had much difficulty placing your-self in the appropriate stage. However, determining what actual amount of risk you should take during each phase is not quite as easy. Table 5.1 provides some guidance on this question.

An individual who perceives himself as fairly aggressive would begin the household formation period at risk level five. As his career flourished and he began a significant savings program, it would be appropriate to increase the risk level to one and to maintain that level through the maximum accumulation period. During his later years, he would probably revert to risk level five, which is more conservative but should still provide an important hedge against inflation. At the other extreme, a very cautious person might find that risk level four is about as aggressive as he ever wants to be. Most investors find that the medium risk

» **Table 5.1 Recommended Risk Levels** «

	Level of Aggressiveness		
Life Stage	High	Medium	Low
Household formation	5	6	7
Early accumulation	1	2–3	4
Maximum accumulation	1	2–4	5
Retirement years	5	6	7

levels meet their needs during all four stages of the investor life cycle.

If you can quickly determine which level of aggressiveness best describes your needs and personality, then the appropriate risk category is dictated by Table 5.1. However, many investors are not really sure where they fit. To help them along, why don't we consider the key factors that influence the amount of risk you should take?

» **Financial Capacity to Take Risk** «

The first matter you need to consider is the relationship between your investment program and your total financial picture. In general terms, an individual who enjoys a secure financial status can afford to take more risk in his investment portfolio than someone whose situation is precarious. Thus, you should consider your circumstances to identify financial variables that may justify your being somewhat aggressive with your portfolio. Several are listed below.

» **Factors That Allow More Risk in a Portfolio** «

- Availability of other assets outside the portfolio
- Potential inheritance
- High level of earned income
- Job security
- Substantial insurance protection
- Capacity to borrow
- Income of a spouse

First, you can certainly afford to take more risk in your portfolio if you have other assets that can serve as a cushion. For example, you may have real estate assets, an interest in a personal or family business, or perhaps a trust fund of which you are the beneficiary. If you are covered by your employer's pension plan, and if it takes away the pressure of saving for retirement, that could allow you to focus your investment program on other goals. Similarly, the prospect of a substantial inheritance provides an alternative source of financial security. Any of these factors gives you added flexibility in assessing your ability to tolerate fluctuations in the value of your portfolio—that is, to assume risk.

Since most of us do not have substantial assets on which we can rely, current income from employment represents the only source of financial security. If your current income is high relative to the assets in your investment program, you can take a significant amount of risk because any serious loss in your portfolio will not impact your current life-style and could be replenished if necessary. Conversely, if you are barely scraping by, you will want to be more cautious about taking risk. In addition to considering the amount of your income, you should also think about your job security. Many individuals who considered their positions secure are now unemployed as a result of severe competition in almost every sector of our economy. If you have any doubts about the safety of your job, you will do well to approach your investment program cautiously, since your portfolio might be called on to feed the family.

Related to the amount and security of your job income is the amount of insurance protection you maintain. If your dependents are well protected by both life and disability insurance, you can afford to take more risk in your portfolio because it will not have to serve as their sole source of income. Finally, you can afford to take more risk if you have substantial borrowing capacity because, in the event of an emergency, you can resort to credit rather than drawing upon your investment portfolio for assets.

Just as some situational factors warrant greater risk in a portfolio, other financial circumstances point one toward greater caution. First, the reverse of any of the factors in the above list might indicate a lower-risk approach. For example, an insecure job or the inability to purchase sufficient insurance represent caution flags. Some additional factors that usually steer one toward low levels of risk are listed below.

»»   Factors That Call for Less Risk in a Portfolio   ««

- Large number of dependents
- High level of personal debt
- Lack of liquidity, no emergency fund
- Poor or questionable health

In simple terms, a single person should be able to take more risk than someone who carries financial responsibility for others. However, this issue can usually be dealt with through insurance and other sources of income protection.

A high level of personal debt entails potential risk to your financial status, since a loss of current income could result in your inability to pay interest due creditors, which could lead to personal bankruptcy. When you already have high risk in your life, it makes sense to have as few other sources of risk—such as that assumed in your portfolio—as possible. Similarly, if you do not have sufficient funds to meet an emergency, your portfolio must serve as your cushion; thus, you should seek stability of principal and relative certainty of return. Finally, an investor's ill health usually represents the most compelling circumstance for cautious risk taking. This situation is generally associated with secure, short-term investments.

Since every person's financial situation is different, no formula can tell you exactly how to evaluate each of these factors. But by considering your circumstances in relation to them, you should be able to quickly gauge whether your financial capacity to take risk is high or low. Knowing whether the several factors in your financial situation point toward high or low risk is important. But we have not yet considered the most important variable: time.

»»   Your Greatest Ally   ««

As an investor, time is your greatest ally. The most important determinant of your financial capacity to take risk is the length of your time horizon. An individual who is saving for a retirement that is still twenty years down the road obviously has a very different point of view from that of a sixty-four-year-old. Time is important for two reasons. First, as the length of your horizon increases, you can have more confidence in the rate of return you will earn. Second, a long time frame gives you plenty of opportunity to recover from a short-term disaster. Let's focus on each of these.

Table 5.2 provides some fascinating information on the performance of stocks for various time periods over the past ninety years. After taking a quick look at it, you might wonder how there could have been eighty-one ten-year periods between 1901 and 1990. This table is based on rolling periods, which means that the first ten-year period was 1901 through 1910, the second was 1902 through 1911, and so on. The same procedure was used to derive the five-year and twenty-year periods.

As you can see, there is great uncertainty regarding the return you will earn over a one-year period. While the annual return averaged 9.4% from 1901 to 1990, the actual in any given year ranged between 54% and −43.4%. However, as the time frame lengthens, the range of annual returns narrows considerably. For five-year periods, returns varied between 28.7% and −12.5%, or a range less than half that for one-year returns. And for periods of twenty years, the range narrowed to the degree that returns fell between 16.9% and 3.1%.

»   Table 5.2   Historical Returns on Stocks 1901–90   «

	1-Year Periods	5-Year Periods	10-Year Periods	20-Year Periods
Number of periods	90	86	81	71
Maximum *annual* return	54.0%	28.7%	20.1%	16.9%
Minimum *annual* return	(43.4)%	(12.5)%	(.9)%	3.1%
Number of periods with negative returns	27	9	1	0

Source: Cambridge Associates, Inc.

These historical results clearly indicate that a long time horizon should give you added comfort that the return you actually
experience should come close to long-range averages. Yet it is
important to realize that considerable variation in returns still
occurs over periods as long as twenty years. It was for this reason
that I suggested in Chapter 3 that an investment program should
be based on forecasts of returns over a thirty- to fifty-year period.

You should also note from Table 5.2 that only one ten-year
period (out of eighty-one) resulted in a loss of money invested
in stocks, and that never has a twenty-year period provided a
negative return. Once again, this should add to your confidence
as a truly long-term investor.

So, now that we know how stocks have behaved in the past,
what about the future? Chart 5.1 provides a graphic display of
the range of returns you might expect. It is based on my long-
range forecast of an 11% average return on stocks, and it assumes that stocks will be about as volatile as they have been in
recent years. This picture is very similar to the pattern illustrated
in Table 5.2. While you can certainly expect considerable fluctuation from year to year, a long time horizon will greatly increase the odds that your actual return will be in the vicinity of
the 11% forecast. Similar charts for bonds or Treasury Bills
would show the same sort of pattern, though the ranges would
be quite a bit narrower. Narrower ranges would result because
these investments tend to be much less volatile than stocks, and
that adds to the predictability of return.

Here's the point: If you are one year away from retirement,
you probably want to avoid high-risk investments because of the
great uncertainty regarding what could happen during the next
year. You do not want to spend your last year prior to retirement
worrying about whether your return will be 54% or −43%. On
the other hand, a thirty-year-old with thirty-five years until
retirement should have a high comfort level that his stocks will
earn an annual return in the neighborhood of 11%.

The second reason that time is so important is that it affords
the ability to recover from a short-term loss. If you are two years
away from retirement and your portfolio declines 50% in the

Chart 5.1   Expected Return Over Various Time Horizons

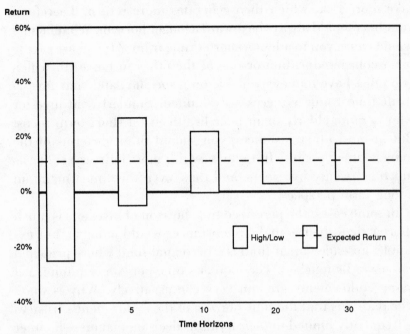

first year, it must double in the next year just to get back to where you were. In contrast, a serious loss during the early stages of a long-term investment plan can usually be recovered without much difficulty. For example, we will assume that your plan calls for you to earn 10% per year for the next twenty-five years in order to meet your ultimate objective. Suppose you do earn 10% for five years but suffer a 25% decline in year six. During the remaining nineteen years, a 12.2% return is necessary to overcome that loss and reach your original objective. In contrast, if the 25% decline occurs in year sixteen, the required return in the remaining nine years is 14.8%. While 12.2% is probably still achievable, 14.8% pushes the outer limits. Moreover, achieving the 14.8% return will require a high degree of risk just at the time that you most likely want to adopt a cautious approach to investing.

How do you know what your time horizon is? You should begin with the assumption that you will invest for the rest of your life and then consider any reasons that you should shorten that time frame. Remember, a longer time frame allows you to take more risk, which then generates more return. Therefore, your bias should always be toward a longer horizon. What factors would cause you to adopt a shorter time frame? If you are saving for a college education or one of the other instances in which you must have money available on a specific date, your investment time frame is necessarily limited. Similarly, an investor who is quite elderly or in poor health has a short-term focus. But in most other instances, you should think in terms of the longest time possible. In today's world, most retirees live for as much as twenty-five years, and thus, even they must maintain a long-term perspective.

In some cases, the perceived time horizon of investors is much shorter than their actual circumstances would indicate. For example, an endowment fund is a perpetual fund whose principal can never be touched. Therefore, its time horizon is infinite. Yet many endowments are run very conservatively. Why is that? The reason is that the time horizon of the endowment's trustees is frequently limited to *their* terms as decision makers—in other words, they do not want to risk a disaster during their tenure. The same is also true of many corporate pension funds, in which the actual time horizon of the fund is close to infinity but it is operated as if the time frame is equal to the career of the pension-fund officer. The point is that frequently the time horizon suggested by an investor's age and financial status becomes blurred by his perceived ability to bear risk. This blurring is a function of investor emotions, which is the other key factor in determining how much risk one should take.

»   Emotional Capacity to Take Risk   «

Assessing your emotional makeup may be the hardest step in the development of an investment program. Some individuals think of themselves as risk takers, but when the going gets tough, they discover that their stomachs weren't as strong as they thought. On the other hand, many investors have an inordinate fear of short-term loss, and this fear causes them to sacrifice a good deal of return unnecessarily.

You might begin by evaluating your basic personality in the most objective way you can. Are you a Type A person, who is frequently impatient and likely to react to external events in a take-charge manner? In times of stress, do you feel compelled to do something? If so, you may want to dampen the risk in your portfolio, because you are a good candidate to get disgusted in a weak market and sell at the bottom.

Are you prone to panic? While it is never easy to answer this question objectively, you ought to think about how you would react to a steep decline in your portfolio. Would you lose sleep over it? Would a decline in your net worth impact your job performance or home life?

One clue to your likely behavior may be the way you reacted to the stock market crash in 1987. As you will recall, all of the news media portrayed an environment characterized by gloom and even outright panic. Financial experts made dire predictions of further declines in the stock market, and many economists opined that the 500-point decline in the Dow Jones average would certainly push the economy into a recession. If ever you had an opportunity to panic, that was it! If you survived that episode in good emotional shape, the odds are pretty favorable that you can handle whatever cards the markets deal you.

Just as your financial needs change over the course of your life, it is perfectly normal for your emotional status to change as well. Early in our lives, none of us acknowledge our mortality, and most of us think that risk only applies to others. Therefore, many younger investors are emotionally comfortable taking a lot of risk in addition to their natural financial capacity to "swing for the fence." Most individuals grow more conservative with age, however, and it is perfectly normal to want to avoid spending one's later years worrying about investments. The point is that it is perfectly normal and acceptable for your emotional capacity for risk to diminish over time. One reason that your portfolio should be adjusted periodically is to reflect these changes in your ability and willingness to bear risk. But you should never decide to become more cautious right after a market decline, and it is equally dangerous to become a gunslinger as the market rises. In either case, you will probably make a serious mistake.

Having considered the financial and emotional factors just described, you should now have a good sense of whether you are an "aggressive," "moderate-risk," or "low-risk" investor. At this point, you need only review Table 5.4 to identify the proper risk level for your stage in the investor life cycle.

Before we proceed with the remaining four steps in creating your program, we should take a quick look at the actual amount of risk and return associated with the level you have chosen. Hopefully, your choice will provide enough return to accomplish your financial objectives without subjecting you to a temporary loss that would unnerve you. But if either the risk or the return side of the tradeoff seems uncomfortable, you will have to reevaluate your choice.

»   Risk:Return Tradeoffs   «

In Chapter 3, I forecasted annual returns on various types of investments ranging from 6% on U.S. Treasury Bills to 14% on small capitalization stocks. Chapter 7 presents an "ideal" or recommended portfolio for each of the seven levels of risk and these portfolios contain between three and five different investment types in various proportions. By combining the return forecasts and the recommended weighting in each asset type, we can estimate the future return on a given portfolio. For example, let's assume that a portfolio consists of 60% stocks and 40% bonds, and further, we expect returns on those two categories of 11% and 8%, respectively. The expected return on the portfolio is 9.8% (11 times .6 plus 8 times .4). Using this approach, Table 5.3 shows the return you can actually expect on each of the seven portfolios.

These rates represent the return side of the risk:return tradeoff. A doctor friend of mine recently suggested that he "wasn't necessarily trying to hit a home run with his portfolio, a 15% or

>> **Table 5.3 Long-Term Rates of Return for** <<
Each Risk Level (Annual Returns)

Risk Classification	Higher Risk – – – – – – – – – – – Lower Risk						
	1	2	3	4	5	6	7
"Best Guess" Return	12.3%	11.7%	11.0%	10.6%	9.9%	9.1%	8.2%

Source: William T. Spitz Estimates

20% return would be fine." Clearly, the doctor is going to be disappointed. There are other approaches to investing that could conceivably achieve these high rates of return, but they do not belong in the core of a long-term investment program. The core of your program should contain portfolios that are highly diversified and provide a very attractive balance between risk and return.

If you calculated specific return targets in Chapter 2, you can now focus right in on the risk level necessary to achieve those targets. For example, the college savings example necessitated a 14.2% return, which can be achieved only at risk level one (if at all), while the retirement savings target of 9.05% could be met by any risk level except number seven. In considering risk levels for your investment program, you should choose one that offers good odds of achieving your return target. Stated another way, a portfolio that is not likely to achieve your goals is risky. If you create a portfolio that is expected to earn 9% per year, it is not very likely to earn 12% unless your assumptions regarding the future prove to be invalid. Using statistical analysis, we can calculate the odds that each of the seven portfolios will actually achieve a certain rate of return. In order not to overwhelm you with numbers, this information is included as Appendix II, which shows the odds that each risk level will earn a return between 8% and 14%. For example, these odds reveal that risk level one offers a 63% chance of earning 10% while number seven provides only a 27% chance. Therefore, if your objective is in fact 10%, you can only get better than even odds of achieving your goal at one of the higher risk levels.

The most important determinant of which risk level is appropriate for you is the amount of short-term loss you could sustain without going into a state of panic. It is virtually impossible to predict what might happen to each of these seven portfolios on any given day or even in any given quarter. No one could have predicted that stock prices would fall more than 20% on October 19, 1987, for instance. But we can make some educated guesses about what could happen over a one-year period.

Table 5.4 shows that portfolio one will lose money about 21% of the time, or in about one out of every five years. So, if you choose this portfolio, you will suffer a decline in your investments on a regular basis. Can you handle this? If not, you should move down the risk scale. At the other extreme, portfolio seven will

» Table 5.4 Probability Analysis «

Risk Classification	Higher Risk – – – – – – – – – – – – Lower Risk						
	1	2	3	4	5	6	7
Odds of losing money in any given year	21%	20%	19%	17%	15%	11%	10%
Odds of losing more than 10% in any given year	7%	6%	4%	3%	2%	1%	NM
Odds of losing more than 15% in any given year	4%	3%	2%	1%	NM	NM	NM

NM = Not Meaningful (less than 1%)
Source: William T. Spitz Estimates

only lose money about 10% of the time, or once in ten years. You should also note that portfolio one will lose at least 10% of its value about 7% of the time, or once every fourteen years, and it could lose at least 15% once every twenty-five years or so. In contrast, portfolios five through seven are quite unlikely to decline by 10% or more. In the broader scheme of things, you should understand that all of these are fairly low risk by most standards, as a result of diversification and careful construction. However, there is still a chance of a good drubbing in a severe market decline. Table 5.5 provides an indication of how bad that drubbing could be.

This table represents a worst-case scenario that is defined as the greatest annual loss that would be expected over a one hundred year time frame. As indicated, portfolio one might decline by as much as 23%. This may or may not sound bad to you, but how would you react if it actually happened? If you could not handle it, you had better look at one of the lower risk portfolios. These losses are not very likely, but they do happen. Therefore, be sure to pick a level of worst-case loss that would not cause you to jump out of the window, as many investors did in 1929.

Perhaps the best way to look at all of this data is to combine both risk and return in a single table so that the tradeoffs involved can be compared directly. Table 5.6 brings together the key factors discussed thus far.

This table may be the most important one in this book, because it graphically demonstrates the tradeoff between risk and return. At one extreme, portfolio one offers the highest potential return at 12.3%, but it is likely to suffer a decline in about one

»»   **Table 5.5   "Worst Case" Losses**   «««

Risk Classification	Higher Risk 1	2	3	4	5	Lower Risk 6	7
Loss	(23)%	(21)%	(18)%	(15)%	(12)%	(8)%	(7)%

Source: William T. Spitz Estimates

out of every five years, and could lose as much as 23% of its
value in a really bad year. At the other extreme, portfolio seven
is expected to lose money in only one out of ten years and its
worst-case loss is fairly modest at 7%. But portfolio seven will
likely earn only about 8.2% per year on average. Remember,
you can't have it both ways!

In most cases, the risk-and-return data presented in Table 5.6
will confirm the risk level you chose after reviewing the investor
life cycle. But what if your chosen risk:return tradeoff does not
provide enough return to meet your needs? Obviously, you will
have to move to one of the higher risk:return combinations. Can
you live with the added risk? Similarly, if your initial choice now
seems too risky, you must move down the risk scale. Can you
still accomplish your financial goals with a lower level of return?
Only you can evaluate these tradeoffs. Remember, your selection
is not to be carved in stone; it is appropriate to review it once
each year and whenever extraordinary events in your financial
life happen. But your choice should change only a few times over
the course of your life and not whimsically—for instance, in
response to what happened in the stock market last quarter.

I want to caution you again that risk taking must be your

»»   Table 5.6   Projected Risk and Return   ««

| Risk Classification | Higher Risk – – – – – – – – – – – – Lower Risk | | | | | | |
	1	2	3	4	5	6	7
Projected return	12.3%	11.7%	11.0%	10.6%	9.9%	9.1%	8.2%
Odds of losing money in any one year	21%	20%	19%	17%	15%	11%	10%
Worst-case loss	(23)%	(21)%	(18)%	(15)%	(12)%	(8)%	(7)%

Source: William T. Spitz Estimates

decision. You should not be overly influenced by what the "typical" investor does. I can think of dozens of exceptions to each of the general guidelines about how much risk is appropriate. For example, retired individuals are normally expected to invest rather conservatively. But the primary hobby of some older people is speculating in the stock market. As long as this speculation is confined to a portion of their assets, this risk is perfectly normal and acceptable. Similarly, some younger people are dead set against taking any risk despite their financial ability to do so. Once again, this stance is perfectly acceptable. So, however you make these difficult decisions, make sure that you have captured your financial and emotional circumstances as well as you can evaluate them.

By now, you should have selected one of the risk:return combinations, which means that you have completed the first of the five steps toward creating and implementing your investment program. You will be glad to know that this first step is by far the most difficult, because you are forced to make some tough choices. At this point, you should know what you are trying to accomplish with your investment program and what level of return will be necessary to achieve your objective. You should also have a strong sense of whether your target is reasonable and achievable. Most important, you now have a good indication of how much loss your portfolio could suffer in a dismal year. If you have done a good job of analyzing your psyche, you should be able to live through this loss when it actually occurs. Clearly, you won't enjoy it, but neither will you panic and make a poor decision.

You are now ready to begin implementing your program. In step two, you will decide which of the many categories of investments should be included in your portfolio, and in step three, you will focus on what percentage of your funds should be allocated to each category. You will be glad to know that I do all of the work for you in each of these steps. But you must pay close attention! The next two chapters hold the keys to achieving both attractive *and* stable rates of return.

>> ——————— **Key Points to Remember** ——————— <<

- The amount of risk you should take is related to your general financial health as well as your emotional capacity to survive a serious market decline.
- The most important single determinant of your ability to take risk is the length of your time horizon.
- Most individuals find that the investor life cycle accurately characterizes their needs, and should, therefore, accept the risk levels recommended in Table 5.4.

CHAPTER 6

A CORNUCOPIA OF INVESTMENT OPPORTUNITIES

A man's wisdom is most conspicuous where he is able to distinguish among dangers and make choice of the least.

—Machiavelli

》》 《《

This book began with a reference to "sensory overload," a state of mental paralysis that can be brought on by too much noise, activity, or information. While virtually every aspect of the investment world entails both excessive and contradictory information, perhaps the most difficult thing to handle is the variety of recommendations that emanates from Wall Street on a continuous basis. During any given week, the financial press quotes a number of experts, each of whom recommends a different type of investment. Most investors are familiar with traditional alternatives such as stocks, bonds, and money market instruments. But what about all of the other categories? Should your portfolio hold gold? What about real estate, commodities, options, and limited partnerships? Obviously, there are dozens of different types of assets, but any portfolio is necessarily limited to a few of them. How do you distinguish between all of these categories and which ones are right for you? Once again, you probably feel a case of sensory overload coming on.

Relax! By carefully choosing a limited number of categories, we should be able to accomplish our objective of achieving attractive rates of return and the maximum stability possible for those rates. As is the case with most facets of investing, selecting the optimal number of investment categories for your portfolio is a balancing act. On the one hand, I have argued vigorously (and I hope persuasively) that diversification is essential, for it is the investor's primary means of controlling risk. This principle calls for the inclusion of a large number of asset classes, or categories, in any portfolio. On the other hand, some investments are redundant in that they do not add any additional diversification to the categories most investors already hold. Moreover, a large number of categories can lead to excessive accounting headaches that prevent you from effectively managing and controlling your investment program. Large pools of capital, such as pension funds and endowments, frequently have as many as a dozen different categories, whereas the average individual investor probably has two or three. While this matter certainly has no right or wrong answer, my own experience as well as a fair amount of research indicates that between three and five classes can provide sufficient diversification. Specifically, I recommend five different asset types for most of the seven risk levels. By carefully choosing your investments, you can capture the bulk of the diversification the big funds enjoy without creating a mountain of paper that keeps you befuddled.

» Criteria for Selection «

The asset classes I recommend later in this chapter were chosen according to three criteria. The first is availability and manageability. Obviously, we only want to consider investments that are available to even the smallest investor. Not only should an investment category be readily available, but it should also involve a minimum of accounting or administrative effort. In other words, it should be easily manageable. For starters, most individuals are precluded from investing in leveraged buyouts, oil and gas, venture capital, and direct ownership of real estate because they require large minimum investments. Similarly, direct investments in oil and gas entail a blizzard of paperwork as well as a variety of complex legal and accounting issues. In contrast, the portfolios recommended in the next chapter can be constructed with as little as $10,000 and can be managed with a few hours of annual paperwork.

The second criterion calls for the selection of a package of investments that offers as much stability as possible. This goal is accomplished by selecting categories whose prices do not move in tandem with one another. In Chapter 4, I cited the example of bonds and real estate as assets whose values tend to move in opposite directions in response to an increase in inflation. As you will recall, a portfolio consisting of both of these assets would be more stable than either one in isolation. You might reasonably ask why you should not simply use these two categories and ignore the rest. After all, since they do tend to move in opposite directions, they should result in a highly stable portfolio. The problem is that the returns on these categories are lower than the returns on other categories. Thus, various combinations of bonds and real estate probably will not produce a return high enough to meet the needs of some investors. Additional categories must be included to give the portfolio extra kick. Unfortunately, the case of bonds and real estate is unusual; most other categories of investments move in the same direction rather than in opposition. To gain sufficient diversification, we are, therefore, forced to include four or five categories, but we will choose those whose price movements have the lowest correlation.

The final criterion is, in some ways, the most important because it revolves around the idea of hedging your bets. As you know, this book is based on the premise that the best way to accumulate wealth is to consistently earn reasonable rates of return while avoiding disasters. If each of us could predict the future, we could easily avoid any looming disaster by an adept change in investment strategy. But few of us are lucky enough to have a crystal ball. Therefore, you must structure your portfolio in such a way that it can survive in any conceivable environment regardless of whether we can foresee it or not—that is, your portfolio must be able to perform acceptably irrespective of the economic and market circumstances. How do you accomplish this? The first step is to identify a range of possible economic environments; then, select for each environment one asset type that has historically performed well in that economy. By including just three asset types in your portfolio it should always be protected from financial disasters—although not necessarily from occasional losses. This "hedge your bets" philosophy of investing was first articulated by the consulting firm of Cambridge Associates, Inc., and is now followed by most large, institutional funds.

»   A Minimum of Three Types of Investments   «

There are as many ways of classifying the economic outlook as there are economists. Is the economy in a growth phase or a recession? Are interest rates rising or falling? Is corporate America enjoying growing profits or are corporate earnings headed south? What about unemployment? Obviously, you can easily wear yourself out trying to come up with the best means of assessing the condition of the economy. But the most comprehensive way of thinking about this issue involves our old friend the dragon. We first assume that the economy can always be classified by one of three conditions: high inflation, low/moderate inflation, or deflation. In fact, Americans have experienced at least two periods of each of these conditions during this century. The next step is to identify one asset class that should do well in each of these different environments. Real estate usually performs well during periods of high inflation, stocks normally excel during periods of low or moderate inflation, and certain types of bonds are winners in a deflationary environment. Therefore, every investor should strongly consider holding at least these three categories to protect their assets. Why don't we go into some detail about each category.

High Inflation

There is no generally accepted rule of thumb as to what constitutes "high" inflation. For our purposes, I define it as a period in which prices are increasing at a rate equal to about twice the historical level of 3.1%. Defined in this way, we can state that there have been three periods of high inflation during this century. In all three, the surge in inflation was accompanied by a rise in interest rates, which, in turn, caused a decline in bond prices. Therefore, bonds almost always provide poor returns during a period of rapid increases in the Consumer Price Index (CPI).

The performance of stocks in high inflation environments has been mixed. From 1916 to 1919, a period when inflation averaged 16.3%, stocks provided an annual return of 5.3%, which means they lost 11% in real, or after-inflation, terms. Similarly, stocks earned 5% annually from 1973 to 1981, but this return represented a loss in purchasing power of 4% after adjusting for inflation of approximately 9%. On the other hand, stocks provided an average return of 10.6% per year during the wartime inflation from 1941 to 1948. After adjusting for consumer price increases averaging 6.9% for that period, the 10.6% gain represented a positive real return of about 3.7%. Because of these variances, we don't really know what to expect from stocks during an inflationary environment, and therefore they cannot serve as a reliable hedge.

One asset class that does provide a hedge is real estate. Investments in real estate usually realize high returns during a period of surging consumer prices. Several characteristics of real estate account for this result. First, an office building or apartment complex usually has a number of different tenants whose leases mature at different times. In just about every year, some tenants are forced to renew. During a period of high inflation, the landlord is often able to increase rents on these maturing leases more rapidly than during a low-inflation environment. While some costs of operating the building also rise with inflation, others are fixed, and that frequently results in an increase in the profits of the landlord. In addition, an increase in the operating profit on a building increases its value and may allow the owner to sell it at a particularly attractive price. The second source of inflation protection in some types of real estate stems from the owner's participation in the revenues of the tenants. For example, the owner of a shopping mall generally receives a base rent plus a percentage of the retailers' sales. In response to rising inflation, for instance, a department store raises prices on the goods it sells. Those higher prices result in higher revenues to the store and also to increased participating rent to the landlord. Finally, inflation raises the cost of constructing new buildings, which, in turn, increases the value of existing buildings. These factors do not guarantee that real estate will always provide an effective inflation hedge. Other critical factors, such as the number of unoccupied buildings, need to be considered. But historically, this asset class has been up to the task.

The last major period of high inflation in the United States was from 1973 to 1981 when the CPI rose at an annual rate of 9.2%. During that period, both stocks and bonds provided lackluster returns, while real estate exceeded inflation by approximately 3.1% per year. The most widely used index of real estate performance recorded annual returns that averaged 12.3% during that period. The two most severe years, 1979 and 1980, were characterized by inflation rates of 13.4% and 12.5%, respectively. The returns on the Frank Russell Company Property Index for these years were 20.8% and 18.1%, respectively.

Real estate is not the only inflation hedge. Some investors use gold, oil and gas, timberland, and even Treasury Bills for this purpose. Why not one of these as opposed to real estate? Let's consider the pros and cons of each.

The discussion in Chapter 3 about linkages between markets pointed out that the return on U.S. Treasury Bills is equal to the inflation rate plus a small premium, or real return. Therefore, the return on Treasury Bills should increase with inflation and provide a potential hedge. Unfortunately, this equation only works if you reinvest all of the income and are exempt from taxes. For example, assume inflation averages 10% and Treasury

Bills yield 11%. If you spend all of the interest income, your principal will be constant, which means that it is losing 10% of its purchasing power each year. Even if you reinvest all interest income, taxes could take a bite of as much as 3.4% (31% tax bracket), leaving a 7.6% net return. In other words, you are still 2.4% behind inflation. Therefore, Treasury Bills can be an effective hedge, but only in certain, restrictive circumstances. Moreover, Treasury Bills provide a very low rate of return over time. Clearly a better hedge would be one that is effective in broader circumstances and provides better returns over a long period of time.

Gold is widely used as a "store of value" during periods of world crisis and is thought to be an effective hedge against inflation. The problem with gold is that its price is extremely volatile. In fact, gold has been considerably more volatile than common stocks over the past ten years. In contrast, real estate tends to be much more stable than many other asset classes. While real estate usually dampens the volatility of a portfolio that consists primarily of stocks and bonds, gold may increase that volatility. An additional problem with gold is that it does not produce any current income, and it actually involves storage and insurance costs if you buy the metal itself. One way around this problem is to buy shares of gold stocks. However, all stocks tend to be affected by what is happening to the market as a whole. That means, therefore, that the behavior of gold stocks is related to both the stock market and the price of gold, so gold stocks do not represent a pure play on gold.

Energy investments and timberland have been successful inflation hedges, but small investors are effectively precluded from investing directly in them. Both of these categories involve large minimum investments and are difficult to manage effectively. It is possible to participate indirectly by purchasing stocks of energy or forest product companies. Again, however, the return on your shares will be heavily influenced by the stock market, which diminishes their role in diversifying your portfolio.

Needless to say, real estate is not without its problems as well. Most small investors are precluded from directly owning properties other than their home. In addition, questions abound regarding the outlook for real estate as a result of significant overbuilding during the 1980s. But, on balance, I believe real estate is preferable to other hedges because it is familiar to most investors, and because it always offers opportunities to earn good returns through property selection and good management irrespective of the economic environment. However, if you prefer one of the other inflation hedges, I would not argue strongly against it. Just make sure that your portfolio includes one of the categories that performs well in periods of high inflation.

Low/Moderate Inflation

Depending upon how you define a "low" inflation environment, the United States has experienced between three and six periods during this century. Just as the performance of stocks has been mixed during high inflation environments, bond returns have been fairly unpredictable during low inflation periods. From 1949 to 1967, inflation averaged about 2% per year, although it fluctuated a good bit around the average. During this period, bonds earned an average of only 1.9% annually, a real, or after-inflation, return of only .1%. On the other hand, bonds provided an annual return of 17.1% from 1982 to 1989, which was characterized by moderate inflation of 3.5%. While not low by historical standards, most investors have learned to live with inflation in the 3–5% range. The bottom line is that bonds do not represent a reliable performer in a low-inflation environment.

Similarly, real estate cannot be considered a good candidate during low inflation. We do not have good historical data prior to 1971, but real estate generated an annual return of 8.7% from 1982 to 1989. While this was an acceptable rate of return, it significantly lagged the return on both stocks and bonds; in fact, it was only modestly higher than the yield on U.S. Treasury Bills.

It is in low-inflation environments that stocks really shine. After adjusting for inflation, stocks earned 12.9% per year between 1920 and 1926, and 13.0% annually between 1949 and

1967. In the most recent low-inflation environment, which lasted from 1982 to 1989, stocks earned 18.8% per annum, or a real return of approximately 14.8%. You should recall that the long-term real return on stocks has been between 6% and 7%; therefore, in all three of these low-inflation periods, stock returns were roughly twice the normal level.

Why do stocks do well in low-inflation environments? Basically, these are periods of stable interest rates and good, steady growth in the profits of corporations. Under these circumstances, investors become increasingly confident that the economy is in for a sustained period of growth, and that outlook makes them more comfortable buying stocks at higher and higher prices. In other words, these are normally periods of widespread prosperity and optimism.

Deflation

Most of us forget that consumer prices do occasionally decline. The last calendar year in which the CPI actually registered a decline was 1954, but there were several periods during this century when prices fell for several years in a row. The most vivid period was from 1926 through 1932 when consumer prices fell a total of 27%, or at an annual rate in excess of 4%. Of course, this period included the stock market crash of 1929 and the Great Depression, which really lasted until the beginning of World War II.

No reliable data exists on the performance of real estate during this era, but it is fair to say that values declined significantly. I probably do not have to remind you that the stock market declined almost 90% from its peak to the subsequent trough. Obviously, neither of these asset classes did much to protect a portfolio during this period of economic collapse.

The bright star in this dismal period was U.S. government bonds. They provided an average annual return of 5.3% from 1926 to 1932. Since consumer prices actually fell by 4.4% per year, the real, or after-inflation, return was about 9.7%. While this level of return is certainly no barn-burner, it was wonderful in the context of the disaster that occurred in most investment types. Bonds perform well in deflationary environments because interest rates almost always decline. Therefore, the prices of bonds rise materially, which adds to the return from interest payments. In this kind of environment, the best performing bonds are noncallable issues with long-term maturities, because they will enjoy the greatest price appreciation.

It is absolutely critical to note that *only* U.S. government bonds provide the safety necessary in an economic collapse. A number of corporations have defaulted on their bonds in recent years, and the leveraged buyout boom of the 1980s will undoubtedly lead to more bankruptcies. Many people are not aware, however, that tax exempt municipal bonds are also subject to default, and in fact, such defaults have occurred during periods of economic stress.

Many investors in high tax brackets purchase municipal bonds because they provide a higher after-tax yield than either U.S. government or high-quality corporate issues. While this strategy makes sense in terms of current income, it is risky from a capital preservation standpoint. These assets are totally at risk in the event of a serious recession or depression. I recommend, therefore, that you seriously consider limiting your bond investments to U.S. government securities. If you follow this advice, you may well end up with a little less after-tax income, but this tradeoff can be viewed as an insurance premium of sorts. As is the case with all kinds of insurance, you do not enjoy paying the premium, but you are elated to have the protection when you actually need it. It may also be possible to avoid the tax problem by placing higher-yielding assets in a tax-deferred fund such as an Individual Retirement Account (IRA). For example, your IRA might consist entirely of government bonds so that interest earnings will not be taxed, whereas your personal portfolio would contain stocks that throw off less current income subject to tax.

You are probably aware that economists are seldom successful in predicting the future, and there is no reason to believe you or I can do any better. We should accept the fact that no one really knows what economic climate is in store for us. The most prudent course, therefore, is to structure your portfolio to survive in any environment. As indicated in Table 6.1, a portfolio consisting of stocks, government bonds, and real estate will always have at least one asset that is performing well and, thereby, should protect you in any environment. For this reason, these three asset categories represent the minimum diversification that should be present in just about every portfolio. Still, other asset categories deserve a place as well. The stocks of foreign companies and small U.S. companies are two important subcategories within the broader category of stocks. These investments afford the opportunity to increase the return on a portfolio while also adding to its diversification. Let's consider foreign stocks first.

»   **Foreign Stocks**   «

First of all, a useful perspective can be gained by viewing U.S. capital markets in the context of the world as a whole. As indicated in Table 6.2, all stocks owned worldwide represent about 42% of the World Market Portfolio, and the U.S. stock market represents only about one-third of the global stock market. In other words, the traditional practice of Americans of investing exclusively in stocks within our own borders is mistakenly narrow because two-thirds of the potential opportunities are being overlooked. Financial theory suggests that your portfolio should

»   **Table 6.1 Performance of Different Investments in   «**
Various Economic Climates

	Deflation	Low Inflation	High Inflation
Stocks	−	+	0
Government bonds	+	0	−
Real estate	−	0	+

+ means good performance; − means poor performance; 0 means uncertain

»   **Table 6.2   World Market Portfolio**   **«**

U.S. equities	14.1%
Non-U.S. equities	28.3
Venture capital	.1
Real estate	7.2
U.S. bonds	17.9
Non-U.S. bonds	26.2
Cash equivalents	6.2
	100.0%

Source: Brinson Partners

have the same weightings as the World Market Portfolio unless you have a compelling reason to do otherwise. Therefore, most Americans could theoretically have as much as 55% of their portfolios invested in foreign stocks and bonds. As a practical matter, few individual investors have any investments outside the United States, so a weighting of 15–20% might represent a comfortable first step. In addition to the theoretical arguments, there are two practical reasons to invest in stocks of companies based outside of the United States.

First, there are reasons to believe that the returns on foreign stocks may be slightly higher on average than the returns on their American counterparts. The returns on stocks are related to the growth of the underlying companies, which, in turn, is impacted by the overall growth in the economy. Several countries in Asia are already enjoying periods of dynamic growth, and many forecasters believe that Western Europe will begin a significant revitalization in the early 1990s. These trends have resulted in higher returns on non-U.S. markets, and it is reasonable to believe that those returns will continue. From 1973 through 1990, the Europe, Australia, and Far East Index (EAFE) reflected annual returns that averaged 12.5%, which compares with a return average of 10.5% on the Standard & Poor's 500 Index. Since 1979, twelve of the major stock markets around the world have provided a cumulative return in excess of that earned on the U.S. market. Interestingly, the U.S. market has provided the highest rate of return among the major world markets in only one year out of the past ten. The bottom line is that investing outside the United States should give your portfolio a little extra kick.

The second reason for owning non-U.S. stocks is that they can dampen swings in a purely domestic portfolio. This effect occurs because stock markets around the world do not ordinarily move up or down in tandem. During the fourth quarter of 1987, which included the now-famous market crash, the U.S. stock market as measured by the Standard & Poor's 500 declined 22.6%. For the same quarter, however, the Japanese market declined 2.5%, the United Kingdom's market fell 15.8%, and Spain's was off 10.1%. The EAFE Index declined only 10.6%, which indicates that markets outside the United States suffered less than half of the damage experienced by U.S. investors. Since 1962, foreign stocks have outperformed their U.S. counterparts in eight of the nine periods in which U.S. stock prices were weak. Foreign stock prices actually rose in two of these periods. The glaring exception to this trend was in 1990, when the U.S. market declined 3.1% while the EAFE Index fell 23.4%. Even so, there were opportunities to make money outside the United States in 1990 as indicated by the fact that the Hong Kong and United Kingdom markets provided returns of 9.2% and 10.3%, respectively. With the growing interdependence of world economies, it is likely that all stock markets will become somewhat more interwined, but the advantages of international diversification should remain largely intact for many years.

How do you invest in the stocks of foreign companies? One way is to purchase American Depository Receipts (ADRs), which are receipts for shares of stock in foreign companies that are held outside the United States. These securities are denominated in U.S. dollars, and more than two hundred of them trade on the various U.S. exchanges. While ADRs do give investors a window on the growth of non-U.S. economies, the fact that they trade on American exchanges significantly reduces their contribution to diversification. Remember, like all publicly traded stocks, ADRs are impacted by what happens in the market as a whole. Therefore, ADRs will look and act like U.S. equities despite the fact that they are equities in foreign companies.

If you are to get the maximum benefit of diversification, you must invest directly in foreign markets. Stocks listed on a foreign exchange do not act like U.S. securities. Unfortunately, purchasing these securities yourself can be a difficult ordeal. When you invest outside the United States, you have to worry about foreign currencies, differing tax laws, and a variety of other administrative hassles. Happily, mutual funds offer opportunities to enjoy a diversified portfolio of foreign securities without any of these headaches.

There are three broad categories of mutual funds that invest in stocks outside the United States. First are "country" funds, which invest only in the stocks of a specific country. In certain countries, foreigners are not allowed to invest directly in securities, which means that the country fund represents the only means of participating in such markets. The problem with buying a country fund is that *you* must make the decision that a given country's market is more attractive than the markets of other countries. Given the complexities of different economies and currencies, I know that I am not competent to make such decisions. But if you are, more power to you.

The second fund type consists of "global" funds, which invest both in the United States and in foreign markets. This structure provides the fund manager with the flexibility to switch money back and forth between the various markets depending upon their relative attraction. If their managers are truly talented, these global funds should provide the highest rate of return among the three fund types. On the other hand, investing in these funds results in your losing control of the structure of your overall portfolio, because the manager, not you, decides how much of your allocation is invested outside the United States.

The third type of fund invests strictly in securities outside of the United States. These "international" funds circumvent the control problem with global funds because you can allocate funds to them in amounts that maintain your desired weighting for non-U.S. stocks. On the other hand, international funds are not as flexible as global funds, a factor that could diminish their return potential. There are never any easy choices in the investment business because every approach has distinct pluses and minuses. In this case, I prefer international funds because the mission of this book is to place you in control of your investment program and that control includes your allocation of funds to U.S. and foreign markets.

»   **Small Capitalization Stocks**   «

At earlier points in the book I referred to "small capitalization" stocks without telling you exactly what they were. The capitalization of a company is equal to the price of its stock multiplied by the number of shares owned by all investors (usually called stock outstanding). In one sense, it is a measure of what all investors think the company is worth—that is, its market value. Capitalization is frequently used as a proxy for company size. The four companies with the largest market value, or capitalization, are IBM, Exxon, General Electric, and Philip Morris. At the other extreme are hundreds of smaller companies you probably have never heard of. Most investors, and particularly professional ones, limit their focus to the 772 companies that had market capitalizations greater than $500 million on December 31, 1990. In total, the stocks of these large companies represent about 89% of the value of all U.S. stocks outstanding. But according to the consulting firm of Wilshire Associates, there are 5,066 publicly traded companies with capitalizations less than $500 milion, and the bulk of them have capitalizations below $50 million. Since most professional investors ignore these smaller companies, one has every reason to believe that many wonderful opportunities remain largely undiscovered.

Many of these smaller companies have attractive financial characteristics as compared to their larger counterparts. A 1991 study by the brokerage firm Goldman Sachs & Company analyzed 1,250 companies and found that the smallest 250 of them were expected to enjoy growth in profits of 18% annually over the next five years as compared to 12% for the 250 largest companies. Stocks in these small companies sold at lower price earnings ratios than stocks in the big companies, an indication of good value. Moreover, these small companies were, on average, financially strong. You don't have to be a professional security analyst to understand that small stocks appear to be a bargain since they offer higher growth potential than the blue chips and sell at lower prices. Small stocks have historically provided a premium return of about 2% over the S&P 500. I believe there is every reason to think that this spread will persist.

Investing in small-company stocks is not without difficulties, however. First, smaller companies are usually associated with stock prices that are quite volatile. This volatility is due to the propensity of smaller companies to be relatively unseasoned, and it is not unusual for them to succumb to poor management, competition, or financial pressure. Moreover, the small stocks tend to be less liquid than large stocks, which means that a rush to buy or sell small stocks can have a dramatic effect on their prices. To be sure, a portfolio consisting solely of small companies is not for the fainthearted! But in the context of a diversified portfolio of several asset types, this volatility becomes manageable for nearly everyone.

An additional problem for the investor is that information is less readily available for small companies. Brokerage firms tend to do most of their research on larger companies that trade actively. So if you choose to select your own securities, you will have to do most of the homework yourself. For those of us who are less energetic, easy access to first-rate mutual funds that concentrate on small stocks provides us with the opportunity to enjoy a diversified portfolio of these exciting companies.

»»   Cash Equivalent Investments   ««

The cash equivalent category of investments includes money market funds, U.S. Treasury Bills, certificates of deposit, and a variety of similar short-term securities. As previously mentioned, most financial planners suggest that everyone should have an emergency reserve of between three and six months' salary in one of these investments. Hopefully, this sum will be sufficient to help you out during a temporary period of unemployment or in the case of an expensive medical problem. Moreover, most disability insurance policies do not begin to pay benefits until after you have been disabled for three to six months. Your emergency reserve should be sufficient to bridge that gap. I agree with the conventional wisdom in this instance and encourage you to build and maintain a reserve in a money market fund or in another readily accessible security.

Beyond the emergency reserve, only the most risk-averse investors with very short time horizons should hold any significant amount of cash-equivalent investments. As was detailed in Chapter 3, these investments have provided the lowest return of any major asset category over just about every time period. I find no reason to expect this pattern to change. My forecast of a 6–7% return in the future suggests that the actual return could be as low as 4–5% for those who pay taxes. Thus, these returns could lag inflation slightly.

These securities do provide safety and liquidity, but these characteristics should be critical only to individuals with very short time horizons. This group might include elderly investors, those with health problems, or unusual cases in which a specific amount of money must be available on a specific date that is close at hand. Longer-term investors who create a diversified portfolio, however, can achieve a high degree of stability without resorting to these low-yielding investments. For this reason, only the lowest-risk portfolio (risk level seven) presented in Chapter 7 will hold any short-term investments.

»»   On to the Next Step   ««

Virtually every portfolio should contain investments in stocks, U.S. government bonds, and real estate. These asset categories

represent the minimum diversification. In addition, most investors will be well served by adding non-U.S. stocks as well as
small capitalization domestic equities. Both of these categories
add increased diversification and stability to the portfolio while
enhancing its return. Various combinations of these five categories can provide you with a portfolio that is as sophisticated and
diversified as most of the large pools of managed capital in the
United States.

Does this mean that you should never hold any other type of
investment? Of course not. Investors have been successful in a
variety of asset types. My goal, however, is to help you construct
a portfolio that will serve as the core of a quality investment
program. Once this core is in place, you will still have plenty of
room to dabble in other investment categories.

We have now completed two of the five steps in creating and
implementing your program. The third step involves the asset
allocation decision—that is, the division of your funds among
the five categories selected in this chapter. Yogi Berra is often
quoted as saying that "baseball is 95% mental, and the other
half is physical." In the investment game, asset allocation is 90%
of the equation, so it is critical to get that decision right before
we focus on the other half.

»»————————— **Key Points to Remember** ————————— «««

- Most portfolios should contain stocks, bonds, and real estate as
  a means of preserving capital in any economic climate.
- The addition of foreign and small capitalization domestic stocks
  will further diversify a portfolio while potentially increasing
  returns.
- Only the most cautious investors should hold money market
  funds beyond their reserve for emergencies.

CHAPTER 7

A PORTFOLIO FOR EVERY INVESTOR

The more you know about yourself as an investor and
the more you understand investment management and
the securities markets, the more you will know what
asset mix is really right for your portfolios, and the
more likely you will be to sustain your commitment
for the long term.

—Charles D. Ellis,
Investment Policy, 1985

»» «««

I have mentioned in passing that approximately 90% of the
overall return on a portfolio is produced by its asset mix. Consequently, whether you buy stock in Apple Computer or IBM really
doesn't matter a lot in the long run. What matters is how much
of your portfolio funds are invested in stocks versus bonds versus
other types of investments.

Most investors find this concept difficult to accept. Their reaction is understandable. After all, every investor is constantly
bombarded with advisers' recommendations to buy ABC stock
and sell XYZ. In contrast, how often have you heard financial
pundits talk in detail about properly structuring an investment
portfolio? Don't forget that Wall Street makes its living by convincing investors to buy and sell. It is, therefore, no surprise that
investment professionals do a poor job of educating their clients

regarding asset allocation. While it is indeed no surprise, the lack of knowledge regarding this topic is a great shame because most individuals are unprepared and ill-equipped to make the most important decision in their financial lives. Before I present information to help you make this critical decision, I should explain why the asset allocation decision is so important.

»   Asset Allocation   «

The risk and return on any given stock is a function of three factors. First, every stock is affected by what goes on in the market as a whole. When the market is rising, most stocks increase in price to a greater or lesser extent, and the converse occurs when the situation is reversed. Second, every company's stock is impacted by what happens to the stocks of similar companies. How does one define "similar" companies? In fact, there are many different ways of grouping similar stocks. The most familiar and constant way that investors group stocks is by industry. For example, when drug company stocks are in favor, most drug stocks earn better returns than the market as a whole. Investors also tend to divide stocks into groups based on how they are impacted by economic trends. For example, an increase in oil prices usually causes the stocks of energy-related companies to rise and those of heavy energy users such as airlines to fall. Other categories frequently used for grouping are "growth" and "value" stocks and "big" and "small" companies. In any case, the performance of every stock is affected by its membership in various groups because market forces impact similar companies in similar ways. The final source of risk and return on stocks consists of factors that are unique to each particular company. The performance of a given stock is affected by its earnings prospects, management, competitive position, and a variety of other variables.

Chapter 4 emphasized the critical role of diversification in controlling risk and suggested that every stock portfolio should hold a large number of issues with representation in many industry groups. In a diversified portfolio, two of the three sources of risk and return disappear. At any given time, several stock groups represented in your portfolio will be in favor while others reside in the doghouse. The divergent returns on stock groups will cancel each other out. Similarly, one specific stock might soar because of a technological breakthrough while another plunges as a result of a product recall. Once again, these high and low returns tend to cancel each other out. In a diversified portfolio of stocks, the individual and group factors largely disappear and the result is that the return is determined primarily by the return on the market as a whole.

The same basic principle applies to bonds. The return on a bond portfolio is influenced by the types of bonds held, their maturity, coupon or interest rate, and quality. But in a diversified portfolio, most of these factors are dwarfed by the impact of interest rates. When interest rates rise, most bond portfolios fall in value to a greater or lesser extent; conversely, a decline in interest rates leads to improved bond returns because bond prices rise. Once again, the return on a given bond portfolio is largely determined by what happens to the market as a whole. Without going into all of the details, this phenomenon is true of most investment categories, and that underlines the need for a diversified portfolio.

The one major exception to the rule may be real estate. Since every property is unique with respect to location, a portfolio of properties may perform differently from the real estate market as a whole. This can be avoided by creating a diversified portfolio, but the cost of purchasing real estate necessitates a huge pool of funds to achieve real diversification. The return on your allocation to real estate, therefore, may not always track the market closely. But factors such as interest rates, economic growth, and inflation impact every property, which means that the overall market for real estate still represents a good proxy for the return you can expect to earn.

We have discovered that your prowess in selecting superior stocks, real estate, and bonds will have relatively little impact on performance since the return on each segment of your portfolio will be determined largely by the performance of its respective market. Therefore, the return on your overall portfolio will be a function of the percentage of your assets that is committed to each category. Fixing these percentages is called the asset allocation decision.

In reality, you must make two different asset allocation decisions. The first is to decide the long-range, or target, asset mix for your portfolio. Sometimes this is called the strategic asset mix. Whatever you call it, the product is the mix of different investments that best meets your feelings about risk and return. If you want to take a "Rip Van Winkle" approach to investing, in which you structure a portfolio and then sleep for ten or twenty years, your strategic mix would need to represent the right combination for the entire period. In the real world, the investor life cycle suggests that because each of us goes through three or four different phases during our investing life, a target asset mix should in fact be good for ten to twenty years. This chapter is devoted to developing strategic or target asset mixes for different investors. Specifically, one structure is recommended for each of the seven risk levels.

The second decision is to set allocation percentages for a tactical asset mix. Your tactical mix is the actual structure of your portfolio at any given time. Many investors allow their actual weightings to fluctuate within a band on each side of the long-range target. For example, if your target weighting in stocks is 60%, you might actually allow it to swing between 50% and 70%. The rationale for this practice is to allow you to take advantage of interim moves in markets without making such a big bet that an incorrect call would kill you. For example, you would lower your equity exposure to 50% if stocks appeared overpriced and then increase it to 70% when the market fell and stocks became attractive at lower prices. The wisdom of this practice is covered in detail in the chapter devoted to the annual update and review of portfolios. But to give you a brief preview, the evidence suggests that it is exceedingly difficult to make successful short-term calls about swings in the stock market. I therefore recommend that you select the appropriate long-range asset mix and stick to it until you move on to a new phase in your investor life cycle. In other words, three or four asset mixes should get you through an entire career of investing.

» **Deriving Target Portfolios** «

One of the reasons many investors are not equipped to make the asset allocation decision is that it takes a fair amount of technical knowledge. Moreover, evaluating alternative portfolios involves a huge amount of number crunching. Hundreds of different types of investments are available and combinations of them are virtually infinite. We are faced, therefore, with the task of selecting seven portfolios (one for each risk level) from literally millions of choices.

In theory, the process is simple enough. For any given amount of risk, one portfolio above all others should provide the highest possible rate of return. If we can identify that portfolio, we have no reason to even consider any other, because it would be inferior. In practice, actually identifying this perfect portfolio is impossible, but there are ways of coming close.

Many investment professionals use an extraordinarily sophisticated computer program called an optimizer to produce target asset mixes. Here's the way it works. First, they enter forecasts of risk and return on each investment category. Second, they estimate the degree to which each category is correlated with every other category. This factor is a measure of the extent to which the prices of investments in any two categories move together. To come close to finding the "ideal" portfolio, they must include most, if not all, investment categories that one could conceivably invest in. Otherwise, the result may not actually be the best portfolio structure. Finally, they enter the amount of risk the investor wants to take. The computer then crunches away until it spits out the best single portfolio for the risk assumed.

While this process sounds straightforward enough, it actually involves a number of problems. First, you must forecast return, risk, and correlation data for every investment category. Just to give you an indication of the magnitude of this problem, a total of 135 different forecasts is required to run calculations for 15 different categories. While some of these forecasts, such as expected returns, are not too difficult to make, others are problematic. For example, how does one go about estimating the extent to which U.S. real estate and Japanese bond prices move together? Frankly, I haven't a clue. A second problem is that computer programs are so precise that small changes in the inputs can meaningfully change the recommended portfolio structure. Given the uncertainty in forecasting future returns, this level of precision is unwarranted. Similarly, the computer analysis may recommend that 2.7% or 3.5% or some other small percentage of the total portfolio should be invested in a given asset class. For small investors, this result is impractical because of minimum required investments in mutual funds and other vehicles. Finally, these programs sometimes spit out bizarre portfolio structures that would be completely unpalatable to most investors. For example, it might tell you that the optimal portfolio for your risk level consists of Australian bonds and pork belly futures.

To get around all of these problems, most advisers place constraints on the computer program to ensure that the portfolio it recommends will be one the investor will find comfortable and reasonably familiar. By doing so, they compromise the process in such a way that the recommended portfolio is essentially known before the computer starts its work. In other words, these advisers jiggle the inputs and constraints until they get the output they want. Such "tampering," however, may be warranted. I agree that a recommended portfolio must be comfortable for the particular investor. But I also find it possible to approach the asset mix problem in a manner that is less complex and more direct than the computer analysis.

First, six of my recommended portfolios consist of large capitalization stocks, small capitalization stocks, foreign stocks, bonds, and real estate. The seventh and most conservative portfolio holds no stocks but adds some money market instruments.

By limiting each portfolio to a maximum of five carefully chosen categories, the whole process is more manageable because only twenty forecasts are needed. Second, all of the weights recommended for the five asset categories are multiples of 5%, and no weighting is less than 5% for any category. Greater precision beyond this level is not called for given the uncertainty of future behavior of different investments. Third, and perhaps most important of all, each of the portfolios is designed to be familiar and comfortable to most investors. You will recall from the last chapter that financial theory would dictate that most Americans have more than 50% of their portfolio invested outside the United States. As a practical matter, virtually no one would be willing to take such a bold step. Therefore, I have recommended weightings in foreign stocks that vary from 5% to 20% depending upon the risk level chosen. The bottom line is that the seven portfolios, while not "optimal" in a theoretical sense, are diversified, well-balanced, and easy to construct.

While my process is considerably simpler and more straightforward than the application of fancy software, I don't want you to think these portfolios were pulled out of the air. Actually, the target asset mixes were chosen as a result of three careful steps. First, based on my own experience and the criteria mentioned, I selected a preliminary asset mix for each risk level. Then, using a computer simulation model, I carefully examined the likely future behavior of each structure and modified each as necessary. Finally, I rounded the weightings in order to make the portfolio mixes easy to work with. The final product is a series of seven portfolios that are likely to achieve reasonable rates of return within the confines of moderate to low levels of risk. Most important, every one of the resultant portfolios is available to even the smallest investor.

»   Recommended Portfolio Structures   «

Table 7.1 shows my recommended portfolio weightings for each of the seven risk levels covered in Chapters 4 and 5. Just to make

»   **Table 7.1   Recommended Portfolio Structure**   «««
                          (% of Portfolio)

Risk Level	1	2	3	4	5	6	7
U.S. stocks	10%	30%	40%	35%	30%	15%	0
Non-U.S. stocks	20	20	15	15	10	5	0
Small capitalization stocks	50	30	15	10	5	0	0
Bonds	10	10	15	25	40	60	70
Real estate	10	10	15	15	15	20	20
Money market securities	0	0	0	0	0	0	10
	100%	100%	100%	100%	100%	100%	100%

Source: William T. Spitz Recommendations

sure we are on the same wavelength, let's focus on risk level four as an example. If this level best represents your risk:return needs, your portfolio should consist of the following asset types and weightings: large capitalization U.S. stocks, 35% non-U.S. stocks, 15%; small capitalization U.S. stocks, 10%; bonds, 25%; and real estate, 15%. This mix represents the long-term target structure of your portfolio; it is intended to serve your purposes until there is a major change in your financial circumstances. Occasionally, you may need to shift some of your funds between categories in order to maintain your portfolio structure. This rebalancing of your assets will normally occur during your annual portfolio review and will be one of your more important management obligations.

A quick explanation of portfolio seven is deserved because it may seem curious. Chapter 6 included a recommendation that virtually every portfolio have a reasonable commitment to stocks, U.S. government bonds, and real estate. You might then ask why portfolio seven does not include any kind of stocks. Frankly, I do not recommend this structure, but I encounter enough investors who do not want to own stocks under any circumstances that I feel compelled to include a portfolio to meet their needs.

You probably do not have any frame of reference that will enable you to judge whether my seven recommended structures are reasonable or not. One way to gain some perspective on this is to check the average structure of the 2,100 largest pension, profit-sharing, foundation, and endownment funds in the United States. In a sense, these funds represent the combined wisdom of America's most experienced investment professionals. The structure of the 2,100 funds depicted in Table 7.2 is probably most similar to that of my risk level four and a comparison of the two yields many similarities as well as some important differences.

This breakdown of assets does not list a separate category for small capitalization stocks, which means they are included in the U.S. stock line. My portfolio number four has a total of 45% invested in domestic stocks (large cap, 35%; small cap, 10%), which compares closely with the 42.1% weighting in the average large tax-exempt fund.

At this point, however, my recommendations for portfolio four diverge significantly from common practice among these funds. First, you will note that I recommend a 15% weighting in non-U.S. stocks as compared with a 4.5% allocation in the typical fund. (Remember, this category represents about 28% of the

» **Table 7.2   Asset Mix of 2,100 Largest Tax** «
Exempt Funds (% of Portfolio)

U.S. stocks	42.1%
Non-U.S. stocks	4.5
Bonds and related	38.9
Real estate	4.7
Money market securities	6.4
Other	3.4
	100.0%

Source: Greenwich Associates, *Investment Management*, 1991

World Capital Market.) I believe the tax-exempt funds will steadily increase their interest in non-U.S. equities and it would not surprise me if their weighting approached my 15% target over the next few years. A second major difference occurs in the real estate weighting. I recommend a 15% exposure as compared with the average fund's weighting of 4.7%. Here I argue that a 4.7% allocation really does not provide much of an inflation hedge and is hardly worth the trouble. Third, the tax-exempt funds hold cash equivalent investments of 6.4% as compared with my recommendation of no weighting whatsoever. Frankly, I do not understand why funds that are essentially perpetual in nature maintain such large positions in low-return investments. Finally, I recommend only a 25% weighting in bonds as compared to the 38.9% allocation in the tax-exempt funds. It's not that I have anything against bonds—they represent one of my three mandatory categories—but in order to fund larger weightings in real estate and non-U.S. equities, investment had to be curtailed in some other category, and the lower return on bonds as compared with stocks makes them the logical choice.

Based on my forecasts of returns on each investment category, I would expect portfolio four to outperform the average tax-exempt fund by about one percent per year. This assertion is supported by calculations of annual returns over the past fifteen years: A portfolio that maintained over the entire period the mix shown in Table 7.2 would have earned a return of approximately 12.7% as compared with 13.7% for portfolio four. I don't want to make too much of this comparison because historical comparisons of this sort are frequently unrealistic and even unfair. Nevertheless, I do believe my recommended structure is superior to similar portfolios widely in use today. I can't assert that these structures are superior to every conceivable portfolio, but I can argue that they represent an attractive balance between competitive rates of return and moderate risk. In addition, most of them should also provide a reasonable level of current income. These points are demonstrated in Table 7.3

Here's why it's important to consider those expected rates. You will recall that I suggested that investors with substantial

» **Table 7.3   Expected Returns and**   «
                Current Income Yields

Risk Level	1	2	3	4	5	6	7
Average total return	12.3%	11.7%	11.0%	10.6%	9.9%	9.1%	8.2%
Current income	3.3%	3.6%	4.3%	4.8%	5.6%	6.8%	7.6%

Source: William T. Spitz Estimates

income needs should select a portfolio that balances current income with attractive total returns in order to survive the ravages of inflation. Three of the recommended portfolios are good candidates for meeting this objective. My estimates in Table 7.3 indicate that portfolios three through five should provide current income ranging from 4.3% to 5.6%; at the same time, they should generate total returns of 9.9–11%. These rates should be high enough to allow someone with current income needs of 6–8% of his portfolio value to meet the income requirements and to enjoy a little bit of growth in principal that partially offsets rising consumer prices.

After reading all of this material, you might reasonably feel you do not have enough money to put together an investment program that includes five different types of investments. Moreover, if you accept my advice that each category should include a large number of individual investments, the whole thing may become more than a little scary. Don't worry. An investment program of this sort can be manageable even for someone with limited assets. This contention, in fact, is central to the work of this book. In the next few chapters, the specific details of implementing everything covered thus far are explained to you.

If I may jump the gun a bit, though, I will tell you that every one of these asset classes is easily available through mutual funds. In fact, several of the larger mutual fund families offer funds in all six categories. It is therefore possible for you to put together any one of these sophisticated portfolios while you deal with only one organization, which should minimize the paperwork required. Many mutual funds have minimum initial investments of $500 for IRAs and $1,000 to $2,000 for other accounts. These modest levels mean that even the smallest investor can participate. Think about it! Even an investor with $5,000 to $10,000 can have a portfolio that does not look much different from that of a billion-dollar pension plan.

»   **Credibility of Recommended Portfolios**   «

One of the characteristics of a successful investor is a high degree of skepticism. As a skeptic, you should be concerned that these recommended portfolios were constructed on the basis of forecasts of future returns on various types of investments. While the projected returns on each of the seven portfolios look reasonable enough and follow the proper pattern, you should still be a little skeptical. In fact, there are two key areas of vulnerability.

First, my forecasts may turn out to be wrong despite the fact that they were based on both historical performance and the changes that have recently taken place in the financial markets. Indeed, I am willing to bet that all seven portfolio forecasts will be either too high or too low. However, I will also bet that the pattern of these returns will be on target. In other words, I am confident that the higher-risk portfolios will outperform their lower-risk counterparts over time.

Second, my forecasts of portfolio returns are based on the assumption that you earn market returns in each asset type. In other words, I assume that *your* stocks, bonds, real estate, and other assets generate the same returns as their respective market indices. If any segment of your portfolio underperforms the market averages, your overall return will lag despite the fact that my forecasts turn out to be accurate. As you will find out in the next chapter, it is actually quite easy to ensure that each component of your portfolio tracks the market. However, even if one segment does not behave as it should, the effect on the

overall portfolio may not be too serious. By combining five different investment categories in each portfolio, the overall return is
likely to be in the ballpark even if one category does not perform
according to expectations.

The bottom line is that there is always uncertainty in the
investment world, and no investment can generate a guaranteed
result. There are no sure things, free rides, or easy answers.
While imperfect, these carefully chosen, diversified portfolios
represent the best job we can do in dealing with the unknowns
of future returns. To add a little credibility to this effort, I
calculated the actual return on each portfolio for the fifteen years
from 1976 through 1990. These returns appear in Table 7.4.
Once again, these calculations assume that each segment of a
portfolio earned the same return as the comparable market index.

First, you will note that this was an extraordinary period for
investors in that returns ranged from 9.9% to 16.4% depending
upon the level of risk assumed. In addition, the volatility of these
portfolios was actually less than that assumed in preparing the
future projections of risk and return. But more important, the
pattern of return was just as it should be: The highest return
was achieved at risk level one, the lowest return was earned by
portfolio seven, and there was a progressive decline in return at
the intervening levels. This should give you some confidence that
we are on the right track.

You are probably more concerned about the actual losses that
these portfolios experienced in down markets. Therefore, lest
you accuse me of only looking at the good times, we should also

» Table 7.4 Actual Portfolio Returns 1976–90 «
(Annnualized)

Risk Level	1	2	3	4	5	6	7
Annual Return (%)	16.4	15.5	14.3	13.7	12.6	11.1	9.9

Source: Ibbotson Associates; Frank Russell Company; Morgan Stanley–Capital International; William
T. Spitz Estimates

focus on bear markets. The worst single year for investors in the postwar period was 1974 in which the Standard & Poor's 500 declined 26.5%, small capitalization stocks fell approximately 20%, and foreign stocks fell by more than 23%. More recently, 1990 was characterized by a decline of 3.1% in the Standard & Poor's 500 Index and by much larger losses on both small capitalization and foreign stocks. Moreover, 1990 represented a miserable year in the real estate market. Table 7.5 provides the return on each of the seven portfolios during these "problem" years.

Once again, these data are comforting. The losses experienced were well within the worst-case returns I had predicted, and the pattern of returns was pretty much in line with expectations. Specifically, the greatest losses were experienced on the higher-risk portfolios while the lower-risk ones fared quite well. In fact, portfolio seven provided positive returns in both periods.

The fourth quarter of 1987, which included the October crash, was the most extreme environment that most investors have experienced. Actually, calendar year 1987 yielded modest positive rates of return on most diversified portfolios, but they are forgotten in the context of the trauma of October 19. While none of us as long-term investors should care about a single quarter's return, I am sure you are interested in how my seven portfolios fared. The results in Table 7.6 tell you that losses ranged from less than one percent at level six to about 16% at levels one and two, but level seven posted a 4.2% gain.

To be sure, losses of 16% in a single quarter are fairly scary. Nonetheless, my portfolios essentially behaved in line with expectations during this difficult quarter. Those investors who

»» Table 7.5 Portfolio Returns in 1974 and 1990 «««

Risk Level	1	2	3	4	5	6	7
1974 return	(16.1)	(17.4)	(15.3)	(12.6)	(8.4)	(1.1)	5.3
1990 return	(15.1)	(11.4)	(6.9)	(5.0)	(1.7)	2.3	5.4

Source: Ibbotson Associates; Frank Russell Company; Morgan Stanley–Capital International; William T. Spitz Estimates

»   Table 7.6   Portfolio Returns—Fourth Quarter 1987   «
(Unannualized)

Risk Level	1	2	3	4	5	6	7
Return	(16.6)	(16.0)	(13.6)	(10.6)	(6.8)	(.4)	4.2

Source: Ibbotson Associates; Morgan Stanley–Capital International; NASDAQ; Shearson Lehman Brothers; Frank Russell Company; William T. Spitz Estimates

could not tolerate a high degree of risk actually experienced only modest losses while the risk takers took a pounding. All of these losses, however, were within the limits I would have expected had I been able to predict such a quarter.

While there are no guarantees that these patterns will continue, all of this data lead me to the conclusion that my portfolios should behave "as advertised." In both up and down markets, the pattern of return has been for the higher risk portfolios to deliver greater returns and higher losses, as the case may be. Similarly, the lower-risk portfolios have been considerably more moderate in their swings.

»   Taxes as a Secondary Concern   «

One of the first rules of successful investing is that taxes are a cost of doing business. In other words, your investment program should be based on sound financial principles and not on tax avoidance.

Prior to their demise, which was caused by the Tax Reform Act of 1986, tax shelters were sold to many investors in the form of limited partnerships. In many cases, even a rookie business analyst could see that the partnership did not make any sense because the underlying project was uneconomic. Stated another way, the partnership existed solely for tax reasons. Given a period of time, economic principles have a way of proving correct; uneconomic projects ultimately fail. Many investors who participated in these partnerships eventually sacrificed their entire investment and, in some cases, now have significant tax problems.

The portfolio structures recommended in Table 7.1 are appropriate for either taxable or tax-exempt investors because they are based on financial principles that are basic yet enduring. Tax considerations were not involved in any way in making these allocations. However, there may be a way to divide your investments among different pots in order to minimize the tax bite. As alluded to in the previous chapter, this strategy involves separating your portfolio into higher- and lower-yielding components.

Let's suppose you chose risk level four, which has the following recommended structure: U.S. stocks, 35%; non-U.S. stocks, 15%; small stocks, 10%; bonds, 25%; and real estate, 15%. Among these five categories, two produce fairly high annual income. Specifically, I have assumed that bonds will yield a current income of 8% while real estate will provide a current return of 6.8%. To minimize taxes, it makes sense to place these two categories in a tax-free or tax-deferred fund. An IRA, a profit-sharing plan, or a 401K, 403B, Keough, or SEP plan could house these two investments, which represent 40% of your overall portfolio. Thus, your current return of 6.8–8.0% from assets in these funds would not be taxed. No taxes of any kind would be payable until you began to draw upon your accumulated balances after retirement. Your portfolio's remaining three categories will provide current yields of only 2–4% each, which means that the bulk of their return comes from appreciation. These categories would be held in your own name and be subject to taxes; however, the tax due on the 2–4% yield will be fairly modest. Capital appreciation will not be taxed until each asset is actually sold, and even then, may be taxed at a lower rate than that levied on current income.

Since every person's situation is different, I can't give you an exact formula to accomplish the task of minimizing your taxes, but I trust that these comments are sufficient to get you started. I do, however, want to reemphasize that you should first select an asset mix that is appropriate for your needs. Then, and only then, should you look for some opportunity to minimize your tax load. If no such opportunities are feasible, implement your program and be happy that you have to pay taxes, because that indicates that you are earning attractive returns.

» **The Nitty Gritty** «

You have now completed three of the five steps in creating your investment program. You know what you are trying to accomplish with your investments and have identified a long-range portfolio mix that seems likely to achieve your goals. At this point, the structure or framework of your plan is in place. It's now time to turn to the specifics of implementing your plan. While it is fine to talk about investment objectives and asset allocation, someone ultimately has to select individual securities. Someone has to identify stocks, bonds, and real estate that represent attractive purchase candidates. Someone has to do the research to confirm that they are indeed attractive. And someone has to actually consummate purchases and sales. Who should that person be?

»——————— **Key Points to Remember** ———————«

- The return on your portfolio is determined primarily by its asset mix.
- Table 7.1 includes one recommended mix for each of the seven levels of risk. All of these portfolios are available to even the smallest investor.
- The recommended portfolios are based on sound economic principles and not on tax avoidance.

CHAPTER 8

WHO WILL ACTUALLY INVEST YOUR PORTFOLIO?

A creditable, if unspectacular, result can be achieved by the lay investor with a minimum of effort and capability; but to improve this easily attainable standard requires much application and more than a trace of wisdom. If you merely try to bring *just a little* extra knowledge and cleverness to bear upon your investment program, instead of realizing a little better than normal results, you may find that you have done worse.

—Benjamin Graham,
The Intelligent Investor, 1973

》》 《《

The majority of this book is devoted to creating the structure or framework of an organized investment program rather than the selection of specific securities. As has been mentioned several times, security selection represents only 10–15% of the investment equation. But that does not mean we should ignore it. Quite the contrary, you need to think about this aspect of your program in the same disciplined, systematic manner that you adopted to select your investment objectives and an appropriate asset mix.

When it comes to selecting securities, you have several choices. First, you can pick your own specific investments if you have the time and ability to do so. Second, you may find it convenient to purchase several of the more than 3,000 mutual funds that are available to American investors. Finally, more substantial investors often hire an adviser to manage a separate portfolio on their behalf.

Prior to electing one of these options, you must first decide whether you want to try to "beat the market"—that is, do you want to outperform the average investor? At first blush, you probably think this is one of the dumbest questions you've ever heard. Of course you want to earn better returns than everyone else! Outperforming the competition is so thoroughly ingrained in our culture that it almost seems un-American to settle for average results. The investment world, however, is unique. Oddly enough, you may well end up outperforming most professional investors by accepting "average" results.

» **The Great Debate** «

A great debate has been raging for more than twenty years as to whether it is reasonable to expect some investors to consistently outperform the stock market as a whole. In other words, can you expect to earn above-average results by turning your assets over to a skilled professional?

One camp argues that a combination of intelligence, hard work, and the disciplined implementation of a coherent investment philosophy should allow some investors to outperform the competition. Intuitively, this position makes sense to most people. After all, hardworking and resourceful individuals can usually outsmart their rivals. It shouldn't be that difficult for a skilled practitioner to select a portfolio of "strong" stocks or bonds that will outperform the thousands of "average" securities that are available. As you can well imagine, most professionals employed in the investment business accept this point of view, and each of them believes that he or she is among the small group of experts who can spot the winners.

The opposing point of view suggests that fierce competition

quickly eliminates any advantage gained by a particular investor. Therefore, no investor is able to consistently outperform his peers; success is only momentary. Even a very knowledgeable player who enjoys periods of good results will reap periods of bad results; and over time, his return will regress to the average of all investors. Stated succinctly, it is unlikely that even skilled investors can consistently beat the market. The majority of the supporters of this position are academics who have developed both a theoretical and empirical case for its validity. This material is an integral part of the finance curriculum taught in every business school today.

It would not surprise me if you are having a tough time seeing the connection between this debate and your investment program. You might even respond that you don't really care which side is correct. In fact, the implications of this debate are significant for all investors. If the second camp is correct in believing that it is almost impossible to outperform the market, then there is *no reason to pay a professional to manage your money.*

According to the second camp, the return earned by a professional investor is unlikely to be any better than that of an amateur, and eventually, the returns of both investors should equal the market's return. However, the professional is paid a fee to manage your money, and other costs arise from the fact that he buys and sells securities on your behalf. If his return only equals the market before these costs, then your net return will trail that of the market after deducting these costs. The bottom line is that even a professional money manager is likely to underperform a representative market index such as the Standard & Poor's 500. Moreover, you can purchase and hold all 500 stocks via an "index fund," which guarantees that you always earn exactly the return on the S&P index. Therefore, a naive strategy of buying and holding a large group of stocks is likely to beat the average professional money manager.

I am sure that you now understand that it is important to decide where you stand in the great debate. If you agree with the first camp, then you should direct your effort toward finding the most skilled professionals available. If you decide that you can't beat the market, then you should opt for index funds. Before turning to the evidence, it will be useful to first consider why the market is so difficult to beat.

»   Efficient Markets   «

The answer is that the stock market is an "efficient market," a term you have probably seen bandied about in the financial press. An efficient market is characterized by a large number of buyers and sellers, by readily available sources of information, and by transaction costs that are not prohibitive. In such a market, the buyers and sellers are constantly analyzing all available information and making "buy" and "sell" decisions accordingly. At all times, the price of a security represents fair value as determined by all market participants. In other words, each security always sells right where it should. Since each security is priced correctly, the market presents no opportunities for any investors to take advantage of; every investor operates on a level playing field.

If a security is always priced correctly, then why does its price change? First, prices change when investors receive and process new information about the company in question. However, given insider-trading laws as well as an army of researchers analyzing data, it is highly unlikely that any particular investor is able to process new information and react (buy or sell) correctly all of the time. The second reason for a change in a security's price is the reassessment by analysts of existing information. In other words, the price might change if enough analysts decided that their earlier interpretation of the data had been incorrect and had triggered a wrong decision to buy or sell that security. Once again, if anyone were able to consistently foresee changes in investors' evaluation of information, it would be a superhuman feat.

This all sounds very theoretical, so let's compare a market that is efficient with one that is not. The U.S. stock market is

characterized by a large number of participants who have access
to an incredible amount of information regarding the economy
and the outlook for individual companies. Many of these participants are highly motivated, experienced professionals armed
with research departments, economists, and data bases. Such
investors do have the capability to analyze security values. While
costs are involved in trading, they are not so large as to prevent
one of these investors from taking advantage of an opportunity
to buy or sell a security deemed to be mispriced. In this environment, any edge gained by an investor is short-lived because his
approach is analyzed and imitated by his competitors, which
quickly takes away his advantage.

In contrast, the real estate market is highly inefficient. In
the first place, each property is unique. Second, determining
precisely what any given property should sell for is a difficult
and expensive undertaking. While some information on prices
is available, most comparisons of properties are distorted by
differing locations and features. At any given time, buyers and
sellers in a specific real estate market are limited. And finally,
the cost of selling one property and replacing it with another
approaches 10% of its value. Obviously, you don't sell your
home and move down the street just because you think the new
home offers a little better value. As a result of all of these factors,
there are periodically great opportunities for a skilled professional with available capital to take advantage of real bargains.

The bottom line is that it is extremely difficult for any investor
to outperform the competition in an efficient market. Whereas
real estate is clearly inefficient, the stock market is undeniably
quite efficient. The only question is whether it is perfectly efficient. This debate will undoubtedly continue for years. The initial academic work on market efficiency studied only U.S. stocks,
but several subsequent analyses indicate that the U.S. bond
market and some foreign markets are also quite efficient. What
about the evidence? The best indications that financial markets
are efficient would be, first, that professional managers fail to
outperform the market consistently, and second, that the average

returns of those managers lag the market return by an amount equal to fees and transaction costs.

» The Evidence «

Unfortunately for professional money managers, the evidence is not very encouraging. First, let's focus on managers who handle the equity portion of large pension, profit-sharing, and endowment funds. According to Indata (a consulting firm), only about 35% of these managers have outperformed the Standard & Poor's 500 Index during the past ten years. In fact, the last year in which more than half of these managers outperformed the market was 1982, and some experts argue that certain special factors that year made even this outperformance questionable. Perhaps most troubling is that the percentage of managers who outperform the market has been trending erratically downward for many years.

The news isn't any better for managers of stock mutual funds. The year 1990 represented the eighth consecutive year that the average equity fund underperformed the Standard & Poor's 500. According to Lipper Analytical Services, the average fund fell 6.27% in 1990 as compared to a 3.1% loss on the index. Over the past ten years, the average fund has trailed the market by 2% per year, which is roughly equal to fees, transaction costs, and other expenses charged to the fund.

Finally, managers have been no more successful in the bond market. Over the past ten years, only about 35% of bond mutual funds have outperformed the Salomon Brothers Broad Investment Grade Bond Index. According to one consulting firm, the SEI Corporation, not a single one of the bond managers it monitors outperformed the Salomon index in each of the last ten years, and only 7.2% of them beat the index in as many as eight of these years.

All of this evidence suggests that even the most astute professional managers are hard pressed to beat the market. Yet I am sure that you have seen track records of managers and mutual funds that showed performance superior to that of the market. And everyone knows that Peter Lynch achieved a stellar record as the manager of the Fidelity Magellan Fund. How do we reconcile these feats with the evidence just presented?

First, most managers enjoy periods when they do outperform the market. The problem is that they do not consistently beat the averages. Their marketing material generally contains performance data covering only the period of superior results. What a coincidence! In addition, a manager will occasionally have a spectacular year, which, even combined with four mediocre years, is sufficient to provide a five-year return in excess of that earned by the market. The message is that you should be duly skeptical of performance information.

Second, a few managers really do have extraordinary records. How is this explained? It could be just luck. If you flip a coin enough times, ultimately you will reach a period when it comes up heads one hundred times in a row. But in truth, a few pros and amateurs are unusually skilled; they are just plain better than the competition. Unfortunately, there aren't many such talents and there are plenty of investors who seek them out. If they really are that good, they probably don't need your money. Therefore, the odds of your finding the few truly skilled players are low considering that more than 10,000 investment management firms and at least 3,000 mutual funds operate in the United States. More than likely, you will pick an "average" manager who will generate returns that trail the market.

Despite this powerful evidence, most people still want to try to beat the market. Recent estimates indicate that only 9% of all funds invested in the 500 stocks of the S&P index is held in index funds. The remaining 91% is caught up in the rat race of trying to beat the competition. My own experience is that the market is quite efficient, and it is extremely hard to find those few truly gifted individuals who consistently outperform. While they do exist, thousands of consultants and pension fund officers are looking to hire them. You really don't have a chance in this game. Therefore, I suggest you adopt the "if you can't beat 'em, join 'em" approach by investing the bulk of your funds in an indexed portfolio.

<h2>»   Index Funds   «</h2>

An index fund is a portfolio that is designed to earn the return on a specific market index by essentially replicating that index. For example, I have previously mentioned that the Standard & Poor's 500 Index is widely used as a proxy for large capitalization stocks. If you had enough money, you could simply buy shares of all 500 stocks in the index in proportions that reflect the index's composition and hold them. By doing this, you would be guaranteed the return on the index. In fact, it is actually posssible to purchase about 300 of the stocks in the index and still have a portfolio that tracks the entire index closely. However, the 300 stocks would *not* be chosen because someone thought they were attractive or offered more potential than the remaining 200. Instead, they would be selected to fairly represent the index as a whole. This takes a little knowledge of statistics to accomplish, but the technology is widely available today.

Here's the point: It is possible to put together a portfolio that will provide exactly the return on any market index. It doesn't take a great deal of expertise to construct an indexed portfolio, and once in place, it requires little maintenance on the investor's part. The great irony is that this kind of simple portfolio has outperformed about two-thirds of the professional investors in the United States.

Why have index funds been so hard to beat? As previously mentioned, the stock market is quite efficient, which makes it awfully hard for any investor to get a leg up on the competition for more than a fleeting moment. Plus, index funds offer several advantages that are structural in nature. First, index funds are always fully invested in stocks. That means they hold no cash equivalent investments. In contrast, most equity mutual funds operate with roughly 5% of their holdings in money market investments at all times. This practice causes an annual return deficit of approximately .25% because stocks outperform money market instruments by at least 5% a year on average. Second, index funds buy stocks and hold them. Changes in the portfolio are very modest and are only made to ensure that the portfolio continues to track the index. On the other hand, traditional mutual funds buy and sell much as 90% of the portfolio *every year*, which racks up commissions and other transaction costs.

Perhaps the most important difference between traditional funds and index funds is fees. Managing an index fund is a rather mechanical process that does not require a high-priced portfolio manager. In fact, most of the work can be done on a personal computer with relatively inexpensive software. The largest indexed mutual fund has an expense ratio of .21%—that is, 21 cents of every $100 invested is withdrawn from the fund every year to pay for investment advisory fees, auditing, and other administrative charges. By way of comparison, the average equity fund has an expense ratio of almost 1.5% ($1.50 per $100). If you take into account the cost of holding short-term investments, transaction costs, and fees, the average fund starts off almost 2% behind the eight ball as compared with the index fund. In a competitive and efficient market, 2% represents an almost insurmountable hurdle.

» **Using Index Funds** «

The asset mixes recommended in Chapter 7 included large capitalization U.S. stocks, small stocks, non-U.S. stocks, bonds, real estate, and money market investments. Index funds are available in four of these six categories. First, I will deal with the two categories in which they are not offered.

Money market funds are mutual funds that invest in short-term, highly liquid investments. Moreover, these funds are strictly regulated with regard to the maturity and the quality of the securities they hold. Therefore, the performance of money market funds falls within a fairly tight band and it is unlikely that any fund's return will vary greatly from the market over time. So there is no need for an index fund of these investments.

Real estate is a very inefficient market in which a skilled professional does have a real chance to beat his competition. First-rate real estate professionals must have expertise in identifying attractive properties, in negotiating their purchase on favorable terms, in managing properties, and finally, in disposing of them at the right time in the cycle. Moreover, given the variety of property types and significant differences in location, it would be virtually impossible to amass a portfolio of properties that was diversified enough to be considered a proxy for the overall market. For both of these reasons, there is no such thing as an index fund in this market, and every real estate investor should attempt to secure the services of the most skilled professionals available.

Index funds are available for investing in the other four categories. Let's consider bonds first. The generally poor performance by bond fund managers makes the case for indexing quite strong, yet I believe it more prudent *not* to index this asset class. Most bond index funds are designed to replicate either the Salomon Brothers Broad Investment Grade Index or the Lehman Government/Corporate Index. Both of these indexes contain corporate bonds, which means that any index fund holds them as well. Remember, we use bonds in your portfolio to hedge against a deflationary collapse. That purpose suggests that your holdings should be limited to U.S. government securities because they are not subject to default in difficult economic times. Therefore, you should either put together a portfolio of government bonds yourself, or invest in one of the many mutual funds that exclusively contain these bonds. More on bonds later.

It does make good sense to invest in index funds for large capitalization stocks, small stocks, and foreign stocks for the reasons explained earlier. Most index funds use the Standard & Poor's 500 Index for the large capitalization category. In the small-stock segment, there is more variation; some funds use the Russell 2000 Index, other funds prefer the smallest 20% of the stocks traded on the New York Stock Exchange, and some organizations construct their own proxy for the small stock market. Frankly, it doesn't matter a great deal which small stock index fund you choose because all will perform well when small stocks are in favor. Finally, most international funds are pegged to the Morgan–Stanley Capital International EAFE Index, which this book uses as the benchmark for non-U.S. equities. Indexed mutual funds in these categories are available from the Colonial Group of Funds, Dimensional Fund Advisors, the Fidelity Group, and the Vanguard Group of Funds, among other organizations.

Many reasons to invest in index funds have been discussed but you should consider one additional factor: Traditional managers must place bets in order to beat the market, and these bets frequently turn out to be wrong. Therefore, actively managed portfolios periodically underperform the market by a *wide* margin. All of the risk parameters specified in Chapters 4 and 5 were based on the behavior of the market as a whole and not on individual portfolios. If your manager makes big bets and loses, your overall performance could be much worse than was indicated in the tables. In other words, if you try to beat the market, you run the risk of a very unpleasant surprise.

Despite the compelling case for indexing, most people will elect to try to beat the market in order to gain the last ounce of potential return. If you opt for this choice, you can select investments yourself, invest in traditional mutual funds, or hire your own manager. Why don't we consider the pros and cons of each option beginning with the wisdom of selecting your own investments.

»   The Case for Managing Your Own Money   «

Why would you manage your own funds? I can think of three potential reasons. First, selecting investments can be a hobby or pasttime that is a great deal of fun. Second, you may believe you have what it takes to do a better job than the professionals.

Finally, it is possible that managing your own funds may lower the cost of operating your investment program.

In my opinion, the only clearly defensible reason to handle your own funds is the first one: *because you enjoy it*. Researching companies, reading about the economic outlook, and trading securities are all interesting and intellectually stimulating activities. But you must be able to devote the time and energy to do it right.

What about the other reasons? First, some individual investors believe they are smarter than the pros and can achieve better results over time. There are obviously arguments on both sides of this issue. Professional investors have access to substantial resources that may not be available to the individual investor, and they devote their full time and energy to achieving good results. Moreover, the pros tend to manage more diversified portfolios than individual investors, and diversification moderates risk. On the other hand, professionals are particularly vulnerable to the "herd instinct" because they are clustered in large cities, attend the same conferences, and read the same research reports. Second, the pros have a fixation on short-term performance, a factor that should give the patient individual investor an edge. Finally, the individual investor does not have to worry about liquidity, or impacting the market, which is one of the drawbacks of larger fund size. After weighing both sides of this argument, I call it a draw: Neither side has an inherent performance advantage.

What about the issue of costs? Mutual funds have annual expense ratios that typically range from 1% to 2% of the funds invested. The true cost of separately managed accounts is probably very similar to that of mutual funds. If you manage your own funds, you will not have to pay advisory fees, but you will have to subscribe to periodicals and research services of one sort or another to help you select specific assets. Moreover, institutional investors are able to negotiate commissions that are substantially below the rates you pay as an individual, even if you use a discount broker. You may also have to pay an accountant to handle some of your paperwork. In the final analysis, it may be a little cheaper to "do it yourself," but I'm not convinced the cost savings are large enough to sway one to self-management.

If you enjoy picking stocks and bonds and are willing to devote the time and energy required, you will want to focus carefully on Chapter 11. It gives you a few clues on how to approach the selection of investments in an organized manner, but it does not purport to cover the subject. Since there are lots of good books on security analysis, there is no reason for me to reinvent the wheel.

Most individuals who choose not to invest in index funds are, in my judgment, best served by entrusting their money to a professional. For all but the largest investors, mutual funds make good sense. These funds number more than 3,000 and every conceivable strategy is to be found among them. Chapter 10 is devoted to mutual fund selection. Once again, there are many excellent sources of information on mutual funds, so my objective is only to get you headed in the right direction. But what about those investors who want a separate account managed on their behalf?

»   Pros and Cons of Separately Managed Accounts   «

Why would you want a separate portfolio managed on your behalf? First, if you are a substantial investor (greater than $5 million or so), it may be cheaper. Whereas the expense ratio on the average equity mutual fund is about 1.5%, a large investor should be able to negotiate fees on a separate account of .5% to .75%. In fact, the cost of managing a billion-dollar pension plan should be under .4% per year.

A second major reason for a separate portfolio is to satisfy a set of unique investment guidelines or an unusual financial circumstance. For example, you may have inherited a block of low-cost stock that you do not want to sell due to sentimental or tax reasons. In this case, you cannot participate in a mutual fund and must establish a separate account. A second issue involves social or moral considerations. Some investors have strong feelings about certain political or social questions that lead them to avoid the stocks of weapons manufacturers, tobacco producers, distillers, and other companies. While socially conscious mutual funds do exist, none of them may exactly cover the issues that are important to any particular investor. Finally, some individuals prefer a separate account because it affords them a sense of importance or prestige; it allows them to feel that they have "arrived."

While you may have one or more of these reasons for a separate account, they also have many disadvantages that you need to consider. First, top-flight money managers frequently have minimum account sizes of $2 million to $5 million. While some managers have lower minimums, it is unusual to find a creditable firm that accepts an account of less than $250,000. Some brokerage firms do have special programs for smaller investors, but they have some distinct disadvantages that I will cover shortly.

Second, separate accounts raise anew the issue of diversification. You are now aware that it is critical to have four or five asset types in your portfolio. Likewise, it is important to have several different organizations manage your funds in order not to be overly reliant on the performance of a few individuals. Unless you have a pile of money, you probably cannot accomplish this kind of diversity with separate accounts.

Finally, separate accounts usually involve a blizzard of paperwork. You receive a steady stream of brokerage statements, confirmations, and tax forms. Moreover, you have to worry about the custody of your securities and a variety of other administrative issues. If you still want a separate account despite all of these drawbacks, a number of alternatives are open to you. Let's consider their pros and cons.

»»   **Types of Advisers**   ««

Some individuals allow a *stockbroker* to manage their funds on a discretionary basis. This avenue probably is the only opportunity for small investors to have a separately managed account.

Moreover, it can be relatively cheap because the broker usually charges no fee for either management or custody of your assets. Instead, the broker is paid a commission on all trades. These relationships, however, are fraught with problems. First, this arrangement has an inherent conflict of interest: The broker only gets paid by executing trades, and a high level of trading activity usually does not enhance the account's return. Second, while some brokers are skilled managers, many have been trained primarily in sales rather than in financial analysis. Moreover, brokers are relatively unregulated in account management, which makes it hard to get a handle on the level of their performance over time. Finally, a small account with a broker almost certainly is undiversified and, therefore, usually lacks exposure to some desirable asset classes.

To get around all of these problems, several brokerage firms have created programs in which they establish relationships with a number of independent advisers who then manage a portion of each account. Here's the way it works. Suppose you open a $50,000 account with your broker. Your account will be divided among three or four different investment managers, each with a different style or approach. In order to remove the issue of a conflict of interest, the brokerage firm will charge you an annual fee based on the market value of your portfolio and there are no separate commissions charged on trades. This fee is called a "wrap fee" because all the costs are blended, or wrapped, into a single charge. The fee is divided among the broker, his firm, and the outside advisers.

In principle, this is an excellent approach to managing money that is not really much different from that advocated in this book. Still, two problems need to be mentioned. First, many of the brokers are not well equipped to give you sophisticated advice in setting your investment objectives and in selecting an appropriate asset mix. But if this book has taken you over that hurdle such advice is not necessary. The other problem is more serious. The fees charged for these programs are often as high as 3% per annum. Since index funds can be had for .25% per year and traditional mutual funds cost about 1.5%, the wrap fees entail and additional 1.5–2.5% that is almost impossible to make up through skillful management.

Another major source of investment management skill is a bank's *trust department*. These usually provide separately managed accounts and commingled trust funds that are roughly equivalent to mutual funds. Banks are highly regulated, and consequently, most trust departments have guidelines and review processes to ensure that each account is managed according to its objectives. Therefore, placing your money with a trust department offers a degree of safety. Traditionally, banks were viewed as stodgy, conservative organizations doomed, at best, to mediocre performance. As a result of severe competition and a loss of business to independent advisers, many trust departments "got their acts together." The better organizations now pay competitive salaries to attract good talent, and some have subcontracted the management of funds to carefully selected independent advisers. As a result of these actions, some banks have established very creditable track records.

If you choose to open a separately managed account with a bank, you may well suffer from the same diversification problems as you would with a broker-managed account. Small accounts frequently are handled by less-experienced officers, and it is difficult to get exposure to small capitalization and foreign stocks. However, commingled trust funds may overcome these problems. Top banks offer a variety of funds that cover the full range of asset classes and styles. Some even offer a range of index funds. By dividing your assets among several funds, you can enjoy the diversified portfolio structures that were recommended in Chapter 7. An additional factor is that because these funds are highly visible and their results are widely reported, commingled trust funds are usually managed by the most experienced professionals.

Finally, you may want to consider an *independent investment manager*. Independent managers are not related to brokerage firms, banks, or any other organization; thus, their sole source of income is the management of accounts. These advisers, therefore, have few, if any, conflicts of interest and exist only to serve the needs of their clients. The primary advantage of working with such a manager is his or her ability to tailor a portfolio to your needs.

Unfortunately, independent managers also present a few problems. First, I have already referred to the problem of large minimum account sizes. An additional issue is that only a few managers have expertise in large capitalization stocks, small stocks, foreign stocks, and bonds. Therefore, you will have to employ several different managers to cover all of the asset classes. Once again, your net worth must be large to make this work. In addition, most managers are not allowed to actually hold securities, so you also have to hire a bank or brokerage firm to act as custodian. Finally, managers usually charge pretty hefty fees for their services.

After covering these multiple options for investing your portfolio, you surely realize that there are no easy answers or solutions in this business. Still, you should be convinced that separate accounts are only appropriate for those who are either quite wealthy or have unusual needs.

»»   It's Time to Make Your Decision   ««

While the investment business seems mysterious and complex, it is actually pretty easy to structure a sophisticated program. At this point, you have selected an appropriate risk level and identified an asset mix that is optimal for it. If you now accept my advice to hold index funds, three key investment categories in your portfolio will be certain to provide returns consistent with the respective market's performance. That result will greatly enhance the odds that your portfolio's overall return will track my long-range predictions. All that now remains is for you to select a method to invest in U.S. government bonds and to choose the best way to invest in real estate. (These topics are covered in Chapters 10 through 12.)

In all likelihood, you will reject my advice and attempt to beat the market. If you make this decision, you should invest in mutual funds that provide the diversification you want and have a relatively low cost. The alternatives to mutual funds are not viable for just anyone. Managing your own money is a time-consuming affair that you should not consider doing unless you intend to make it your primary occupation or hobby. Finally, separately managed accounts have major drawbacks—minimums and fees—that make them inappropriate for all but the largest investors.

The only investors who have any chance of beating the market are those who apply an investment philosophy in a disciplined manner. All the rest are chasing their own tails. If you opt to try to beat the market, you need to understand and be comfortable with the investment philosophy to be employed, whether by you or your hired manager. The next chapter discusses the investment approaches widely used today and highlights their primary advantages and drawbacks.

»» _____ **Key Points to Remember** _____ **««**

- Markets are so competitive that even the pros have a tough time outperforming market indices.
- By investing in index funds, you will earn the "market" return and are likely to outperform most of the professionals.
- Mutual funds represent the best way to invest for all but the largest investors or those with unusual needs.

CHAPTER 9

INVESTMENT
PHILOSOPHY

Every successful investment manager I know has a sensible, logical investment approach and he sticks to it.
—H. Bradlee Perry,
The Babson Staff Letter, 1982

》》《《

Despite the difficulty in beating the market, a few professional investors have established truly superior track records over long periods of time. Warren Buffet, John Templeton, Peter Lynch, and John Neff are titans in the investment management industry. All four are among that small group of documented winners. While each has a different approach to selecting stocks, all four have one thread in common: Whatever their approach, it is applied in a disciplined and consistent manner. Each of these successful investors can tell you exactly what attributes he looks for in selecting a stock, and *every* stock in his portfolio will meet these criteria. Managers who flit from one approach to another are the proverbial generals fighting the last war; they are always one step behind and doomed to failure. It is not always easy to apply a chosen philosophy on a consistent basis. Investment approaches shift into and out of favor. And every investor goes through periods of poor results and great tension. But the true pros stick to their philosophy despite pressures to change, and ultimately, they earn the best returns.

138

Why is an investment philosophy so important? First, the thousands of publicly owned companies generate a staggering array of potential equity investments. Investors are continually bombarded with buy and sell recommendations from brokers, newsletters, and financial pundits. How in the world can anyone sort through all of these recommendations? In the absence of an organized approach to stock selection, the task of putting together a portfolio is monumental. Historically, bonds were viewed as fairly simple investments that did not require a great deal of analysis. The market has changed, however, and now offers junk bonds, mortgage-backed securities, and myriad other complex fixed-income securities. Consequently, bond investors now face the same difficulties as their equity counterparts in choosing among too many options.

A second reason for a structured approach is the necessity for diversification. You will recall that an equity portfolio can be fully diversified with as few as twenty holdings so long as they represent a variety of industry groups. Therefore, a successful stock picker must focus on not only the relative attractiveness of the stocks being considered for purchase, but also the effect they will have on portfolio diversification. This takes organization and control.

Finally, investors must always deal with their emotions and the herd mentality. Unless an investor develops a set of rules or criteria for selecting stocks and bonds, he or she is vulnerable to both "hot tips" and the risk of panic when things go the wrong way. The bottom line is that you need to develop an investment philosophy if you decide to select your own investments. Likewise, if you choose to depend on a professional, you must understand and be comfortable with his approach to selecting your investments.

Some professionals argue that picking stocks is an art, not a science. Others suggest that a well-defined approach makes stock selection too rigid. Frequently, these assertions represent excuses for poor performance or a justification for high levels of compensation. Picking stocks *is* an art. But it is an art that must be practiced within the framework of a flexible investment philosophy.

»   **Equity Investment Philosophies**   «

In simple terms, every equity investor must have an opinion regarding what makes certain stocks outperform others and must organize his or her research efforts to identify stocks with those characteristics. Were you to listen to fifty different portfolio managers discuss their approach to picking stocks, you might initially think that you had heard fifty different philosophies. On further analysis, you will realize that most practitioners follow one of two basic approaches, or frequently, some combination of the two. They are commonly called "growth" and "value." Let's consider the growth approach first.

Growth Stock Investing

Investors who practice the growth philosophy seek to capitalize on the relationship between the growth of a company and the performance of its stock. The fundamental tenet of the growth approach is that the best performing stocks will be those in which the underlying companies enjoy above-average growth in earnings and dividends. Actually, there are several variations on this basic theme. Some investors look for companies that have the ability to enjoy above-average growth for a long period of time. Others are more interested in companies that are experiencing a sudden burst in earnings even though this growth may not be sustainable. In either case, the key ingredient is growth.

Why do some companies have the ability to grow faster than others? There are dozens of books on management that attempt to identify the key factors leading to corporate success, so it would be presumptuous of me to suggest I know the whole answer. But a few factors that almost everyone agrees on can be cited. First, some companies have superior technology that allows them to dominate their markets. This criteria is obviously of particular importance in evaluating the computer and drug industries as well as other research intensive businesses. Second, excellent products and superb marketing can create a consumer franchise that is very difficult for competitors to threaten. For example, the dominant position of Nabisco products as well as the strength of Reynolds tobacco justified the huge price that was paid for R.J. Reynolds in the now famous takeover by Kolberg, Kravis, and Roberts. Third, some companies, such as Federal Express, create a new industry as a result of an insightful or creative idea and rise to dominate later rivals. Finally, many companies dominate their markets because they are the low-cost producers of their products. This efficiency in operations allows them to price their products aggressively and gain significant market share. As you would expect, the common thread among all of these examples is excellent management.

Knowing these success factors, how does one identify potential growth stocks? One easy clue may be companies that have grown rapidly in the past. In other words, strong companies tend to stay ahead of the pack. Beyond that, growth stock investors look for companies that have gained leadership positions in each of their markets, because a top position usually brings with it a large share of that market. Also, growth companies often show a high level of spending on research and development and the proven ability to bring new products to the market. Finally, most growth companies have strong balance sheets that allow them to finance future growth.

All of these indicators of growth companies are somewhat abstract. To bring the concept of growth investing closer to home, we can review an actual list of securities that I borrowed from a growth stock money manager. While every growth portfolio will be different, this list gives you a good sense of what a quality growth portfolio looks like.

Abbott Labs
Automatic Data Processing
Banc One
Bandag
Borden
Bristol-Myers Squibb
Community Psychiatric
Con Agra

Deluxe Corp.
Walt Disney
Dun & Bradstreet
Equifax
Food Lion
John Harland
Melville Corp.
Merck
Reuters
Safety-Kleen
Sara Lee
Sigma Aldrich
Super Valu Stores
Upjohn
UST
Wal-Mart Stores
Waste Management

While you are probably not familiar with all of these companies, Borden, Walt Disney, Sara Lee, and Wal-Mart Stores are essentially household words to most Americans. The entire list of twenty-five companies represents a variety of industries, and virtually every one of them occupies either the number one or two position in its industry. Over the past five years, both earnings and dividends of these companies have grown about 50% faster than the average rate for all companies on the stock market, and many analysts expect them to enjoy premium growth in the future.

Since there is no such thing as a free lunch in the investment business, you should ask why everyone does not buy these stocks, given their growth characteristics. The answer is that they sell for a premium price. Most investors use the price earnings ratio (P/E) of a company as one measure of its valuation level. The P/E tells you how much you are paying for each dollar of the company's earnings per share. For example, a company whose stock trades at $25.00 would be selling at a P/E of 12.5 assuming that its earnings per share is $2.00. As a frame of reference, the

P/E on the Standard & Poor's 500 has averaged about 14 over the past sixty years. The list of twenty-five growth stocks sells on average at a P/E that is 30% greater than the average of all P/Es on the market. In other words, they are 30% more expensive than the average stock. The tough part of being a growth stock investor is deciding whether the above-average growth that these companies enjoy justifies their premium price in the market.

Now that you have a basic understanding of this approach, the next question is whether it works or not. A recent study by Goldman Sachs compared the returns on high growth stocks with those of low growth companies during the period 1977 to 1989. In each year they calculated the returns on stocks in the twenty industries that enjoyed the largest increase in corporate earnings over the prior year, and compared them with the twenty industries that experienced the poorest growth. The stocks of the higher growth industries enjoyed superior returns in twelve out of the thirteen years; on average, they provided an annual return of 25.9% as compared to 6.6% for the laggards. The high-growth industries also outperformed the market in those twelve years: Their 25.9% return exceeded the market's average return by about 11% per year. These data suggest that the ability to select companies that will enjoy strong growth in earnings should allow an investor to outperform. The tough part of the job is recognizing this impending growth before other investors do.

As is the case with every facet of investing, the growth stock approach has both pluses and minuses. First, the pluses: Growth stocks are exciting companies that are usually characterized by innovation and articulate, visionary management. A second advantage is that their dominance of market segments frequently allows them to survive a difficult economic environment in good shape. Finally, many of America's great fortunes have been made by buying and holding the stocks of these leading companies.

The principal drawback of growth stocks is that, because they carry high expectations and sell at lofty prices, they are subject to sudden drops in value. Having paid a premium for predictable and sustainable growth, investors have little patience with a disappointment in performance. If a growth company stumbles, watch out! When one of these companies reports earnings that are below expectations, there is usually an immediate and severe decline in its stock price. Some years ago, the brokerage firm of Kidder Peabody nicknamed these "torpedo stocks" because they sink like a ship in response to bad news. Therefore, if you follow the growth approach, you have to be prepared to mentally and financially withstand an occasional calamity in your portfolio. Your diversified investment program should allow you to weather the event financially. Your ability to survive the emotional trauma is another issue.

Technical Analysis

Before moving to the value approach, I need to spend a moment on technical analysis because it is a distant cousin of growth investing. Technical analysis is the art of trying to forecast future stock behavior based on past stock price patterns. The idea is simple enough: Stock prices change because investors make decisions to buy and sell. Being creatures of habit, individuals make their decisions in the same manner time after time. It is not necessary to understand how they make these decisions, we need only know that they always use the same logic. By looking at charts of stock prices, therefore, one should be able to pick out patterns that occur over and over again. By learning to identify these patterns and by noting what happens after each appears, one can predict future stock price behavior when any particular pattern next appears.

Business scholars hold technical analysis in very low esteem because it is a free-flowing art form without a clear set of rules. Most academicians argue that it is impossible for anyone to outperform the competition using this technique because others can recognize the patterns just as easily and quickly. In other words, since lots of investors can see these patterns beginning to develop, their implications are already reflected in stock prices. While many professionals will not admit to using this technique, most actually do to a greater or lesser extent.

Technical analysis is distantly related to the growth approach because it tends to focus on companies whose stocks are "hot." Technicians look for stocks that are showing "relative strength," which means that they are outperforming others. They also look for stocks whose prices have broken through previous "highs," for such movement is a sign of momentum. Finally, technicians are interested in stocks that are "under accumulation" because that means they are becoming increasingly popular on Wall Street.

The catchwords for both growth stock investing and technical analysis are momentum, action, volume, and enthusiasm. As you will see, *value* stocks represent the antithesis of each of these concepts.

The Value Approach

Value investors believe that a good analyst can determine the value of any company. It doesn't matter whether the company is a "good" or "bad" business or whether it is growing rapidly or slowly. In every instance, the company's stock has a fair value. The value investor analyzes a number of companies and then buys those stocks that are selling at the steepest discount to his appraisal of the companies' worth. Michael Price, who manages a successful value fund called Mutual Shares, says that he tries to buy stocks in which the price represents only 50% of its true value. The key to being a successful value investor is the ability to dig into a company's finances to determine what it is really worth.

How does one estimate the value of a company? The easiest way is to find similar companies that are growing at about the same rate as the company being analyzed. The price-earnings ratios and other valuation measures of the comparables can then be applied to determine a fair value. While many practitioners do follow this approach, it is difficult to discover undervalued situations because everyone else is using the same yardstick. If you are to gain an advantage over other investors, you must dig deeper. The most successful value investors are those who have the energy and ability to discover hidden assets. For example, some companies carry real estate on their books based on their original cost when the actual market value is much greater. In fact, I am familiar with one instance in which the true value of a retailer's land is equal to the price of the stock. In other words, you get the retail business for free. In other cases, accounting policies can understate the value of inventories, and some companies have a hidden asset in the form of an overfunded pension fund. Analysts frequently underestimate the value of strong consumer franchises as reflected in financial statements. Finally, many investors are so afraid of owning a company in bankruptcy that they undervalue the stocks of companies in financial distress.

Value players tend to focus on companies in mature industries that are overlooked by Wall Street. The best bargains are found in companies that are totally out of favor, and not in stocks that are in vogue. The value investor must be willing to go against the grain to buy stocks that everybody else is selling. For this reason, value investing is often referred to as a "contrarian" strategy. It takes courage and independence to practice that strategy successfully.

The growth portfolio shown previously contained several leading companies in industries such as drugs, retailing, consumer products, and business services. In contrast, consider the portfolio structure of the Windsor Fund, a mutual fund of the Vanguard Group, as outlined in its 1990 annual report.

Virtually every one of these investments is in a mature industry that growth players would find mundane and uninteresting. To place this portfolio in the proper context, you must remember that 1990 was characterized by the savings and loan crisis as well as deep concerns regarding the viability of the banking and insurance industries. Yet almost 29% of the portfolio was invested in banks, savings and loan, and insurance stocks. Now that's contrarian investing!

Whereas growth stocks usually sell at "premium" prices, value stocks, by definition, sell at a discount. Most value-oriented portfolios have below-market P/Es, and it is not unusual for

»»	Windsor Fund Industry Weightings, 1990	««
	Airlines	7.4%
	Autos	11.8
	Banks	14.2
	Building	1.3
	Chemicals	8.9
	Utilities	2.1
	Data processing	.9
	Insurance	8.5
	Metals	10.4
	Oil	2.5
	Paper	1.5
	Retail	.8
	S&Ls	6.0
	Steel	3.2
	Telephones	3.8
	Misc & cash	16.7

them to provide more current income in the form of dividends. Without getting into detail, value stocks also sell at a discount according to the price-to-book value and price-to-cash-flow ratios, two other valuation measures also used by professional analysts.

We have seen that the growth stock approach can generate superior returns. What about the value philosophy? It can also produce superior results. Table 9.1 details the performance of value stocks as measured by the P/E.

As indicated, low P/E (or value) stocks outperformed high P/E stocks in each of the last five decades. Moreover, the value stocks outperformed the market in each of these time periods.

The primary advantage of the value approach is limited downside risk. When you buy a stock that is totally down-trodden and out of favor, the odds of a severe decline are pretty low. On the other side of the coin, the stock carries substantial upside potential if other investors notice its value. During the 1980s, many of the takeovers were of value companies whose prices did not reflect the true value of their businesses. The primary risk in value investing is boredom—that is, out-of-favor stocks can

»   **Table 9.1   Annualized Total Return by**   «
Price-Earnings Ratio Quintile
P/E Quintile

Decade	Lowest	Highest	Market
1940s	18.0%	10.8%	16.2%
1950s	22.8	17.3	18.7
1960s	15.2	9.3	11.0
1970s	15.3	7.2	10.5
1980s	19.9	13.5	14.9

Source: Dreman Value Management, L.P.

stay out of favor. When the market is flowing along, it takes great discipline to remain invested in a group of dogs that are not performing. An additional drawback is that it is not exciting to talk at cocktail parties about your steel stocks when your growth-oriented friends are discussing their biotechnology and computer companies.

»   **Which Approach Is Right for You?**   «

The evidence presented thus far suggests that both the growth and value approaches have worked over time. It is not really all that surprising that two seemingly opposite strategies have performed well. It confirms the statement made at the outset that investors with widely varying approaches have been successful by following their disciplines consistently. As it turns out, neither the growth nor value approach is inherently superior. But investors seem to fall in love with one approach for a couple of years only to change their mind and revert to the other method.

The consulting firm of Cambridge Associates maintains a proprietary data base of more than 600 investment managers who are classified according to their approach to investing. Table 9.2 compares the annual returns earned by the "growth" and

»   **Table 9.2   The Cyclical Nature of Common Stock   «**
           Investment Philosophies

Year	Annual Return Growth	Value
1975	31.2%	<u>34.3%</u>
1976	24.0	<u>31.5</u>
1977	.9	<u>3.4</u>
1978	<u>14.4</u>	11.2
1979	<u>29.9</u>	25.6
1980	<u>41.1</u>	28.7
1981	.7	<u>7.7</u>
1982	<u>28.3</u>	27.7
1983	19.3	<u>26.9</u>
1984	1.6	<u>9.6</u>
1985	<u>32.4</u>	31.6
1986	<u>18.5</u>	17.4
1987	<u>6.5</u>	3.7
1988	12.8	<u>20.1</u>
1989	<u>32.6</u>	24.9
1990	<u>−.3</u>	−4.6
Average Compound Return 1975–90	17.2	17.1

Source: Cambridge Associates, Inc.

"value" managers in their universe over the past sixteen years. For each year, the best performing strategy is underlined. As you will note, both strategies have earned a similar rate of return over the entire period, but there is a tendency for one to outperform the other for two or three years before the tide changes.

So where does that leave you? It is important to remember that the objective is to earn attractive rates of return on your portfolio and to achieve the greatest possible degree of stability. The best way to accomplish this objective is to have *both* the growth and value approaches represented. Specifically, I recommend that you consider investing the large capitalization stock portion according to the value approach and the small capitalization stock portion according to the growth discipline. Since this strategy will result in a bias toward value stocks in most portfolios, you might also place the non-U.S. equity segment on the growth side. If you are energetic and willing to keep up with a little more paperwork, it makes sense to have both growth and value represented in each stock segment in your portfolio. In other words, you could select a total of six different mutual funds, two for each of your three equity categories. (I will discuss this concept in more detail in Chapter 14.)

If you choose to select your own stocks, you will find it impossible to employ more than one approach. To be successful, an investor must limit his scope to a single strategy that is implemented consistently. Therefore, you will first need to decide which segment of the portfolio you want to manage, and then decide on your own version of the growth or value philosophy. The remaining two stock categories should then be committed to mutual funds in a way that combines the two philosophies for the right overall balance. You now know everything that is required to be a good steward of your equity funds. Why don't we turn to bonds.

»   Approaches to Bond Management   «

In the last chapter, I suggested that you not use index funds for the bond portion of your portfolio because that entails exposure to corporate bonds, which are subject to default. Instead, you should consider a fairly passive strategy that does not require any particular expertise to implement. It is called the ladder approach.

Under this strategy, you confine your purchases to U.S. government bonds and split your funds among various maturities. For example, you might invest 20% of your fund in five-year bonds, 20% in ten-year bonds, and 20% each in bonds maturing in fifteen, twenty, and twenty-five years. This allocation results in an average maturity of fifteen years, which is long enough to generate attractive returns in a period of declining interest rates brought on by deflation. At the end of five years, the first bonds will mature and the proceeds can then be invested in a twenty-five-year bond at then current rates. Likewise, each five years subsequently, another group of bonds will mature and their proceeds can be reinvested in new bonds. The ladder approach does not involve any forecasting because the maturity of the portfolio remains essentially constant over time. If the fifteen-year average maturity is too long for you, the same basic structure can be created for any range of maturities.

The primary advantages of the ladder approach are that it is easy to implement and does not require any particular expertise. In addition, the periodic maturity of a portion of the fund allows you to reinvest some of your money at higher interest rates. This reinvestment offsets some of the effect of rising inflation and interest rates. The ladder approach also has two potential disadvantages. First, this strategy may not work very well for small investors, because purchasing small amounts of government bonds is both inefficient and costly. It is particularly difficult to implement when bonds are bought with money contributed to the portfolio on a monthly or quarterly basis. Second, this strategy does not allow for any value to be derived from investment management skill. For both of these reasons, many investors should consider a professionally managed fund of one type or another.

»»   **Active Bond Management**   **««**

There are three basic approaches to adding value through active management of a bond portfolio. The first is called *interest rate anticipation*. In essence, this approach is based on forecasting interest rates. Some bonds experience a greater change in price than others in response to a change in interest rates. Specifically, bonds with long maturities and low coupons (for example, zero coupons) are much more volatile than those with the opposite characteristics. Therefore, a bond investor who expects interest rates to fall will switch into volatile securities because they should enjoy the greatest increase in prices. Similarly, a forecast of rising interest rates should cause the investor to move to short maturities and high coupon rates. In simple terms, investors who follow this strategy must accurately forecast interest rates and structure a portfolio that will take maximum advantage of this forecasting skill.

The second major approach is called *sector rotation*. Suppose the difference in interest rates between higher- and lower-quality bonds is normally one percent. If, for whatever reason, the spread narrowed to .5%, the rotator should concentrate in high-quality bonds, because this small difference will not pay him sufficiently to step down in quality. If the spread then widened to 1.5%, he would shift back to lower-quality issues in order to capture the extra yield. Sector rotators also move back and forth between U.S. Treasury Issues and U.S. Agency Paper. They trade between traditional bonds and mortgage-backed securities such as Government National Mortgage Association, or Ginnie Maes. And they switch between shorter and longer maturities depending upon the yields available in each area. But in every case, sector rotation does not rely on an interest rate forecast; it simply attempts to find better value in another sector.

The third strategy for bond management involves *active trading*. Suppose General Motors bonds maturing in ten years yield 9%, while Ford bonds with the same maturity yield 9.05%. By selling the GM bonds and buying the Ford, the trader is able to pick up .05% in extra yield. If the trader is able to pick up small increments on each transaction, he may be able to earn a superior return on the overall portfolio without having to make a big bet on interest rates. Without getting into a number of complex strategies, trading opportunities exist between futures and the underlying bonds as well as between other similar issues. Needless to say, these opportunities are only available to sophisticated traders who can execute their transactions at very low cost.

» **Which Bond Strategy Is Right for You?** «

Once again, it is logical for you to ask which of these strategies is appropriate. It is important to remember that your portfolio holds bonds to generate strong returns in a deflationary environment and that long-term U.S. government securities best serve this purpose. Based on this premise, you should discard the sector rotation strategy because it involves periodic forays into lower quality and corporate bonds. However, a strategy of rotating among different types and categories of U.S. government securities is perfectly acceptable. What about interest rate forecasting? Based on both academic research and the track record of professional bond managers, it is hard to place much confidence in anyone's ability to forecast interest rates. I would, therefore, be wary of funds or managers who make major bets on the direction of rates. It is fine to make modest shifts in maturity or coupon levels in anticipation of a change in rates, but these moves should not be of the "all-or-nothing" variety. Finally, trading strategies represent a low-risk way of adding modest amounts of value.

The bottom line is that the bond portion of your fund is designed to generate current income, a measure of stability, and protection against an economic collapse. In light of these objectives, I would choose either the ladder approach or an actively managed U.S. government bond mutual fund that avoids major changes in maturities and adds modest amounts of return through trading and rotation strategies. If you are wealthy enough to afford a separately managed account, either one of these two approaches is also appropriate.

» **Consistency is the Key to Success** «

If you follow my advice and index the bulk of your portfolio, quite a bit of the information in this chapter will be of only passing interest. But if you want to beat the market, the only way you have any hope of succeeding is to consistently follow a sound investment philosophy. Hence, in the next chapter I stress that one key criterion is a clear and consistently applied approach to investing. Then, in Chapter 11, I help those of you who want to select your own investments to get started.

You will be interested in knowing that you now understand as much about investment philosophies as many individuals who are in charge of large pools of capital. In fact, many consulting firms are paid substantial fees to help large pension funds structure their portfolios and select appropriate managers to fill "growth" and "value" slots. You have now finished the first half of a similar task; you have designated a portion of your portfolio for each stock investing philosophy. With this knowledge, let's move on to selecting the mutual funds that will actually fill each slot in your portfolio.

» _____ **Key Points to Remember** _____ **«**

- An investor's only hope of "beating the market" is to consistently apply a sensible investment philosophy.
- Most equity approaches represent a variant of either the "growth" or "value" philosophies.
- Every equity portfolio should have roughly an equal balance between these two approaches.
- The bond component of your portfolio should be limited to U.S. government securities and should be managed without placing major bets on the direction of interest rates.

CHAPTER 10

MUTUAL FUND
SELECTION

The strongest principle of growth lies in human choice.

—George Eliot

》》 《《

Whether you decide to "index" your portfolio or attempt to "beat the market," you have some tough choices to make. Hundreds of organizations offer mutual funds, and at last count, more than 3,000 individual funds were available. Mutual funds come in all shapes and sizes, and virtually every conceivable investment philosophy is applied by one or more of them. In addition to the sheer number and variety of funds, potential investors must cope with the fact that mutual funds aggressively promote their performance records as do the financial planners and brokers who sell them. Moreover, several business publications provide annual rankings of funds, and some newsletters claim superior results in giving advice as to when to shift from one fund to another. Once again, we are dealing with too many choices, too much information, and too many recommendations—all of the conditions that cause sensory overload.

The only way to avoid this demobilizing syndrome is to go about the selection of funds in an orderly, businesslike manner. The approach that I describe is essentially the same as that followed by America's largest pension plans in choosing their investment managers. In this chapter, I establish three criteria that you should use to differentiate among funds, and I outline a simple process of elimination that will allow you to narrow portfolio candidates down to final choices. I also provide a number of good reference sources for additional information on fund selection. Moreover, I even go so far as to offer four lists of funds to get you started. But at that point, you are called on to do a little work. Fair enough?

It would be easy enough for me to simply give you a list of my favorite funds. However, if you are going to be truly in control of your own financial destiny, you must be able to evaluate, select, and monitor each segment of your portfolio. My objective is to help you make intelligent decisions by effectively using all of the resources that can enlighten those decisions. Before turning to the actual process for evaluating and selecting mutual funds, a little background on funds is in order.

»   Open-End Versus Closed-End Funds   «

First, you need to be aware of the differences between two broad varieties of mutual funds. The most common and familiar variety is the "open-end fund," which allows investors to enter and exit the fund on a daily basis. Here's how it works. At the close of trading each day, the fund calculates the market value of each of the securities held and totals them to determine the value of the entire portfolio. This market value is then divided by the number of shares of the mutual fund outstanding and the result is called the net asset value (NAV). The fund then processes all orders received that day to purchase new shares and to redeem existing shares; each such transaction is based on the NAV, which is the share price on that day. In other words, on any business day, new investors buy into the fund and existing shareholders cash out at the same share price.

Open-end funds have three key aspects that you should remember. First, the number of shares of the fund is unlimited. The size of the fund can change dramatically over time as investors decide to purchase or redeem shares. Second, you purchase or redeem your shares directly by placing an order with the fund itself. No broker or other middleman is involved. Third, the purchase price is determined by the net asset value. Although some funds add a sales charge to the NAV, it is still fair to say that the share price reflects the value of the securities held by the fund.

A "closed-end fund" is much different in its structure. These have a fixed number of shares outstanding, and this number does not change. For example, let's assume that a new closed-end fund is created and that 5 million shares are sold to the public at an offering price of $10 each. After paying legal and underwriting expenses, the fund manager has a little less than $50 million to invest in securities according to the fund's adopted philosophy. Once the fund manager invests all of the proceeds of the offering, the closed-end fund does not deal with purchases and redemptions. Instead, shares in the fund are traded on one of the stock exchanges or in the over-the-counter market. Rather than contacting the fund itself, therefore, purchasers or sellers must place orders with a stockbroker just as if they were buying shares of IBM or General Motors. For an investor to buy shares in a closed-end fund, some existing shareholder must be willing to sell shares, just as is the case with all other stocks.

Thus, the most distinctive feature of closed-end funds is that their share prices are determined by supply and demand. In other words, a closed-end fund trades at whatever price investors are willing to pay. It is not at all unusual, therefore, for that price to be different from the fund's net asset value. During 1990, the Germany Fund traded at a large premium to its value due to the initial euphoria surrounding the reunification of East and West Germany. During the same year, closed-end, junk-bond funds sold at big discounts to their value because of pessimism regarding the outlook for that type of investment. Why should a fund trade at a large discount or premium to the value of the securities held? There really is no good explanation other than that investors react emotionally as a result of fear and greed.

Which of these two varieties of mutual funds is more appropriate for your portfolio? Neither type is inherently superior and both have pros and cons. In the early stages of your search, you should be indifferent between the two types and have several of each among your candidates. You should also apply the same criteria to evaluate both types of funds. However, when you get to the point of making your final selection, two additional criteria need to be considered. First, closed-end funds may be inefficient and costly for small investors who are adding to their portfolios on a monthly or quarterly basis since they are purchased through a stockbroker who charges a commission on each trade. In contrast, no transactions costs are involved in purchasing and redeeming shares in a no-load, open-end fund.

Second, a more important concern is the relationship between the closed-end fund's share price and net asset value. Specifically, the closed-end fund may be more attractive if it is selling at a discount. For example, suppose you have narrowed your search for a small capitalization stock fund to two candidates; one open-end and the other closed. Let's assume that both have a similar investment philosophy, comparable track records, and in fact, are invested in similar holdings. If the closed-end fund happens to be selling at a 10% discount to its NAV, you would clearly select it because you would, in essence, be purchasing the same portfolio 10% cheaper. The laws of economics say that this bargain should not happen, but it frequently does, so why not benefit from it? Before turning to specific criteria for selecting funds, I want to explain two overriding principles that should guide you through the selection process.

»   "Keep It Simple, Stupid"   «

By constructing a portfolio that includes up to five different investment categories as well as several different philosophies, you end up with a diversified, sophisticated investment program. Accordingly, you have no reason to select mutual funds that involve highly specialized or esoteric approaches. Such approaches are employed in funds like "sector" funds, "country" funds, and a variety of funds that use complex option and futures strategies. Avoid them! You should also avoid "balanced funds" that invest in both stocks and bonds, because you coincidentally turn over the asset allocation decision to someone else when you buy into such funds. Instead, the mutual funds you select to fill each portfolio slot should practice straightforward, fundamental approaches. Look for funds that have well-articulated growth or value strategies that they have implemented in a consistent and successful manner.

» **Control Your Costs** «

It is awfully hard to beat the market. The odds are against your selecting one of the winning funds despite the good deal of time and effort you expend to do so. But one thing you can do to impact your investment performance is to control your costs. Mutual funds entail two types of costs: sales loads and operating expenses.

Whereas no-load funds are sold through advertising without a sales charge, load funds are marketed primarily by stockbrokers and financial planners who receive a sales charge, or load, as compensation for their services. Sales charges take many different forms. Traditionally, the buyer pays the charge at the time of purchase in the form of a price that is equal to the net asset value plus the sales load. This form of sales charge is readily visible, because the share offering price and NAV are quoted side by side in the newspaper. The difference between the two amounts represents the load. Loads range as high as 8.5% of the dollars invested. To deal with investor resistance to these charges, however, Wall Street has developed several less obvious means for funds to levy fees. First, some funds do not charge an entry fee; instead, they charge an assessment if you withdraw during the first couple of years after purchase. This is often referred to as a back-end load. Second, many funds use what is called a 12B1 plan in which a portion of the income earned on the fund is siphoned off every year to pay for marketing expenses and sales commissions.

Both load and no-load funds also have annual operating expenses that include the cost of shareholder reports, legal and auditing fees, and administrative overhead. In the case of no-load funds, all of the cost of marketing the fund falls under the heading of operating expense. Most important, both types of funds entail investment advisory fees that are paid to the organization managing the fund in return for investment expertise.

Should you purchase funds that involve sales charges? The simplistic answer is no. First, one reason that some people buy load funs is that the salesperson is available to give advice on structuring a portfolio. After reading this book, you won't need additional advice, so there is no reason to pay for it. A second justification often given is that the annual operating expenses of no-load funds are higher than those of the load funds. It is argued that an investor is better off paying the onetime sales charge than incurring these higher annual fees indefinitely. In fact, there is little or no difference between the annual expenses of the two fund types, and if anything, no-load expense ratios may be a little lower. In other words, the sales charge is a pure add-on. Finally, some salesmen assert that load funds perform better than no-load funds and that this advantage more than compensates for the sales charge. But alas, there is *no* convincing evidence that this higher return is the case.

One could simply state that sales charges should always be avoided; however, it is more appropriate to base a conclusion on a complete analysis of fund costs. A reasonable approach is to spread the sales charge over a period of time, say five years. Therefore, one-fifth of the load is added to the annual expenses in order to determine a true cost of investing in the fund. For example, assuming a sales load of 5% and an expense ratio of 1%, the true cost of the fund would be 2% (5% divided by five years plus 1%). Both the expense ratio and the schedule of sales charges are clearly indicated in the prospectus. Only in this way can load and no-load funds be compared on an apples-to-apples basis. A study that calculated costs in this way was prepared by Lipper Analytical Services and was reported in the 1990 annual report of the Vanguard Funds. The Lipper study found that the total cost of the average mutual fund was 1.7% per year. Yet the average cost of the highest-cost funds was 2.72%, and the lowest-cost funds averaged .77%. In other words, there was almost a 2% annual difference between the highest- and lowest-cost funds! Equity funds have costs slightly higher than bond funds, but the range of annual costs is huge in both instances.

It is reasonable to ask whether costs really matter very much. The efficient markets argument that was presented in Chapter 8 asserted that it is difficult for a fund to consistently outperform the competition. Therefore, the performance of any given fund should approach the average of all funds over time. But that result is before deducting the cost of operating the fund. After all costs, the difference in performance of two different funds generally approximates the difference in their respective costs. Simply stated, a fund with an expense ratio that is .5% greater than the competition should underperform by .5% per year on average. Let's assume you invest $10,000 in a fund and average a net return of 10% for thirty years. At the end of the period, you will have $174,494, assuming the reinvestment of income and ignoring taxes. In another fund whose higher expense ratio reduces your net return to 9.5%, your future value will be $152,203, which is almost 13% less. Costs do matter! In fact, the majority of the top-performing funds tracked by Lipper over the past ten years have below-average expense ratios. It is not a coincidence. The bottom line is that you should always opt for funds with lower expense ratios unless you have *very* compelling information to suggest that higher-cost funds will generate enough extra performance to more than cover the cost differential.

» Criteria for Mutual Fund Selection «

With these general comments in mind, why don't we turn to the specific criteria that should be used to select a fund. In my opinion, three criteria are of primary importance. First, you must have confidence in the organization that manages the fund. Second, a fund should have a clear, well-articulated investment philosophy that you understand and are comfortable with. Finally, the fund's track record should be consistent with its investment approach, and its performance should be superior to that of its peers. Many investors ignore the first two criteria and focus only on performance results. This shortcut is a serious mistake that often leads to disappointing returns and the need to go through the selection process all over again. Why don't we begin with the fund's sponsor.

»   What to Look for in a Mutual Fund Organization   «

Turning over your life savings to someone is obviously a big step. Mutual funds are carefully regulated by the Securities and Exchange Commission (SEC), so you need not worry about fraud or theft. But you are vulnerable to fallout from a fund's administrative problems and poor performance; therefore, you should carefully analyze the strength of the organization that will manage your money. Most of the factors you should consider are simple, commonsense items that apply to any business relationship.

First, a mutual fund organization should be committed to that business and have the resources necessary to manage assets in a first-class manner. In order to make this judgment about a particular organization, you should consider the number and variety of funds offered, total assets under management, the longevity of the firm, and the number of its investment professionals, including research analysts, portfolio managers, and economists. You should also be interested in the administrative or "back office" capability of the organization. You would do well to check with friends, brokers, accountants, attorneys, and other sources regarding the timeliness and accuracy of confirmations, quarterly statements, and the like. Several business publications now rank fund groups, such as Fidelity and Vanguard, in addition to their individual funds. While you need to conduct your own independent review, these rankings represent a good place to start your search for a top-flight organization.

A second critical factor is the experience and capability of the person who actually manages the fund. The ideal situation occurs when the same person has managed the fund for a number of years. In this instance, the performance record is truly indicative of the manager's expertise. In contrast, you should have reservations about a fund in which there has been turnover of key personnel. Since the investment business involves art in addition to science, the chemistry between professionals within a firm is very important. A portfolio manager who performs well in one organization may do poorly in another. Finally, if the portfolio manager is himself a significant investor in the fund or if his compensation is heavily tied to its performance, that is an important consideration. All other things being equal, you should select a fund in which you and the fund manager are in the same boat.

A third consideration is the size of the fund. The investment world is different from corporate America in that bigger is *not* necessarily better. Quite the contrary, the performance of mutual funds tends to be inversely related to size. In other words, big funds do not perform as well as their smaller competitors. The primary reason for this phenomenon is market impact. As a fund increases in size, it tends to move the prices of stocks or bonds as it buys and sells them and this movement often damages performance. One way around this problem is for the fund to purchase small positions in a large number of securities. Unfortunately, this may also decrease returns because the manager's time is diluted by having to stay on top of the financial details of a large number of companies.

How big is too big? The U.S. government bond market is so immense that one buyer or seller does not have any impact. Therefore, size is not an issue in the selection of a bond fund. The same is true of money market funds. Among stock funds, the answer to the size question depends upon the types of securities purchased and the strategy employed. On the one hand, a large

capitalization, value-oriented stock fund can safely operate with
$5 to $7 billion, because it purchases shares in large companies
at a time when other investors are selling them. On the other
hand, a small capitalization growth fund is hard pressed to
generate superior returns when assets exceed $500 million. Ob-
viously, these are rules of thumb that have been successfully
violated by the Magellan Fund and others, but most experts
agree that "small is better" in this segment of the investment
business.

A final note on a mutual fund's organization involves diversification. I have mentioned that some mutual fund organizations
offer all five kinds of the funds necessary to fill the slots in your
portfolio. *But I suggest that you not limit your fund choices to
one organization.* Instead, it is prudent to employ two or three
different fund groups in the management of your portfolio. For
example, you might select funds for large capitalization stocks
and government bonds from one group and choose funds for
small capitalization and international stocks from one or two
other groups. Why is this diversification important? Suppose a
mutual fund group forecasts a decline in interest rates. This
forecast will influence the investment decisions of each of the
funds it offers. Should that forecast turn out to be incorrect, the
performance of all of that group's funds could suffer in varying
degrees. By investing in the funds of several sponsors, it is unlikely your portfolio will be seriously impacted if one group zigs
when it should have zagged.

» Investment Philosophy «

If you choose index funds for your portfolio, you can skip this
section; the return on each segment will simply mirror its respective market index. But as you learned in the last chapter, the
only hope you have of beating the market is to select mutual
funds that employ a clear and consistently applied philosophy.
Mutual funds are often labeled according to the type of securities
they invest in—such as equity, small company, international

equity, or government bonds. These labels should be sufficient
to identify a broad list of funds that could fill each of the slots
in your portfolio. But you will recall that your equity portion
should contain funds that balance your investment between the
growth and value philosophies. Unfortunately, most reference
sources do not label funds according to these terms. How then
do you know a growth or value fund when you see one?

Before you purchase shares in a mutual fund, the fund sponsor
is required to send you the fund's "prospectus," a legal document
that contains a great deal of financial and management information about the fund. Since these documents can be difficult to
read, you might want to study *An Investor's Guide to Reading
the Mutual Fund Prospectus* (copies are available from the pub-
lisher: Investment Company Institute, 1600 M Street, NW, Suite
600, Washington, D.C. 20036). Every prospectus has a section
devoted to the fund's investment objectives and policy. A careful
reading of this information should tell you whether the fund
follows the growth or value approach. If you want to take a
shortcut, you can consult a variety of mutual fund reference
sources that provide excerpts from the prospectus as well as a
good summary of the key information you need to know. (I list
a few of these sources later in connection with researching your
fund prospects.)

By reading the appropriate information in the prospectus (or
reference source), the growth or value bias should come through
clearly. For example, the investment objective of a value fund
might read: "The objective of the Acme Value Fund is to outperform the Standard & Poor's 500 Index by selecting stocks of
out-of-favor companies that are selling below their true value."
Similarly, the objective of a growth fund might be stated as:
"The Acme Growth Fund attempts to earn superior returns by
selecting stocks in companies that are expected to enjoy rapid
growth in earnings and dividends due to their leading technologies, favorable market positions, and superior management." If
the language is not conclusive, you may be able to determine the
strategy employed by looking at the actual securities held by the
fund. Those securities are always listed in a fund's annual report

and are usually grouped by industry. The information in Chapter 9 should have given you a good sense of the type of securities that appear in growth and value portfolios. Growth portfolios will be heavily concentrated in high technology, health care, and selected consumer product companies. Value portfolios are likely to contain companies in more mature industries, such as those represented in the Windsor Fund (see Chapter 9).

The process for evaluating the investment philosophy of a bond fund is identical. Remember that you should limit your candidates to U.S. government bond funds that do not make major bets on the direction of interest rates but rather add value through trading and rotation within the government sector. In keeping with the "keep it simple, stupid" admonition, I would avoid funds that attempt to increase current income by engaging in options transactions and similar strategies.

» Investment Performance «

The tendency of most investors to focus on short-term performance leads inevitably to dissatisfaction and, ultimately, to a decision to change strategies at just the wrong time. In the case of mutual funds, problems begin with the investor's selection criteria. Frequently, investors pick the fund with the highest return over the past five years under the false assumption that these good results indicate unusual skill on the part of the fund manager. In fact, excellent returns in recent years do not tell you much of anything. What is wrong with recent performance as a means of selecting funds?

First, if the fund manager has since left, those exceptional results may be largely irrelevant. How well will the new manager do? Luckily, many of the publications that rank funds now include information on the longevity of each fund's manager. Second, recent results may simply represent good luck and say nothing about the manager's ability. A third trap has to do with consistency. It is possible for a fund to have one extraordinary year that results in an excellent five-year average return despite the fact that the other four years were fairly mediocre. Finally, investment styles come into and go out of favor on a regular basis. A fund reporting strong results may simply be enjoying one of the periods in which its style is in favor. For example, most growth managers outperform when the growth philosophy is in vogue. This does not necessarily indicate skill, and in fact, this fund may have actually underperformed others with the same approach.

For all of these reasons, it is critical that you evaluate performance information in the proper context. What should you look for? First, if the fund manager has changed during the past five years, you are probably better off focusing on the performance of other funds offered by the same organization. In addition, I would focus on the qualitative criteria, such as the strength of the organization and the investment philosophy that the fund will employ. If the manager has been in place for a long period of time, you should evaluate the fund's record over several market cycles, which suggests a minimum time frame of five to ten years. A long time period lowers the odds that luck was a significant factor in the results attained.

Second, look for consistency: First-rate funds should perform reasonably well in both up and down markets. No fund will outperform the competition every year, so you must not have unreasonable expectations. However, you can expect a clear pattern of consistent returns, not a seesaw between good and bad results. Most of the publications that rank funds examine their performance in both rising and falling markets. *Forbes* actually gives each fund a grade in both environments. This information makes it fairly easy to gain a sense of whether a fund manager is disciplined and organized in his approach to investing.

Finally, you must evaluate each fund within its investment context. For instance, a small capitalization stock fund should not be compared with the Standard & Poor's 500 Index, because the performance of large and small capitalization stocks diverges significantly over short periods of time. Similarly, it isn't fair to compare returns between growth and value strategies. Fund performance for each strategy should be evaluated against the returns in the appropriate column in Table 9.2. For example, a value fund that lost 4% in 1990 lagged the Standard & Poor's 500 by .9%. But a 4% loss was actually superior to the -4.6% return earned by the typical value manager; in one sense, that represents above-average performance.

In summary, I want to reemphasize the importance of evaluating mutual fund prospects in the proper context. While most investors focus almost entirely on different fund track records, the *real* pros spend most of their time on the other criteria of organizational strength and disciplined philosophy. Anyone can look at track records and see those that are better than the competition. The real question is whether all ingredients are in place to allow those track records to remain strong in the future. If you are a small investor in mutual funds, you may find it difficult to make some of these judgments. But you need to muster your willpower against being seduced by good recent returns of alluring funds. Your efforts to evaluate all of the criteria I discussed will pay dividends over the long haul.

» **The Selection Process** «

The actual process of choosing a fund is not as difficult as you might think. The best way to approach this problem is through a process of elimination in which you begin with a list of candidates and, by using the criteria just described, narrow it down to a couple of finalists and, ultimately, to a single choice.

The best way to start is by scanning several of the various publications that rank funds. Among others, *Business Week*, *Financial World*, and *Forbes* magazines provide mutual fund surveys that include performance data, fee information, and risk analysis for a large number of funds. Funds are classified by their investment objective and ranked within these different groupings. These rankings are based on performance data that are adjusted for risk and take into account returns in both good and bad markets. A good way to begin is to select a group of funds in each category (large capitalization stock, small capitalization stock, international stock, and U.S. government bonds) that are ranked highly by at least two of these surveys. Since each publication has its own methodology, a high ranking by several organizations should give you a sense that a particular fund deserves a hard look. You should also draw on every other potential source of recommendations. I would ask friends for suggestions, scan the financial press, listen to investment programs on radio and television, and so on. The personnel office of your employer also may have some valuable advice as a result of research done to select profit-sharing or 401(k)-fund vendors. Then, too, brokers and financial planners will gladly provide you with suggestions, although they almost certainly will recommend load funds. One way or the other, you should compile a list of five to ten candidates in each asset category.

Armed with this list, your next step is to head to your local or regional library to do a little serious research. Many publications provide excellent information on a variety of funds, and at least a few of these should be available in most libraries. Generally, these reference sources cover the fund's investment philosophy, parent organization, fees, and performance history. Several of these services also provide a list of the securities held in the portfolio; others include detailed information on the fund's portfolio manager. Among these services are:

Donohues Mutual Fund Almanac
The Mutual Fund Encyclopedia
Mutual Fund Values
Standard & Poor's/Lipper Mutual Fund Profiles
Wiesenberger Investment Companies Service

Undoubtedly, I have omitted a few other excellent services that you may find, but these should get you started.

Next, select a couple of these references and carefully read the information on each of the candidates on your lists. This should allow you to eliminate some contenders and to draw a tighter focus on others. The reasons you might eliminate funds from your consideration are varied. Some of the funds on your list probably entail high fees or sales charges, and one or more may have experienced a change in management. Either of these factors may be sufficient to knock a candidate out of the running. Upon reaching a certain size, some funds no longer accept money from new investors. Obviously, you don't want to spend any time analyzing a fund that is not available. You may also find that some funds have unclear investment approaches or a philosophy that does not fit into your portfolio comfortably. Finally, a review of the fund's performance can raise a red flag. Hopefully, a review of each fund according to the three criteria I recommend will be sufficient to narrow the list to two or three finalists in each asset category that your portfolio needs.

At this point, contact the distributor of each of the finalists and ask them to send you a prospectus and annual report. These documents should be reviewed carefully to confirm that all three of the criteria are satisfied. In particular, you should focus on the fund's investment philosophy to ensure that it fits comfortably into your portfolio structure. When comparing performance records, don't forget to subtract the total cost of investing in the fund in order to ensure an apples-to-apples comparison. The final decision should be based on all of the factors we have reviewed, and it is largely a subjective judgment. While I would not take this process lightly, neither would I lose any sleep over it. By proceeding in a step-by-step manner, the odds of your picking a disaster are pretty low. Moreover, your portfolio will contain between three and five funds, so even a bad choice should not be devastating to the combined return on your portfolio.

To help you get started with the selection process, I gathered four lists of funds from the most recent annual rankings made by *Forbes* and *Business Week*. The funds included in the large capitalization stock, international stock, and U.S. government bond categories received the highest grade from at least one of these two rating services, and most were highly ranked by both magazines. Due to the extended period of poor performance by small capitalization stocks, none of the funds listed were highly ranked by either service. I therefore selected several of the better known funds in this category for your consideration. The prospective funds identified in each category were:

» U.S. Government Bond Funds	U.S. Stock Funds «
AARP GNMA	Dodge & Cox Stock Fund
Benham GNMA	Fidelity Growth & Income
Federated GNMA	Franklin Growth Fund
Fidelity Government Securities	IAI Regional Fund
	Investment Co. of America
T. Rowe Price GNMA	Lindner Fund
Scudder GNMA	Mutual Beacon
Value Line U.S. Government Securities	Phoenix Growth
	Strong Opportunity
Vanguard Fixed Income GNMA	

» International/Global Stock Funds	Small Company Funds «
Europacific Growth	Acorn Fund
Kleinwort Benson International	Dreyfus New Leaders
Oppenheimer Global	Evergreen Fund
T. Rowe Price International	Fidelity OTC
Scudder International	Janus Venture
Sogen International	Pennsylvania Mutual Fund
Templeton Foreign	T. Rowe Price New Horizons
Vanguard Trustees-International Equity	Scudder Development

I want to caution you not to limit your candidates to those shown on my lists. Remember, managers change, organizations change, and funds change. Therefore, you must go through the fund selection process yourself using the most current information available.

»»   Pitfalls   ««

While I can't give you a prescription for success in picking funds, I can point out a few pitfalls you should avoid. Four have been mentioned in the course of this chapter, but they are sufficiently important to merit a reminder. First, it is a serious mistake to place too much emphasis on a fund's recent performance. Second, it is critical that your evaluation of fund performance properly accounts for all expenses. Third, you need to be aware of a change in the management of a successful fund. Finally, you should never confuse excellence with luck or the fact that a particular investment style was in favor.

One less obvious trap involves the merger of several mutual funds. Frequently, small funds are merged because their operating costs become prohibitive below a certain threshold. In this instance, the shareholders benefit because expense ratios decline with the consolidation. However, it is not unusual for a fund with poor performance to be merged into another fund (sometimes a smaller fund) with relatively good results. In this instance, the surviving fund displays the track record of the better-performing fund, and the poor track record simply disappears. Yet it is possible that the personnel who were responsible for the poor record are placed in control of the new entity. This restructuring is all perfectly legal, but it points out once again the danger of overreliance on performance data as the primary selection criterion.

Finally, you must pay attention to fund size. I have already cautioned you to be wary of extremely large funds. You should also be careful of funds that have experienced a great deal of growth in assets. A small fund that generates excellent performance is likely to experience a major inflow of dollars from new investors as well as satisfied shareholders. Unfortunately, the portfolio manager may be forced to alter his strategy to accommodate the additional assets. In addition, the pressure to invest a constant influx of new funds may cause him to relax his disciplines.

» **Separate Managers** «

In Chapter 8, I presented the pros and cons of establishing
your own account with a money manager, and I hope you are
convinced that this approach only makes sense for large investors
or those with rather unusual needs. If you do fall into one of
these categories, how do you go about selecting a manager? In
essence, the process is identical to that followed in picking a
mutual fund.

Some investment consultants describe the criteria for picking
managers as "the four Ps." First, you must have a high degree
of comfort with the *people* involved. Second, the firm must have
an intelligent investment *philosophy*. Third, that philosophy
must be implemented through a disciplined *process*. Finally,
the firm must have good *performance*. The primary difference
between this approach and the mutual fund process is that you
can evaluate your prospective manager face to face. You should
meet several times with the person who will actually manage
your account and make sure the chemistry is good. Does that
person understand your needs? Is he or she willing to tailor
the portfolio to meet your objectives? Can you communicate
effectively with him or her? Since the main advantage of your
own account is the personal touch, make sure that you will be
an important and valued client of the firm.

Once again, the best way to actually pick a manager is through
a process of elimination. Brokerage firms, financial planners,
lawyers, and accountants are all sources of candidates. You
might ask your wealthy friends for recommendations, and there
are services that rank money managers. Radio and TV shows as
well as the financial press often highlight managers, but since
they tend to focus on "hot" managers, you should guard against
being overly influenced by this publicity. Once you develop a list
of candidates, contact the firms and ask for their marketing
material. In general, their brochures will be easier to read than
a mutual fund prospectus. One reason is that these firms are not
subject to the same level of regulation as a mutual fund. By

reviewing this information, you should narrow the list to a couple of finalists. As mentioned, you should visit each firm to discuss the handling of your account and to evaluate the firm's four Ps. It is also helpful to ask the names of some current and *former* clients you can contact. How well satisfied are they? Finally, make your selections with particular emphasis on the chemistry between you and the key personnel at the firm.

» Rounding Out Your Knowledge «

If you chose to invest in mutual funds, you need only learn about real estate investing and you will have sufficient knowledge to implement four of the five steps in your investment program. Real estate is covered in Chapter 12. The next chapter is devoted to the selection of individual stocks and bonds. While it will be of direct interest only to those who intend to personally manage their assets, I encourage you not to skip this chapter because a good understanding of security selection will improve your ability to evaluate both mutual funds and separate managers.

» ———— Key Points to Remember ———— «

- Three criteria should determine the mutual fund you select: the sponsoring organization, the fund's investment philosophy, and its track record.
- The best way to select a fund is through a process of elimination in which you begin with a list of candidates and narrow it ultimately to a single choice.
- You should begin with the assumption that the lowest cost funds are superior.

CHAPTER 11

SECURITY SELECTION

The "average" analyst will probably fare about the
same as the average member of any other profession.
But for the outstanding man—who combines native
ability, a flair for the subject, and a courageous, independent spirit—the sky is the limit.

—Benjamin Graham, David L. Dodd, Sidney Cottle,
    & Charles Tatham, *Security Analysis,*
    Principles and Techniques, 1951

》》 《《

I have argued that the only investors who should bother to select
their own investments are those who want to make investing a
hobby to which they devote a good deal of time, effort, and
mental energy. All of the data presented in Chapter 8 demonstrate that professionals have a tough enough time beating the
market despite their high level of intelligence and their commitment of full work time and considerable resources. If you decide
to enter the fray, therefore, you must prepare yourself to do so
in an organized and disciplined fashion.

It has been suggested that the only hope you have of achieving
above-average returns is to develop an investment philosophy
and implementation process that you follow through thick and
thin. Further, I stated that most approaches to selecting stocks
are variants of either the growth or value philosophies and that
active bond managers follow one or more of three different strategies. Finally, Chapter 9 included a description of the ladder

approach to investing in bonds, which is a simple strategy for those who are not interested in trying to beat the market.

With all of this background in mind, the next question is how you should manage *your money*. Which portion of your portfolio should you manage and which should be turned over to professionals? Which of these various investment philosophies make sense for you? And how do you actually go about selecting stocks or bonds? As has been mentioned, this book is not a manual on security analysis, but I do want to provide enough information to create a framework within which you can handle your own investments.

At the outset, we should agree that certain investment categories offer virtually no opportunity for your management. First off, it is impractical for you to invest the non-U.S. equity portion of your fund. The majority of the professionals in this country have neither the information nor expertise to invest in foreign stocks; hence, a part-time analyst doesn't have a chance. Second, given the availability and low cost of many mutual funds, there is no reason for you to bother investing directly in money market securities. Finally, direct investment in real estate is impractical for all but the largest investors; thus, most individuals should consider a commingled vehicle such as a partnership or a Real Estate Investment Trust (which is covered in Chapter 12).

These eliminations leave three asset categories that you can manage yourself: large capitalization stocks, small capitalization stocks, and bonds. In general, I recommend that you manage only one of these three segments. It is difficult enough to perform well in any single market; outperforming the competition in two or three different categories borders on the impossible. Since the ladder approach to investing in bonds is a "buy and hold" strategy that does not require much work, you should be able to manage both the bond segment and one of the stock segments if you use a bond ladder. But if you want an actively managed bond portfolio, stick to managing only one category yourself, be it bonds or stocks.

Two criteria should determine your choice of a portfolio segment and how you manage it. First, you should select a segment that is comfortable, familiar, and intellectually stimulating. For example, many investors choose to manage their small capitalization growth stocks, because the prospect of discovering "the next Xerox" is both exciting and challenging. The second criterion is more important; it concerns your own strengths and weaknesses.

»   **Gaining an Edge**   «

For you to justify managing your own investments, you must believe that you are better at something than other investors. Remember, the average investor is likely to generate below-average returns after adjustment for transaction costs and other expenses. Therefore, it makes sense to index your portfolio unless you are an above-average investor. In other words, you must have an "edge" on the competition in some area of capability.

It is obviously difficult for any of us to make an objective judgment regarding our own capability. It is awfully hard to accept that we are neither smarter nor more clever than the next guy. But the investment business is populated with intelligent, educated, and highly motivated professionals. Can you look in the mirror and honestly say that you have some skill or insight that the others do not? If so, plunge ahead! Otherwise, index funds or traditional mutual funds make good sense.

What are some possible edges? I believe it is convenient to divide potential advantages into two groups. First, a number of basic skills are required to become a successful money manager. If you are simply better than average at one or more of these skills, you may be able to outperform the competition. Second, some individuals gain an advantage by investing differently from the crowd. In my opinion, it is unlikely that you fall in the first group, but the second offers a ray of hope.

Let's begin by considering all of the skills that are involved in successfully managing money. First, to a greater or lesser extent, most money managers rely on an economic forecast. As you probably know, the track record of professional economists is pretty dismal. While there isn't much hope that you or I could do much better, there is clearly an opportunity for an above-average forecaster to whip the competition. Similarly, market timing offers a means of greatly increasing returns. According to a study by Cambridge Associates, $100 invested in stocks in 1900 would be worth $337,061 at the end of 1990. If that investment had been held out of the stock market during the worst three years of this time period, however, the original $100 investment would be worth $1,285,674. While there is certainly great potential value in market timing, very few, if any, investors have been able to document a successful track record of such timing over a long period of time. But if you have this ability, you indeed possess a valuable skill. Finally, it is possible to outperform others by having an unusually good "feel" for the market. Whether you call it instinct, trading skill, technical analysis, or the "black art," the ability to profit from changes in market trends is certainly a great advantage.

All of these skills are related to the general economic and financial climate. Another whole set of skills is required for one to successfully analyze individual companies. First, some analysts have an unusually good understanding of technology and are well positioned to determine which specific companies will be able to capitalize on it. Similarly, analysts who are particularly in tune with a given industry should be able to predict which leading companies will come out on top of the competitive heap. Other analysts with above-average accounting skills are often able to dissect a company's financial statements and discover hidden or undervalued assets. Some investors spend the bulk of their time assessing new consumer products and trends as a means of identifying rapidly growing companies before others catch on. Finally, Wall Street's intense focus on a company's reported earnings should give an unusually accurate forecaster a leg up because stock prices frequently respond to earnings surprises.

The problem with all of these areas of expertise is that they fall in the mainstream of Wall Street's efforts. Large brokerage firms and money managers have economists, research analysts, and portfolio managers who possess many of these skills to some extent. In addition, these firms have massive computer power and large data bases that are devoted to the ends of economic forecasting, market timing, and technical analysis. Research analysts develop significant expertise in every facet of the industries and companies for which they are responsible. In addition to frequent visits to the companies themselves, these analysts talk to customers, suppliers, competitors, trade associations, and so on. In other words, they are on top of their industry. Given all of these factors to overcome, you have only a slight chance to gain an edge over the competition by playing its game.

But you may be able to beat the professionals by doing something different. Perhaps the easiest way is to invest in a different arena. Money managers and mutual funds generally invest in medium to large companies. A prime reason is that they cannot invest enough money in a small stock to justify the amount of analysis that must be done to stay on top of it. Even managers who specialize in "small" companies tend to invest in companies with capitalizations between $100 and $500 million. Yet more than 3,500 publicly traded companies in the United States have capitalizations under $50 million and these small companies are largely ignored by Wall Street. By focusing on these stocks, you may be able to find some truly undiscovered bargains. Because they are eschewed by Wall Street, you must do a lot of the research yourself, but this study can be a fascinating and rewarding way to spend your free time. You may also be able to get unusual insight by concentrating on a few small local companies to which you can gain access to management.

Another way you can gain an edge is to invest in complex or unusual securities that most investors are hesitant to own or too lazy to analyze. A good example involves payment-in-kind (PIK) securities. A number of companies were taken private during the 1980s in leveraged buyout transactions. The shareholders of these acquired companies were often given a combination of cash and PIK securities as payment for their shares. In many cases, these former stockholders did not want to own the PIK shares and dumped them on the market immediately, which depressed their prices. As a result, the dividend yields on many of them reached 25% and a huge opportunity was created for investors with good analytical skills and a little courage.

What was wrong with these securities? First, the majority of the purchase price in the buyout usually consisted of cash, so each investor was left with relatively few shares of the PIK. Why bother! Second, many investors were legitimately concerned about the viability of the acquired company given the new level of debt. More important, PIK securities pay their dividends in the form of additional shares rather than in cash. For example, an investor who owned 100 shares of a 10% PIK would receive 10 more shares each year. The problem was that the investor had to pay taxes on the dividend despite the fact that he did not actually receive any cash. For all of these reasons, many investors said "who needs it." Whenever this occurs, great buying opportunities are created.

Finally, it is possible for you to outperform the market by taking a "contrarian" approach. In other words, when Wall Street moves "in a herd" to an extreme position, investors who take the opposite tack can often earn enormous returns. To be a successful contrarian, however, takes great courage and a particularly independent spirit; it is, therefore, emotionally demanding as well as mentally challenging. A good example of a contrarian opportunity occurred during 1990. As you will recall, the national savings and loan crisis was burgeoning as was concern about the viability of the U.S. banking and insurance industries. The result was a panic in which major investors sold every stock in their portfolios that had even a remote connection to the financial world. While some of these companies were, in fact, in big trouble, many excellent financial concerns were tarred with the same brush. In this kind of environment, a contrarian investor has the opportunity to buy wonderful stocks at bargain-basement prices.

Obviously, I am not the first person to recognize the kinds of opportunities just mentioned. Many investors do attempt to avoid the herd to find overlooked opportunities. By definition, these investment areas are out of the mainstream, and that provides you with some hope of gaining your edge.

At this point, you need to decide what it is that you are able to do better than the competition. Whether you are simply more skilled than the typical analyst or choose to invest in a different arena, you must have some advantage. Be honest with yourself! If you really can't identify a particular strength or unique strategy, revisit the chapter on selecting mutual funds. Remember also that you can outperform most of the pros with a portfolio of index funds. But if you can convince yourself that you have an advantage over the crowd, the next step is to make sure that you make maximum use of it.

» **Organizing for Success** «

The key to picking your own investments successfully is to design a strategy that takes advantage of your skills and that avoids decisions in areas in which you have no expertise. Many investors are unsuccessful because they try to do too much. For example, some of my friends attempt to time markets, select stocks, and trade options. And these individuals are employed in fields other than the investment management profession. It is hard enough to be really good at any of those much less all three. Therefore, you should confine your activity to a narrow area of focus. Why don't we consider a few examples.

First, let's assume you have no particular skill in selecting individual stocks and bonds, but you are convinced that you have above-average knowledge of the economic and market outlook. You can adopt a strategy in which you move money back and forth between a money market fund and an indexed stock fund depending upon your assessment of the outlook for stock prices. In this instance, you maximize the impact of your market-timing skill without having to pick specific stocks, which you have predetermined is not your strong suit. Similarly, why don't we assume that you are exceptionally good at translating the economic outlook into the best industries to include in your portfolio. But once again, you have no special ability for actually picking individual stocks. By moving your funds into sector mutual funds that correspond with your forecast, you can capitalize on this skill without bothering to analyze individual companies. Finally, if your skills lie in forecasting interest rates, why should you invest the time necessary to carefully analyze one individual bond versus another? Instead, you can invest in long-term U.S. Treasuries when you expect a decline in interest rates and move to money market securities when you expect rates to increase. In each of these situations, it is easy to craft a strategy that takes advantage of your skill without requiring you to make decisions for which you are not qualified.

At the other extreme, many research analysts believe they are talented at analyzing individual companies but distrust their ability to forecast the economy or the market. If you are like this group, you should not bother to time the market; rather, you should always remain fully invested in stocks and bonds according to the long-range target weightings you have established. Instead of trying to forecast the economy, you should devote your time to finding attractive stocks. Similarly, if you have no skill at forecasting interest rates, it makes sense to keep the maturity of your bond portfolio constant and to focus on under-valued market sectors' or particular issues.

To summarize what we have covered up to this point, it is critical that you determine your edge. Once you have identified your leg-up on the competition, it is easy to decide which portfolio segment you will manage and what philosophy will be employed. The remaining segments can then be invested in either index funds or traditional mutual funds. It is also important that you remember to keep a balance between growth and value investments if you opt for active management. The actual strategy you employ should take maximum advantage of your edge without requiring you to make any decisions outside your area of expertise.

⟫ Time-Tested Maxims ⟪

Regardless of the approach you take, your adherence to a couple of time-tested rules will save you from unnecessary pain and agony. First, don't ever forget about diversification. The greatest single mistake that most investors make is to place too many of their eggs in one basket. As has been mentioned, a stock portfolio needs at least twenty holdings to be adequately diversified, although as many as forty or fifty is preferable. But it is not sufficient merely to have a large number of holdings; they must cut across a number of industry and market sectors. The only exception is a U.S. government bond portfolio, since credit quality is not an issue.

Second, don't forget about costs. In Chapter 10, I illustrated the effect of costs on mutual fund performance, and the same principle applies to managing your own funds. Active trading will make your broker happy but will do very little for you. Therefore, negotiate the lowest possible commission rates and trade only when you have compelling reasons to believe a new-found security should replace one of your existing holdings. How many rich traders do you know? Probably very few. America's great fortunes have been made by buying and holding stocks in excellent companies.

⟫ The Stock Selection Process ⟪

Let's assume that you believe your edge lies in analyzing individual companies, and that you have developed your own philosophy and criteria. How do you actually go about the process of picking stocks? As was the case in choosing mutual funds, stock selection is a process of elimination. Thus, you must begin with a list of candidates. First, you should be able to develop some ideas of your own. Yogi Berra pointed out that "it is amazing what you can observe just by looking." Do you see companies in your daily life that have innovative or unique products and services? Are some companies in your area growing rapidly? If you are sympathetic to the growth approach, ask yourself questions of this sort and you may uncover some potential winners. Similarly, value-oriented investors should comb the financial press for companies and industries that are clearly out of favor. All you have to do is look for the grim headlines. Another source of value ideas is the "new-low" list published in many newspapers. This listing identifies all stocks then trading at their lowest price during the past fifty-two weeks.

In addition to your own ideas, you will be deluged with recommendations from brokers, financial publications, and investment gurus. Try to immediately reject those stocks that do not meet your criteria so that you keep the process under control. Finally, good sources of candidates are the many different computer screens that are available. The Value Line Investment Survey ranks a large universe of companies in terms of timeliness and safety. This service is available in most libraries or you can subscribe for a modest annual fee. Many brokerage firms screen their data bases for companies that are growing rapidly or whose stocks are unusually depressed. Other organizations, such as Ford Investors Services, use sophisticated valuation tools to identify companies whose low stock prices do not reflect their growth rates. One way or another, you should emerge from this first step with a list of candidates that on the surface meet your growth or value criteria.

Your next step is to do the homework necessary to decide whether these stocks are as attractive as they appear to be and to determine which ones offer the greatest potential. This involves reading annual reports, brokerage reports, and industry analyses. In addition, good analysts talk directly to a company's management as well as industry experts and competitors. All of this seems like a lot of work, and in fact, it is. Unless you are ready to commit to this level of involvement, you might want to rethink your position on mutual funds.

Finally, from the prospects that survive your scrutiny, you must select a group of stocks that constitute a diversified portfolio and meet your investment philosophy. Once done, you should write down the key criteria that caused you to pick each stock along with any important assumptions that were involved in those choices. You should also set a price target or objective for each holding—that is, your profit expectation. This information allows you to monitor your stocks and, at a future point, often provides a cue as to when to sell. For example, you probably will want to sell your shares of a stock that hits its target. This practice represents good discipline because it prevents a "round-trip"—that is, where you enjoy a large profit from a stock's rise only to have it evaporate when its price recedes to your original cost. Second, it is often prudent to sell if one of your critical assumptions is invalidated. For example, a company's failure to launch a new product may well cause you to sell a stock if the primary reason for owning it was to benefit from the additional earnings that product was expected to generate. Finally, you may want to replace one of your existing holdings with a wonderful new stock idea that offers superior potential. If none of these reasons occur, maintain your existing portfolio—remember, unnecessary trading is very costly.

Selecting stocks requires time, effort, and good sources of information. If you are up to the challenge, I suggest you read a couple of books on this topic and consider taking a formal course where available. The "bible" of this subject is *Security Analysis, Principles and Technique* by Graham, Dodd, Cottle, and Tatham. I also recommend *The New Contrarian Investment Strategy*, by David Dreman, and Peter Lynch's *One Up on Wall Street*. So much for stocks. Let's briefly consider bond strategies.

»»   Managing Your Bond Portfolio   ««

Very few individuals have access to the information necessary to do a good job of rotating among bond sectors, and even fewer can take advantage of bond-trading opportunities. Therefore, only two approaches to self-management are worth considering. First, you can move back and forth between long- and short-term bonds based on changes in your interest rate forecast. Since

I am quite skeptical of anyone's ability to do this successfully, I believe that investors who choose not to purchase a bond mutual fund should opt for the bond-ladder approach.

You will remember from Chapter 9 that this ladder strategy involves spreading your funds among bonds of four or five different maturities, holding them until the first maturity, and at that time, reinvesting the proceeds. This is a simple, passive strategy that requires virtually no expertise and little effort. The key question is what range of maturities is appropriate. It is important to recall that long-term, noncallable, U.S. government bonds best protect your portfolio in the case of a deflationary economic climate. This suggests that a long average maturity is desirable. On the other hand, most investors are nervous about committing to long-term securities. How do you reach a compromise?

The most important determinant of the amount of risk you should take is your time horizon. It makes sense, therefore, to tie the maturity of your bond portfolio to your time horizon. If you will not touch your funds for twenty years, a reasonable approach is to structure your bond portfolio with an average maturity of about twenty years. This could be accomplished by investing 20% of your funds in each of five maturities: ten, fifteen, twenty, twenty-five, and thirty years. On the other hand, an investor with a five-year time horizon should spread his funds among maturities ranging from three to seven years. The advantage of these ladder structures is that they give you some exposure to longer-term bonds that provide the best protection in a deflationary environment, while they also limit the risk to a level that is in accord with your needs.

»» Choosing Your Broker ««

Even if you decide to manage your own stocks or bonds, you will need a broker to execute your trades. It is also convenient to allow your broker to hold your securities, collect dividends and interest, and do a good bit of the accounting work required.

How do you select a broker? The type of broker you choose should depend upon the particular scope of services you need to manage your investments. If you intend to do all of your own research and have access to other sources of information, then you should look for a broker who will execute your trades in the cheapest possible manner. In comparing brokers' charges, be sure to ask about "hidden" costs, such as low-activity fees and service charges in addition to commission rates. It is also important that the broker automatically invest any idle cash held in your account. You should make sure that those balances earn competitive interest rates. Most do-it-yourself investors find that a discount broker meets their needs.

But if you intend to rely on your broker for research and recommendations, a different relationship is called for. In this case, you need a full-service firm, and the personality of the broker becomes important. Selecting a full-service broker is similar to selecting a money management firm, even though you will call the shots. What is the reputation of the firm's research department? Does the broker make effective use of the firm's resources? Is his philosophy compatible with your own? Does he or she understand your needs and seem ready to recommend securities that meet those needs? Finally, is there good chemistry between the two of you, and will you be an important client?

A more important factor that many investors ignore is the financial strength of the brokerage firm. Most brokerage firms belong to the Securities Industry Protection Corporation (SIPC), which insures up to $500,000 in each client's account but no more than $100,000 in cash. Make sure your broker is a member of SIPC. You must realize, however, that this insurance has limitations. It does not protect you from some types of fraud. While there are specific laws against manipulative or fraudulent selling schemes, the recovery of funds in these cases is often difficult. SIPC does protect you against the firm's bankruptcy, but it may take several months to recover your assets. The moral of this story is that you should choose a broker with great care. The firm should have an excellent reputation, a strong balance sheet, and membership in SIPC. Moreover, make sure you keep your account's assets below the SIPC maximums, and keep complete and accurate records to document your holdings and transactions. While we're on the subject of brokers, should you purchase securities on margin?

»   **Buying on Margin**   **«**

More adventurous investors often buy stocks "on margin," which means they borrow a portion of the purchase price from a brokerage firm. The details of margin accounts are fairly complicated, but the basic idea is pretty simple. Suppose you are able to put up $500 and purchase securities valued at $1,000—the other $500 represents a loan from the broker. If the securities you purchase rise in value by 10%, you earn $100, which represents a 20% return on the $500 you put up. Unfortunately, the math works the same way on the downside. In other words, the use of borrowed funds increases both the potential return and loss on your investment. In fact, if the security declines significantly, you may lose more money than you actually invested.

The approach to investing outlined in this book should yield attractive returns and a good night's sleep. In contrast, the use of margin provides anything but a good night's rest. I believe ardently that the use of borrowing should be practiced by only the most aggressive and sophisticated investors. It has no business in a core portfolio. Chapter 14, however, does include a few other aggressive strategies for those who find my basic approach a little too tame.

»   **Down the Home Stretch**   **«**

This chapter is only a quick overview of the complicated world of picking stocks and bonds. Hopefully, it has given you a sense of direction that will guide you through your apprenticeship as a security analyst.

Whether you chose to invest in index funds, traditional mutual

funds, or your own securities, you are now in a position to
implement the bulk of your investment program. In the next
chapter, I deal with the real estate segment of your portfolio.
Real estate investing seems unfamiliar and a bit scary to small
investors, especially those whose experience has been confined
to purchasing private residences. But that is no reason to forego
real estate. You have several options among convenient vehicles
that allow even the smallest investor to participate in this asset
class. More important, you have already developed most of the
knowledge that is necessary to choose your real estate investment
vehicle.

»» _____ Key Points to Remember _____ ««

- Managing a stock portfolio correctly is a tough job that requires
  a major commitment of time and energy.
- If you hope to outperform other investors, you must have an
  "edge" on them in some area of capability.
- Organize your efforts to take maximum advantage of your
  "edge" while avoiding decisions in areas in which you have no
  expertise.

CHAPTER 12

REAL ESTATE

I am of the opinion that the boldest measures are the safest.

—Adm. Horatio Nelson

》》 《《

The late 1980s and early 1990s were characterized by the savings and loan debacle and weak real estate markets in most areas of the country. Against this backdrop, most investors would agree that buying real estate is indeed a bold measure, but not many would be comfortable with Admiral Nelson's statement that "the boldest measures are the safest."

During the five years ending in 1990, the most widely used measure of the performance of real estate, the Frank Russell Index, recorded an average annual return of just 5.1%. While hardly disastrous, this return was disappointing as compared with both other types of investments and inflation, which averaged 4.1% over the same time period. As often happens, many investors have concluded that the poor recent experience means that real estate will never again provide attractive returns. Large pension plans are standing in line to withdraw from pooled real estate funds in which they invested only a few years ago. At the same time, banks are so shell shocked that it is difficult to arrange financing for even the most well-conceived real estate projects. And the general consensus is that some markets will take years to work out of their oversupply of properties.

Clearly, the current problems in the real estate market are

serious, and it may well be the case that returns remain modest
for the next few years. Given this outlook, the key question then
is whether *this* is the time to invest. Fischer Black, a noted
academic and partner of Goldman Sachs, has said, "The market
does just as well, on average, when the investor is out of the
market as it does when he is in. So he loses money, relative to a
simple buy-and-hold strategy, by being out of the market part
of the time." While this comment was made in reference to the
stock market, it applies to all types of investments. The truth is
that no one really knows whether *any* time is the "right time"
to invest. Therefore, if real estate deserves a place in your portfolio, then it makes sense for you to always maintain a significant
weighting in this asset class. As I argued in Chapter 6, real estate
serves as a hedge against inflation; in Chapter 7 I called for real
estate to be given a portfolio weighting between 10% and 20%
depending upon the risk level chosen. These two propositions
show the importance of this asset class to your investment program.

» Real Estate and Inflation «

Since real estate is relatively unfamiliar to many investors, we
should begin with a few of the fundamentals. Real estate serves
as an inflation hedge by generating high returns during periods
of rapid increases in the Consumer Price Index (CPI). This phenomenon occurs for three reasons.

First, most types of rental buildings have more than one tenant, and leases are frequently staggered so that some come up
for renewal each year. During a period when the prices of all
goods and services increase rapidly, the landlord is usually successful at gaining significant increases in rents. As leases are
renegotiated at higher rental rates, the revenues of the landlord
increase. In this type of environment, some of the costs of operating the building also increase. But others, such as mortgage
payments, are fixed. The bottom line is that the landlord's profits
usually increase. Since the market value of a building is related

to its operating profits, the owner reaches the enviable position of either continuing to collect his growing income or selling the property at a nice profit. In a period of rapid inflation, the most effective hedge is provided by properties that have very short leases; their expirations allow rents to be adjusted to changing prices more quickly than long-term leases. Mini warehouses and apartments are particularly desirable, therefore, because their leases normally range from one month to a year.

A second source of inflation protection in some types of real estate is what is called "participating rent." The leases for most types of retailers call for the landlord to receive a base rent plus a percentage of the sales revenues generated by the tenant. In other words, the owner of the property benefits from every item or meal sold by a department store or restaurant. In an inflationary environment, the retailer is forced to raise prices on his goods in order to compensate for increases in his costs. While not always immediate, price increases ultimately result in increased revenues that, in turn, provide the owner with a greater level of participating rent. Once again, rising consumer prices improve the profitability of shopping centers and other types of retail property, and this enhanced profitability increases their value in the real estate market.

The final source of protection stems from increases in replacement cost. A burst of inflation usually leads to increases in the price of land. In addition, rising wages and increased prices of building materials raise the actual cost of construction. Both of these factors significantly increase the cost of developing a new property, and this effect, in turn, enhances the market value of existing buildings. While the first two sources of inflation protection apply to specific property types, the replacement-cost factor results in higher values for all categories of real estate.

While real estate is generally an effective inflation hedge, it is by no means guaranteed to serve this purpose. What can go wrong? First, a significant oversupply of property can make it difficult for landlords to raise rents despite a surge in consumer prices. The significant oversupply of office space in most areas makes this counterforce a real concern today. Second, different

types of properties (e.g., office, retail, apartments) behave differently, since each responds to a unique set of supply and demand
variables. If these variables are not favorable, it is entirely possible for you to be invested in the wrong property types in the
wrong areas. Finally, real estate markets vary significantly from
one region to another. If you are heavily concentrated in the
wrong region, the inflation protection may prove elusive.

By reviewing what can go wrong, we can learn some simple
lessons that prevent a great deal of heartache. First, diversification is absolutely essential. If returns are to be predictable, a
portfolio of real estate must be diversified by property type and
geographic focus. Second, real estate is management intensive.
Successful investors must carefully analyze each property type
in each market. In addition, they must have excellent negotiating
skill as well as the ability to effectively operate a property once
it is purchased. Finally, a time comes in the life of each property
when it is appropriate to sell. The manager must recognize this
time and dispose of the property at the highest possible price.

Needless to say, few investors have all of these skills. It makes
sense for most individuals, therefore, to turn their money over
to an organization of real estate professionals who will make
these critical decisions on their behalf. In the interest of providing
something for everyone, however, this chapter covers the full
range of real estate investments. One way or another, we will
find the right one for you.

» Home Ownership «

Owning a home continues to represent the cornerstone of the
American dream. At least historically, home owners have enjoyed a good return on their investment and the deductibility
of mortgage interest is one of the few remaining tax shelters.
Moreover, even families with fairly modest incomes have been
able to build significant net worth through the leveraged growth
in equity that home ownership provides. Finally, there is certainly an intangible value that all of us place on owning a little

piece of the rock. For all these reasons, persons who expect to remain in the same community for at least five years will generally benefit from owning a residence as compared with renting one. Investing in a home is better than no exposure at all to real estate. Home ownership, however, is a less-than-perfect way to participate in the real estate market. Why is this the case?

First, a private home does not generate any current income; in fact, the mortgage, tax, utility, and insurance payments result in a net cash drain. All of the return on a home, therefore, comes in the form of appreciation. Changing residences involves substantial costs and a great deal of emotional trauma. The bottom line is that it is difficult to actually realize the return on your home. In contrast, most types of rental property generate income during the first year after purchase that usually falls between 6% and 10% of the dollars invested. Moreover, this income can be expected to grow over time with increases in rents, and there is always the possibility that the property can be sold at a future date to realize a significant capital gain.

The more important problem with confining your real estate portfolio to your home is that it is undiversified. In fact, it is the ultimate of undiversified portfolios in that it consists of one property in one region. In general, residential real estate does represent an inflation hedge because of the replacement cost factor. But it is entirely possible that *your* home will not achieve this goal. If your area has experienced overbuilding or a loss of jobs due to declining business activity, the price of your home may not keep up with inflation. A better alternative, therefore, is to invest in real estate through a means that generates some current income and offers far more diversification than home ownership.

»   Ownership of Income-Producing Properties   «

The most straightforward way to participate in the real estate market is to purchase income-producing property. Apartment buildings, offices, retail properties, and warehouses all produce

current income, and they benefit from the inflation hedge characteristics described above. An additional advantage of direct ownership is control. You can structure a portfolio to meet your
needs, and you are free to buy and sell properties in response to
changing circumstances.

Unfortunately, this strategy is unavailable to all but the heavy-
weight investors who can swing the large sums of capital it
requires. While smaller investors do occasionally buy properties
directly, this strategy is not much of an improvement over home
ownership. The problem is that a modest portfolio may have
sufficient funds to purchase one or, at the most, two small properties. Usually, these holdings are located in the investor's home-
town to facilitate their management and control. Moreover, it is
likely that the investor understands only one type of property—
for example, duplex housing or strip shopping centers. The end
result is an undiversified portfolio that is likely to suffer from
inexperienced, part-time management. The average investor
can, however, circumvent all of these problems. Most investors
can be well served by participating in a real estate vehicle or fund
along with many other individuals who have similar objectives.
Three such vehicles are readily available. The first is called the
limited partnership.

Limited Partnerships

A partnership is a collection of investors who pool their funds in
order to purchase a portfolio of real estate. Normally, all but a
few of these investors are "limited" partners, which means they
have no control over the affairs of the partnership and their
liability is limited to the amount of their investment. The partnership also has one or more general partners who are actually
responsible for the purchase, management, and disposition of
real estate. Since the general partner is in charge, he is responsible for acting in the best interest of all the partners and is liable
for breaches of this fiduciary duty. The partnership does not
itself pay any taxes on income or capital gains, but each partner
must report his share of the income or losses generated.

This structure has two principal advantages. First, by pooling their funds, the partners are able to construct a portfolio that is much more diversified than any single partner could achieve on his own. Second, all partners have the opportunity to benefit from the skill of the general partner. Frequently, the general partner is an organization with a large staff of real estate professionals who have the expertise and resources to manage a variety of properties on a national basis. A less important, but nonetheless real, benefit is that the general partner handles all of the administrative details of the partnership, including the preparation of tax forms.

Unfortunately, limited partnerships also have several real or potential drawbacks. First, most partnerships are created for terms of approximately ten years. The general partner buys properties during the early years, manages them over a period of years, and attempts to sell them at the optimal time. In any case, remaining properties are sold during the last year or two of the partnership's life, the proceeds are distributed to the partners, and the partnership is then dissolved. Here's the rub. Many partnerships do not allow a limited partner to withdraw for *any* reason. Even if a partner is allowed to sell his interest, the buyer demands a big discount from its true value. Second, as a limited partner, you have no control over partnership activities and are largely at the mercy of the general partner. Needless to say, the combination of a total lack of control and a ten-year commitment should lead you to select your partners carefully.

The third drawback is that a partnership is usually what is called a "blind pool." The partnership documents describe in general terms the investment philosophy and strategy to be employed, but they will not specify which properties will be purchased. Moreover, no guarantee is given that the general partner will follow the approach outlined in the prospectus. In short, you are totally dependent on the skill and integrity of the general partner, and your investment is very much an act of faith.

The final problem with partnerships is the level of fees. Each of the limited partners pays his share of legal, printing, and miscellaneous organizational costs. Partnerships are often sold by stockbrokers and financial planners who receive a fat commission for their trouble. Moreover, the general partner is frequently paid a fee to investigate, evaluate, and actually purchase each of the partnership's investments. In some cases, these front-end fees alone total as much as 20% of your investment. As if this weren't bad enough, the general partner is paid ongoing fees to manage the partnership, and he frequently participates in any profits earned. After taking all of these expenses into account, the limited partners may not earn satisfactory rates of return despite a reasonably good job of investing by the general partner.

I do not want to state categorically that you should never invest in a real estate partnership. But I do want to emphasize that you should evaluate these opportunities *very* carefully. Do a good bit of homework on the record of the general partner, make sure you are comfortable with the strategy that will be employed, and take a hard look at the schedule of fees you will pay. Also, don't pay any attention to the returns that are projected; they are meaningless. If those cautions scare you away from partnerships, you may want to consider a Real Estate Investment Trust (REIT), which overcomes some of the problems associated with partnerships, although they have their own drawbacks.

Real Estate Investment Trusts

A Real Estate Investment Trust, or REIT, is a corporation that is formed to own and operate properties for the benefit of its shareholders. By law, a REIT must have at least a hundred shareholders and must derive at least 75% of its gross income from real estate activities. In addition, a REIT must distribute 95% of its income to shareholders in the form of dividends. As long as it meets these and some other technical requirements, a REIT is exempt from corporate income tax. Instead, each shareholder is taxed directly on the dividends received. While a REIT is a corporation, it is quite similar to a closed-end mutual fund in most respects.

Within the limitations established by the IRS, REITs actually vary considerably in structure and objective. With respect to structure, some REITs are privately held, which means there is no market for their shares. Others trade on the New York and American stock exchanges and in the over-the-counter market. Some REITs are expected to stay in business indefinitely while others are designed to be liquidated at the end of a specified period. Finally, some trusts invest only in one type of property, others are diversified.

Different kinds of trusts also have different investment objectives. A "mortgage" REIT makes loans to real estate projects and is designed for investors who are interested in a high level of current income. "Equity" REITs actually purchase properties with the expectation of earning attractive total rates of return over a long period of time. Finally, "hybrid" trusts use both strategies. In a later section, I provide you with some guidance on how to sort through all of these alternatives.

Real Estate Investment Trusts provide many of the same advantages as limited partnerships. First, by combining the resources of many investors, both vehicles provide the opportunity for a diversified real estate portfolio. Second, both REITs and partnerships entail only limited liability for individual investors—an important shield in our litigious society. Third, the REIT is managed by professional real estate investors who act in the same capacity as the general partner in the partnership format.

In addition to these shared advantages, REITs provide some unique benefits. To begin with, the shares of more than one hundred REITs are publicly traded, which means that you can purchase or sell their shares at any time—so a REIT's shares are infinitely more liquid than an interest in a partnership. As the owner of REIT shares, you receive annual tax documents that are very similar to those provided by a mutual fund. In contrast, partnerships generate a variety of complex and unfamiliar paperwork that may force you to hire an accountant to assist you in preparing your tax return. Finally, the fees paid to the manager of a REIT are usually much more reasonable than those involved in a partnership, so more of the return on the real estate accrues to you.

Unfortunately, REITs also have several drawbacks, primarily those related to the fact that their shares are publicly traded. Returns on real estate are much more stable than those on either stocks or bonds, so the addition of real estate assets to a traditional portfolio of stocks and bonds reduces the overall level of volatility. But since shares in REITs are much more volatile than the underlying real estate held, they diminish the calming effect a real estate allocation would have on the total portfolio. You should recall that real estate prices tend to move in the opposite direction from stock and bond prices. Once again, those offsetting movements have a stabilizing effect on the portfolio. But because REIT shares are publicly traded securities, their prices tend to move in concert with other stock prices. And this movement reduces the diversification benefit of real estate ownership.

Finally, stock prices are impacted by a variety of forces that have little or no connection with the intrinsic value of the underlying companies. In the case of a REIT, the price of its shares fluctuates considerably despite little change in the performance of the real estate owned. A good example occurred in 1990 when the price of the average REIT share fell more than 28%. Yet actual properties, as measured by the Frank Russell Index, returned 1.2% that year. What was going on here? Investors became so pessimistic regarding the outlook for real estate that they dumped REIT shares irrespective of the performance of the underlying properties. For all of these reasons, REITs are less desirable than outright ownership from a portfolio point of view.

Another major drawback of REITs is that their shares tend to trade at prices that are 10–30% less than the real value of the underlying properties owned. This discount occurs because most REITs have an infinite life, so properties may be held for an extended period without actually realizing any appreciation. Purchasing and holding shares, therefore, does not guarantee that you will participate fully in any appreciation on the real estate portfolio. In contrast, a limited partnership must ultimately be dissolved, which means that each property is sold and the proceeds distributed—in other words, each partner is sure to receive his share of the value of the properties. In an attempt to circumvent this problem, many REITs in recent years have been structured with a fixed term. At the end of this term, the REIT will be liquidated in virtually the same manner as a partnership—more on that later.

One practical problem with REITs is that you purchase shares through a stockbroker. If all of your other assets are invested in no-load mutual funds, it may not be worth your while to establish a relationship with a broker just for this small piece of your portfolio. The final real estate vehicle for commingled investing gets around this problem.

Real Estate Security Mutual Funds

A Real Estate Security Mutual Fund is a conventional open-end fund. The distinctive feature of these funds is that they do not buy real estate directly. Instead, they purchase the securities of other corporations that, in turn, have substantial real estate holdings. Frequently, these funds buy shares in REITs that are judged to be particularly well managed or selling at a significant discount to their true value. In addition, they invest in companies that are engaged in a variety of businesses but which also have real estate holdings apparently unrecognized by other investors. For example, forest products companies and railroad companies are sometimes valued on the basis of their primary businesses while their vast real estate holdings are largely ignored. Similarly, even unprofitable hotels or casinos may have underlying real estate values that exceed the price of their stocks.

The primary advantages of these real estate funds are liquidity and flexibility. As a conventional mutual fund, investors can enter and exit at will. Remember, selling shares of a REIT entails a brokerage commission, whereas no such cost is involved in redeeming mutual fund shares. Also, since the mutual fund buys only publicly traded securities, its net asset value is always a "fair" representation of the true value of the assets. As was mentioned, REIT shares often sell at major discounts to their worth. Finally, the fund's investment guidelines usually give the portfolio manager the latitude to invest in a variety of companies and industries. That latitude provides, theoretically, the opportunity for superior results.

The drawbacks of funds are very similar to those of REITs. First, the fact that the fund invests in publicly traded stocks means that it behaves more like a stock than a piece of real estate—that is, your portfolio loses some of the stabilizing benefits of investing in real estate. Then, too, ownership of non–real estate companies such as hotels and railroads adds a variety of other factors to the investment equation. This is another way of saying that a mutual fund of this type is not a pure real estate play.

»   Which Vehicle Is Best for You?   «

In real estate, as in most sectors of investing, no investment vehicle is perfect, each option has significant pros and cons. Direct ownership of a diversified real estate portfolio is the purest play, but this option is only available to large investors. The rest of us must consider one of the pooled vehicles. After carefully weighing the pluses and minuses of each of the three types of commingled funds, I recommend REITs for most investors. Clearly, they have drawbacks, but careful selection of several well-managed REITs provides even the small investor with a diversified real estate portfolio without the necessity to commit to a nonliquid partnership that entails inordinately high fees. I want to emphasize the words *careful selection.* Real estate trusts come in all shapes and sizes, so it is important to develop a set of criteria and a process for their selection.

»   What to Look for in a Real Estate Trust   «

You will recall that there are two broad categories of REITs: mortgage and equity. *Mortgage* REITs make loans or mortgages to real estate projects, and the return to the shareholders of the REIT is related to the interest earned on these loans. *Equity* REITs are actually property owners that benefit both from the current operating income earned by the properties held and any appreciation in their market value that is realized. It is important to understand that inflation protection is derived from the ownership of properties that generate improved profits and increase in value as inflation rises. A lender does not benefit from inflation. Quite the contrary, the value of a fixed-rate mortgage decreases during a period of rising inflation and interest rates. Therefore, you should focus your search primarily on equity REITs. As has been mentioned, some REITs are actually "hybrids" that encompass both properties and loans in their portfolio. This mixed structure is likely to provide a reasonable balance between current income and potential appreciation. But if you select a hybrid REIT, the bulk of the portfolio should consist of direct ownership of properties. Within the universe of equity and hybrid REITs, what criteria should you apply in the selection of candidates for your portfolio?

The first and foremost criterion is diversification. I am probably beginning to sound like a broken record, but it is impossible to overstate the importance of this basic principle. Many REITs, for instance, invest solely in one region or property type. While one of these trusts may be attractive as a specialty investment, it is not suitable as your core real estate holding. Rather, you need to select one or a combination of several trusts that can provide your portfolio with sufficient diversification.

Diversification of real estate should be considered from every aspect. The first point of the diversification issue involves geography. Obviously, your portfolio should have representation in as many different regions as is feasible. No simple formula exists to tell you how a portfolio should be divided among different areas. Some help is gained, however, from the figures in Table 12.1, which break down a large universe of institutionally owned properties by region. In simple terms, this table shows how large pension plans have invested their real estate portfolios.

Still, the issue of geographic diversification is actually more

>>   **Table 12.1   Property Location (% of Universe)**   <<

South	24.9
Midwest	19.5
East	21.4
West	33.6
Canada	.6
	100.0

Source: Institutional Property Consultants

complicated than regional exposure. I am familiar with a REIT that owned properties in: Dallas, Denver, New Orleans, Oklahoma City, and Tulsa. At first blush, representation in these five cities appeared to offer adequate diversification. But all of these cities are heavily impacted by the oil and gas industry, and each was severely penalized by the collapse in oil prices in the early 1980s. As a result, all of the properties performed badly at the same time, and the share price of the REIT declined by about two-thirds. Therefore, not only should the REIT's properties be located in different regions, but those regions should be impacted by different economic trends. For example, you should avoid a REIT whose portfolio shows a concentration in cities that are heavily dependent on federal spending and, in particular, those that rely primarily on defense contracts.

The second point about diversification involves property type. Remember, apartments, office buildings, retail malls, and warehouses are subject to different economic variables; each of these property types experiences its own cycle. Once again, knowing how large pension funds divide their money among different categories is useful. Table 12.2 reveals this mix.

Property type and geographic dispersion are the two most important criteria for diversification, but still other ways of looking at this issue should be considered. It is desirable to have a balance between larger and smaller properties, representation in both central business districts and suburban areas, and exposure to each stage in a property's life (development, fully leased, rehabilitation). Because of these multiple factors, I can't give you

» **Table 12.2 Property Type (% of Universe)** «

Office	30.9
Retail	23.4
Residential	15.0
Industrial	18.9
Other	11.8
	100.0

Source: Institutional Property Consultants

a simple description of what constitutes adequate diversification. The best general statement to keep in mind is this: The more your real estate investments are spread out in accordance with all of these measures, the more predictable and stable will be the return and the less likely will there be a disaster.

The second critical issue after diversification is the quality of the trust's management. Later in this chapter, I list reference sources that provide information on REITs, many of which provide evaluations of management and rankings as to quality and financial strength. The most objective way of evaluating a trust's management is to look at its track record. Specifically, the price of a REIT share is heavily influenced by the dividend it currently pays and the prospect for future dividend growth. You will find it informative, therefore, to look at a long history of a REIT's dividend payments, and in particular, you should look for steady increases. Significant cuts in the dividend paid represent a red flag. A good source of dividend information is the trust's annual report, which can be secured by calling or writing the company. In addition to reviewing the dividend history, you might also read management's description of its investment strategy and carefully review the details of the properties owned by the trust. Finally, you should analyze the expenses charged against the trust's income to help determine whether it is managed efficiently. This information is also contained in the trust's annual report and most of the reference sources provide a basis for comparing different trusts.

A third important consideration is the amount of leverage the REIT is allowed to use. In other words, how much money can it borrow to purchase properties? The use of borrowing offers investors the opportunity for higher rates of return, because the trust can purchase more properties for each dollar invested by the shareholders. However, leverage also increases the risk of property ownership. An unleveraged property that experiences a high vacancy rate or other operating problems may provide a disappointing rate of return, but such events ordinarily do not place the investors' capital at great risk. In contrast, poor performance by a highly leveraged property could lead to foreclosure and a total loss of principal. How much leverage is too much? While there is no simple answer, many real estate experts suggest that you be wary of trusts with a debt that is greater than "two times equity." Stated another way, the debt on a REIT should not be more than 66% of the combined market value of its properties. Personally, I feel more comfortable when debt is between 25% and 50% of the properties' total value, and shareholder's dollars constitute the balance. It is also important that you weigh the kind of debt the trust has on its books. Long-term, fixed-rate mortgages provide the trust with a predictable level of interest expense. In contrast, short-term or floating-rate debt could subject it to serious problems in the event of a large increase in interest rates.

Another factor worth considering is the existence of an exit strategy. As previously mentioned, REIT's shares often sell at discounts of 10–30% of their appraised value partly because the disposition of properties is indefinite. To avoid this problem, many REITs in recent years were formed as "finite life" trusts, which means that their properties will be sold and the trusts liquidated at the end of a specific time period. The risk in this approach is that the liquidation phase of the REIT's life could coincide with a downturn in the real estate cycle and result in the sale of properties at unnecessarily low prices. On the other side of the coin, the price of the REIT's shares should approach its true value as the liquidation phase begins. This should give each shareholder the full benefit of any appreciation that the properties have enjoyed. Since "finite" REITs are relatively new, their performance has not yet produced evidence as to how well the strategy works. Nonetheless, I am attracted to this structure because a well-managed trust should be able to maximize the return to its shareholders by having an orderly strategy of asset disposition.

Finally, it is worth your while to check the price on a per share basis of the trust versus its appraised value. You should recognize at the outset that the appraised value simply represents an estimate of the true value of the properties held. Professional appraisers use a variety of criteria and methods to estimate the value of a property, but in the final analysis, a great deal of judgment is inevitably involved. Consequently, you have no guarantee that a property can be sold for its appraised value. The message is, therefore, that appraised values should be viewed with respectful skepticism. Given these caveats, why not compare share price with share value and purchase a trust selling at a big discount? You should, of course, first carefully analyze several REITs according to all of the criteria discussed. Once you identify several finalists, refer to one of the industry reference sources to find an estimate of the value of each trust. All other things being equal, I would opt for those trusts whose shares sell at the largest discount.

»   How to Actually Select a Real Estate Trust   «

In all likelihood, real estate investing in general and REITs in particular are relatively unfamiliar to you. If so, a good first step is to do some background reading. I recommend *Real Estate Investment Trusts—The Low-Risk, High-Yield, Asset-Growth Opportunity* (published by the New York Institute of Finance, 70 Pine Street, New York, NY 10270). This relatively short book covers most facets of investing in REITs in a straightforward, understandable manner. In addition to useful background information, it includes descriptions of fifteen publicly traded REITs as well as names and addresses of approximately a hundred additional trusts. Once you have a good basic understanding of this investment area, you can turn to the job of actually selecting the right REITs for your portfolio. The process is identical to the one you employed in selecting mutual funds.

The first step is to identify a list of candidates. As has been mentioned, several publications and services evaluate and rank REITs. Two that are available in most libraries are the *Value Line Investment Survey* and *Moody's Investors Service*. Probably the best industry source is a newsletter called the "Realty Stock Digest" (published by Audit Investment, Inc., 139 Summit Avenue, Montvale, NJ 07645-1720). Finally, several brokerage firms have research analysts who follow the REIT industry. In most cases, these firms maintain a list of recommended trusts that you can peruse. When reviewing these materials, you should remember to focus on equity and hybrid trusts and to pay particular attention to their portfolio diversification.

Once you have compiled a manageable list of candidates, the next step is to contact each trust and ask for annual reports and other shareholder information. Using this trust material in conjunction with the information from brokerage firms and the investor services mentioned, carefully analyze each REIT on your list. In addition to diversification, you must apply the other criteria for selection, including management and financial strength, the amount of leverage, the existence of an exit strategy, and the discount to appraised value.

As was the case with mutual funds, your final decision is largely a matter of "gut feel." A single REIT is rarely sufficiently diversified to meet my standards; hence, I suggest that you choose two or more for your portfolio. For example, an ideal package might include two diversified trusts combined with a smaller position in a specialty vehicle such as New Plan Realty (a trust that has been notably successful at buying community shopping centers, primarily in the Northeast). Such a combination should provide both diversification and a little extra sizzle. Once again, I do not want to let you off the hook by giving you

a list of my favorite picks. But the following list of REITs that
are recommended by some industry experts represents a place
to start:

BRE Properties
MGI Properties
New Plan Realty
Vanguard Real Estate Fund I

To give you a sense of what constitutes an "attractive" REIT,
I actually analyzed one of these four recommended trusts. Table
12.3 shows what I found. First, the trust holds nine properties
that are diversified by property type and geography.

Diversification looks good on both counts. Second, I checked
the trust's dividend history and found that the dividend had
been increased in each of the past three years. Currently, the
dividend provides in excess of a 9% yield on the REIT's share
price. Third, I found that outstanding debt represents only 18%
of the market value of the portfolio, which is well within the
guidelines I recommended. Lastly, this trust is a "finite life"
REIT that is scheduled to liquidate its properties between 1994
and 1999. Since the share price of the trust is currently 20%
below the appraised value of the properties, the "finite life"
feature should provide substantial capital appreciation beyond
the 9% current yield.

» **Table 12.3 Portfolio Diversification** «

Property Type	% of Portfolio*	Geographic Region	% of Portfolio*
Retail	20.1	East	19.3
Industrial	32.2	West	41.9
Office	28.4	South	28.6
Residential	19.3	Midwest	10.2
	100.0		100.0

*Market value

>> **Invest Like the Pros** <<

You now are ready to actually set up your investment program. If you have absorbed everything covered to this point, you know what you are trying to accomplish with your investments, how to structure a portfolio, and which investment vehicles to use. Moreover, you have developed a reasonable level of expertise in evaluating money managers, REITs, and mutual funds. In fact, you are now more knowledgeable than many of the professionals who are responsible for investing sizable pools of capital.

Once you actually set your program in motion, you can sit back and enjoy the miracle of compound interest. Unfortunately, your work never totally ends, because you must monitor your progress toward attaining your investment objectives and because your needs will change over the course of your lifetime. These factors necessitate a yearly review of your program. By following the approach outlined in the next chapter, however, your annual review will be short and painless.

>>————— **Key Points to Remember** —————<<

- Real estate generally provides an effective hedge against high inflation.
- Despite recent problems in the real estate market, you should maintain your exposure because no one knows whether *any* time is the "right time" to invest.
- Real Estate Investment Trusts provide a low-cost means of creating a diversified real estate portfolio.
- The process of selecting a REIT is identical to the one you employed in selecting mutual funds.

CHAPTER 13

THE ANNUAL UPDATE AND REVIEW

I have discovered that all human evil comes from this,
man's being unable to sit still in a room.

—Blaise Pascal

»» ««

Wall Street, by its very nature, is a beehive of activity. The market goes up and down, brokerage firms put out buy and sell recommendations, corporations announce their quarterly earnings, and newly released data send the economists back to the drawing board. This perpetual commotion spawns a continuing temptation for investors to make changes in their portfolios. It is awfully easy for you to fall into the trap of believing that the sure path to riches can be found in your broker's latest tip or by switching to a mutual fund that is supposed to be "hot" this year. Moreover, the lure of activity is not limited to individuals; the pros are equally guilty. Mutual funds buy and sell as much as 100% of their portfolios in any given year. In other words, the average length of time they hold a security is just one year. And even large pension funds, which are handled by experienced financial types, hire and fire money managers on a regular basis. So much for long-term investing!

If you step back from this financial fray for one moment, you quickly realize that the primary beneficiaries of all of this whirlwind activity are brokers and consultants. And guess who foots the bill. You do! Wall Street makes its living by executing trades and doing deals. In contrast, investors make money through discipline and patience. If you commit to a long-term strategy, you are not going to jump on the action bandwagon. Rather, by carefully selecting your investment vehicles and sticking with them, you are going to accumulate assets slowly and consistently.

But this strategy does not mean that you should be rigid about your portfolio or oblivious to what is going on in the financial world. Quite the contrary, you must regularly review your investment objectives and monitor your progress toward achieving them. A significant change in your personal circumstances or a fundamental shift in the capital markets may cause a realistic need for you to alter your plan. But any modification should be the result of careful deliberation and not a reaction to the most recent swing in the market. Therefore, it is critical that you learn to review your program in an organized and systematic manner. As was the case with the development of the plan itself, the best place to begin your review is with your investment objectives.

»   **Reviewing Your Investment Objectives**   «

You began this odyssey in Chapter 2 by listing your broad financial goals in simple English. In all likelihood, your list included one or more fairly specific objectives, such as accumulating money for a child's education, and one or more general objectives, such as putting aside money for a rainy day. Once these goals are in place, they tend to remain relatively unchanged over many years. After setting goals, you translated them into a specific risk:return combination that best met your needs. This was a difficult decision in which you were forced to evaluate the tradeoff between comfort and return. Many of the key ingredients in this decision are subject to change. Consequently, your portfolio may evolve with the passage of time despite the fact that your broad objectives are constant. Why don't we consider the key factors in the risk:return decision to understand what might change?

First, you were required to make some assumptions in order to calculate the rate of return necessary to achieve your objectives. One or more of these assumptions may turn out to be incorrect. For instance, the college savings example assumed the cost of an education would increase at a rate equal to the Consumer Price Index plus 2%. Further, it also assumed that you could contribute $325 per month to the program. For present purposes, let's say you began that program about five years ago. In recent years, college costs have actually risen at a rate equal to the Consumer Price Index plus 3–4%. Obviously, a continuation of this trend will result in your accumulated money being insufficient to foot the increased bill. Similarly, you will come up short if you have been unable to consistently make the $325 monthly payment. In either case, something has to give. In simple terms, you have the choice of changing either your college plans or your investment strategy. If you decide to adopt a more aggressive portfolio structure in hopes of overcoming the shortfall, you likewise will have to assume considerably more risk. Hence, you would want to review Chapters 4 and 5 before making this decision lest you take on more risk than your financial status or emotional makeup can tolerate.

Second, even if none of the assumptions go astray, something else may have occurred that alters your ability or willingness to bear investment risk. For example, a significant increase in your compensation or an unexpected inheritance might induce you to take more risk in your portfolio. On the other hand, a deterioration in your health, increased number of dependents, or poor career outlook would usually call for lowering your level of risk. Another possible change is that your time horizon has shortened. For example, a decision to accept an early retirement program would significantly affect your investment strategy.

Finally, it is natural for you to change your attitude about risk as you progress through the investor life cycle. While some investors are willing to roll the die throughout their lives, most become increasingly concerned with the preservation of capital and peace of mind as they move into successively later stages in life. It is difficult to tell you when you will make the transition from one phase to the next, but it is normal for you to have two or three changes in attitude over the course of your investing life.

If you are to adjust your portfolio to changes in your life, you must reexamine your investment objectives once each year. The process should be identical to the one you followed when you initially drafted your objectives and selected your risk:return combination. But this review process should become easier with each successive year. Once you learn to evaluate your psyche and you understand all the factors involved, the actual decision is straightforward. The most likely outcome of most of your annual reviews is that nothing has changed during the past year. Therefore, it seems reasonable to begin with that assumption. You should then reconsider all of the factors that determine how much risk you should take. The key items are your level of financial security, time horizon, and emotional makeup. If nothing has changed relative to these risk factors, you can stick with your current strategy and move on to a review of your progress toward achieving your objectives. But if something has changed, you know what to do: select a risk level appropriate to your changed capability; check Table 7.1 for the portfolio structure recommended for that level; then move your assets from one category to another to create the mix recommended for that portfolio.

»   When Should You Review Your Program?   «

A cardinal point that has been stressed several times is that you should never change your investment strategy in response to a recent move in the market. For example, the worst time to tone down the level of risk in your portfolio is right after a decline. Similarly, you don't want to become a gunslinger when the market is hitting new highs. The best way to avoid this trap is to confine all strategy changes to those that can be justified only after an annual review of your entire program. So, when should you make that review? It really doesn't matter when you actually do it; the key is to avoid acting precipitously. It does make sense, however, to conduct your annual review on roughly the same date each year. I personally find it convenient to review my portfolio in late February or early March for three main reasons. First, virtually all mutual funds, retirement plans, and separately managed portfolios are valued on the last day of the calendar year, but this information is generally not available until several weeks into the first quarter. By waiting until all of your valuations are in hand, you can get a true picture of the assets in each segment of your fund. Second, most funds are evaluated on their performance during the calendar year, and this information also does not become available until several weeks following the end of the year. Finally, many profit-sharing plans make their annual contribution during the first quarter, and additions to IRA and Keough plans are due on April 15. By reviewing your portfolio's structure and performance earlier, you are in a position to allocate these contributions intelligently.

»   Rebalancing Your Portfolio   «

In most cases, your annual review of investment objectives will reaffirm your current risk:return combination, which dictates that the recommended portfolio mix should also remain unchanged. Therefore, you need only rebalance your portfolio. The concept of rebalancing is simple enough. During the year, the weightings in your portfolio will drift away from your original allocations because different markets invariably provide different rates of return. Let's consider a simple example in which half of a portfolio is invested in asset A and the other half in B. Suppose the returns during the year were 20% and 10%, respectively. If the beginning investment was $100 in each, asset A now has a value of $120 and B is worth $110. On a percentage basis, A now represents 52.2% of the portfolio and B is 47.8%. Rebalancing is simply the act of returning the weights to their original values. In this case, you sell $5 of A and reinvest it in B, and the two assets revert to equal weight at $115 each.

Now that you understand the concept, let's see how rebalancing works in a realistic case. Say you had selected portfolio four and began the year 1990 with the weightings recommended for it as follows:

»	Portfolio Weightings	«««
	Large capitalization stocks	35%
	Non-U.S. stocks	15%
	Small capitalization stocks	10%
	Bonds	25%
	Real estate	15%
		100%

The actual returns during 1990 on each of these markets were as follows:

»	Return	«««
	Large capitalization stocks	(3.1)%
	Non-U.S. stocks	(23.4)%
	Small capitalization stocks	(21.6)%
	Bonds	6.2 %
	Real estate	1.2 %

Let's further assume that your portfolio was initially valued at $25,000 and that you actually earned those very returns during 1990. Table 13.1 shows how the portfolio looked at the end of the year and details the changes that must be made to return it to the original weightings—that is, to rebalance.

The figures in the right-hand column tell you that funds must be withdrawn from the large capitalization stock, bond, and real estate categories and reinvested in the non-U.S. and small capitalization stock segments. In other words, some buying and selling is necessary to rebalance this portfolio for the next year.

But another alternative may be feasible. If you add to your

» **Table 13.1 Portfolio Rebalancing** «

	1990 Beginning Value	% Return	1990 Ending Value	Target Weight %	Target Weight $	$ Change
Large capitalization stocks	$8,750	(3.1)	$8,479	35	$8,311	($168)
Non-U.S. stocks	3,750	(23.4)	2,873	15	3,562	689
Small capitalization stocks	2,500	(21.6)	1,960	10	2,375	415
Bonds	6,250	6.2	6,638	25	5,935	(703)
Real estate	3,750	1.2	3,795	15	3,562	(233)
Total	$25,000		$23,745	100	$23,745	

portfolio every year, you may be able to accomplish your rebalancing without actually selling anything. Instead, you can direct the new cash to the correct segments. Let's take the present example with the additional assumption that you are lucky enough to be able to add $5,000 to the portfolio at year end. Table 13.2 illustrates the rebalancing process in this case.

As indicated, the $5,000 is distributed among all five categories in order to return to the correct weightings.

You might reasonably ask why it is necessary to bother making these small adjustments. The answer is that the simple act of rebalancing a portfolio may add as much as .5% per year to the return on its assets. While this may be surprising, the rebalancing process is in reality a disciplined means of "buying low" and "selling high." Though I occasionally get things confused, I believe that this is what good investors are supposed to do. All kidding aside, rebalancing does accomplish the elusive objective of timing different markets. Here's how it works. From Table 12.2 you will note that the rebalancing process calls for selling a portion of the large capitalization stock, bond, and real estate categories where returns in 1990 were (3.1)%, 6.2%, and 1.2%, respectively. The funds derived from these sales are then redeployed to non-U.S. and small capitalization stocks whose value declined 23.4% and 21.6%, respectively, during 1990. In other

»   Table 13.2   Portfolio Rebalancing with Cash Flow   «

	Ending Value	Target Weight		$ Change
		%	$	
Large capitalization stocks	$8,479	35	$10,061	$1,582
Non-U.S. stocks	2,873	15	4,312	1,439
Small capitalization stocks	1,960	10	2,875	915
Bonds	6,638	25	7,185	547
Real estate	3,795	15	4,312	517
Total	$23,745	100%	$28,745*	$5,000

*$23,745 plus $5,000 addition

words, you are selling investments that had performed reasonably well and replacing them with others that had performed poorly. This process does not necessarily add value to your portfolio every year. In this example, your portfolio's performance will be penalized by reducing your bond position if this asset provides the highest return in 1991 as it did during 1990. But on average, you come out ahead by selling high and buying low. Some large funds rebalance monthly or quarterly. Other funds do not follow a fixed schedule but instead wait until one category's weighting has moved off its target by at least 5%. I promised you at the outset that managing your program would not require much effort on your part; however, the rebalancing aspect may involve some administrative or commission costs. The faithful practice of annually rebalancing your portfolio lets you take advantage of the added performance without representing a burden.

»   Rebalancing Versus Market Timing   «

One implication of this approach is that you should maintain a constant asset mix unless you decide to change your investment objectives. Among all of the recommendations in this book, the desirability of a fixed portfolio structure is the most difficult for many individuals to swallow. After all, every investor is subjected to a constant stream of recommendations from market gurus indicating that *now* is the time to buy stocks, sell real estate, lengthen bond maturities, or whatever. Timing enthusiasts argue that there is tremendous opportunity to profit from swings in the markets and that you are foolish not to take advantage of it. Even those investors who are not enticed by short-term timing strategies have a hard time accepting the idea that a given portfolio mix is right for every environment. How can any portfolio be suited for all seasons when markets change and new investment vehicles appear on the scene? Shouldn't you take advantage of new opportunities? Why don't we deal with each of these issues?

In theory, the opportunity to profit from astute changes in portfolio mix is tremendous. In a previous chapter, I mentioned that a study by Cambridge Associates found that an investor who had the good fortune to be out of the market during the three worst years between 1901 and 1990 would have ended up with almost four times as much money as a buy-and-hold strategy would have produced. What I did not tell you was that, if the investor had missed out on the three best years during the same period, the ending value of the portfolio would have been reduced by more than 70%. The moral of the story is that if you play the market-timing game, you had better be right. In fact, the best-known study on market timing, a work by Nobel Laureate William Sharpe, indicated that an investor must make correct timing decisions about 75% of the time in order to beat a buy-and-hold strategy. Remember, the stock market is highly competitive, and a large number of practitioners use highly sophisticated approaches to market timing. Although managers do make a good call here and there, few if any professionals have been able to document a long track record of successful market timing. If the pros can't do it successfully, there is no reason to think you can have much better luck.

Many investors also have a great deal of difficulty accepting that a given asset mix will remain optimal for a long period of time. Most would concede that the recommended weightings in

Table 7.1 look reasonable. But I often hear concerns that they will become outdated at some point. Isn't it dangerous to become wedded to a particular structure? Shouldn't an investor respond to structural changes in the capital markets? The answer to such questions is that it is indeed dangerous to be overly rigid in one's approach to investing; however, it is equally, if not more, dangerous to respond to recent trends in the markets. From my perspective, the most destructive words in the vocabulary of investors are "it's different this time." The relentless fact has been that it is rarely "different this time." Even if a fundamental change occurs in the markets that will render your portfolio obsolete, it is likely that you will not recognize it until long after the fact. The problem is that it is awfully difficult to tell the difference between the temporary distortions that occur routinely in all financial markets and the truly fundamental shifts. Therefore, the most sensible way to manage a long-term investment program is to base its structure on the long history of known relationships between risk and return. Unless you have a great deal of evidence that one of these relationships has changed permanently, you should not tinker with the weightings advised in Table 7.1.

The bottom line is that you should carefully select an asset mix that is in tune with your investment objectives and stick to it until your circumstances change. Don't try to second-guess the markets. Be especially wary of those who would have you alter your strategy because the "world has changed." Rebalance your portfolio once a year, and spend the rest of your time watching it grow. The final step in your annual review is to conduct a brief analysis of investment performance.

» An Overview of Performance Analysis «

Most investors have a preoccupation with short-term performance. This form of myopia is just as prevalent among "professionals" as it is among the small players. Senior corporate officers often complain that Wall Street's intense focus on short-term results forces them to make decisions that may not be in the best long-term interest of their company. Yet while bemoaning this sorry state of affairs, these same officers are quick to fire their pension-fund managers when they have a quarter or two of "bad" results. The development of sophisticated analytical techniques and the availability of cheap computer power have only exacerbated this trend. For a modest price, you can hire a performance measurement company that will provide a huge computer printout containing minute details on the monthly or quarterly performance of your portfolio. This pervasive focus on short-term results is, in my opinion, destructive to our economy as a whole, but I will leave it to the industry statesmen to articulate this impact. This performance mania, moreover, can also wreck havoc with an investment program and I do want to explain how you can avert that damage to your investment plan.

As I have pointed out several times, every investment approach and every fund manager experience periods of good and bad performance. Even such legendary investors as Warren Buffet and John Templeton go through trying times, and these droughts often last several years. If you decide to change funds following a short period of unsatisfactory results, the odds are good that you will sell "at the bottom." Having suffered through the poor returns, you will not be in those funds to enjoy their recovery. Moreover, most investors replace a poor performer with a fund that has enjoyed good returns over the past five years. This move almost guarantees that the next few years will be disappointing because of the tendency of all investors to have both good and bad periods of performance. Thus, you will shortly want to swap funds yet again. So, changing funds is not likely to enhance your returns, and it may even penalize performance. Finally, some real costs are involved in switching gears. You may trigger some unintended tax consequences, and frequently, you will incur commissions of one kind or another. For all of these reasons, you must guard against letting your analysis of short-term performance lead you to respond prematurely.

But, of course, you would be just as imprudent to ignore the annual returns on your funds. Therefore, my objective in the sections ahead is to help you analyze your performance in the right perspective. The most important indicator of the success of your investment program is whether your portfolio is generating the returns necessary to achieve your defined financial goals. If you aren't meeting your goals, who cares how well your investments are performing versus others? Obviously, it is not satisfying to underperform other investors. But you should worry about the competition only after you have determined that your program is on the right trajectory.

»   **Meeting Your Target Return**   «

The end result of the process of setting your investment objectives was a target rate of return and its associated level of risk. Whether you calculated the return necessary to achieve a specific financial objective or backed into your target return from the risk perspective, you established a benchmark against which to measure your progress. Your benchmark is *not* to measure your prowess as an investor or selector of funds; it is meant to tell you whether or not your program is on track. So you should begin by comparing your actual return with your target return for various periods. Most investors look at the past one, three, five, seven, and ten years. In addition, you should look at the entire period since the inception of your program.

If your actual return has been equal to or greater than your target, you have no reason to spend any more time on this issue. You can move on to a quick analysis of your standing versus the competition, which is a second measure of your portfolio's performance. But what if your return has not met expectations? Obviously, a low return for a one -or two-year period is of little consequence, so you need not become concerned unless your performance has lagged for three to five years. But even then, there may not be any reason for great worry. Why not?

In Chapter 2, I explained how to calculate a real target rate of return by subtracting the assumed rate of inflation from the anticipated total return on the portfolio. Now, to assess your actual performance, you should subtract the actual rate of inflation for each year from the total return you have earned each year and then compare the results with the real target. It may well be that everything is still on track. For example, assume that your target rate of return was 10% and that inflation was expected to average 5%. In other words, you needed to earn a 5% real return to meet your objectives. If the actual return on your portfolio for the time period was 9% per annum, your initial reaction is likely to be one of concern and disappointment. However, suppose inflation averaged only 4% over this time period. As it turns out, you have actually achieved your real return target of 5%, and your program remains on track.

Unfortunately, you may experience a long period in which you underperform your objective even after adjusting for inflation. If your goal is fairly general, such as saving money for a rainy day, then an extended period of underperformance versus a target rate of return is not the end of the world. You probably have no reason to do anything differently. But if your goal is highly specific, such as saving money for college, poor results may force you to alter your plans. Time may be running out.

»   **Adapting to Change**   «

What do you do when the actual return on your portfolio is not likely to reach your original objective? To illustrate this situation, let's return to the college savings example outlined in Chapter 2. After making several assumptions, we calculated that you needed to accumulate a portfolio of $144,600 over the next thirteen years. Based on monthly contributions of $325, we discovered that you must earn an absolute (or total) return of 14.2% annually in order to generate this sum.

Let's assume that five years have passed and the actual return on your investments has averaged only 10% per annum. Assume also that the actual inflation rate has averaged 5%, the assumption on which the program was based. Therefore, both the absolute and real return are short by 4.2% (14.2% less 10% and 9.2% less 5%). At this point, you have several choices. First, you can stick with the program and hope the return improves over the next eight years. If the markets cooperate, you might be able to achieve your initial objective. If the 10% return continues, however, your ultimate portfolio value will be just $101,457, which leaves you $43,143 short. Another solution might be to change your investment strategy in an effort to produce a higher rate of return. Unfortunately, the 10% return for the past five years makes it an uphill battle: An average return of 15.95% will be necessary over the next eight years to reach the original target. You will recall that the 14.2% target was already at the high end of the range of possible returns, so 15.9% is just about off the charts. Moreover, you can imagine the amount of risk that you would have to take in quest of a return of this magnitude. Other possible strategies you could adopt include: select a less expensive school; borrow money to make up any shortfall; ask junior to pitch in by getting a job; and kick in more than $325 every month.

While it is certainly no fun to face decisions such as these, I would prefer to be in a position to adjust my plans along the way rather than to reach junior's freshman year in a state of blissful ignorance. By reacting early and combining a few of these alternatives, you stand a good chance of financing a college education without too much pain. Remember, investing is a long-term proposition, so don't overact to either good or bad performance over short periods of time. Yet at the same time, don't be afraid to adjust your plans if performance problems persist to the point of threatening your objectives.

» Performance Analysis «

Whether you manage your own money or participate in one or more mutual funds, you want to know how each segment of your portfolio is doing versus both market indices and other managers. Indeed, many investors spend the bulk of their time and effort on this second component of their performance review. While you should include performance comparisons in *your* review, you should regard it as being far less important than determining whether you are achieving your target return.

In Chapter 8, I recommended that you invest in index funds as passive portfolios designed to achieve the same return as a given market index. By purchasing any of them, you can be assured of earning the corresponding market's return, give or take a little. Alternatively, if you select either securities or funds in an attempt to beat the market, you should reasonably expect to outperform the market index. In either case, the first step in this second phase of your review is to compare the return on each segment of your portfolio with the appropriate market index. By the way, how do you know what the return on your portfolio is? If you hire a manager or invest in a mutual fund, quarterly and annual returns will be reported to you. But if you invest in securities directly, you may have to calculate your own return. To do so, add the year-end dollar value of your portfolio to any dividends or interest received during the year and subtract the beginning dollar value. This represents your total return in dollars, which should then be divided by the beginning value to determine a percentage return.

Comparing your return with a market index seems easy enough, but first you must decide which index is appropriate. Dozens of different market indices exist, and each one is constructed differently. While experts like to argue about which index is the most representative of a particular market, I frankly don't believe it makes a lot of difference. Since you are not going to expend a great deal of energy analyzing performance, the easiest course is to use those benchmarks that are the most widely available to investors. The market indexes that you will find convenient to use are:

»» Category	Index ««
Large capitalization U.S. stocks	Standard & Poor's 500 Index
Small capitalization U.S. stocks	NASDAQ Composite Index
Non-U.S. stocks	Morgan Stanley–Capital International EAFE Index
Bonds	Lehman Government/Corporate Index
Real estate	Frank Russell Index

The first four indices are reported in all major financial publications within the first week after each calendar quarter. The Frank Russell Index, because it is based on the performance of a large universe of properties, is generally not reported until roughly two months after the end of each year.

After recording each index's return for the year, your performance review should be limited to a quick comparison of your return in each category with the appropriate market index. You cannot expect to beat the index every year; no one does! But consistent underperformance in any category relative to the benchmark should lead you to switch funds or rethink the alternative of index funds. Remember, you can be guaranteed market returns at low cost by "joining" the market and giving up trying to beat it.

Most investors are also interested in how their performance compares with that of similar investors. Comparisons of this sort are fraught with peril because of differing styles, client objectives, and in some cases, plain luck. Nevertheless, no one wants to feel left behind. If you invest in mutual funds, it is fairly easy to find out where each of your funds stand. In all likelihood, every fund will provide competitive information in its annual report (particularly if the news is good). Lipper Analytical Services does detailed performance analysis of a large number of funds, and this information is widely reported in the *Wall Street Journal* and other investor publications. *Forbes* and several other magazines provide updates on fund performance in addition to their annual mutual fund surveys. Also, the mutual fund reference sources listed in Chapter 10 provide a great deal of comparative information about the performance of various funds. In addition, a variety of companies rank the performance of money managers who handle separate accounts. Among the best known are the Frank Russell Company, CDA Investment Technologies, and SEI. The best way for you to get this type of information, however, is directly from your money manager.

As was the case with the comparison against market indices, I recommend that you take only a passing glance at this information. If your fund or manager is in the ballpark, don't worry about it. Only a sustained period of poor performance versus similar managers warrants your serious concern. Even then, you should try to understand *why* your manager has underperformed, lest you pull the trigger at just the wrong time. This brings us to the question of when you should change managers or funds.

» When Do You Change Horses? «

I am frequently asked whether it makes sense to withdraw from a fund that has not performed well over a short period and move to another that seems to offer more promise. The short answer is no. In fact, you should change funds or managers only rarely; moreover, the reasons for change often are not related to investment results. In the spirit of full disclosure, I must tell you that my view on this matter does not represent common practice. While most investors pay lip service to the virtue of long-term investing, in reality, few practice it. There is, in the real world, a cottage industry of investment consultants who generate fees by helping large pension funds hire and fire managers. Many of these funds even terminate their managers after only one or two quarters of poor performance. This kind of "instant correction" is costly and nonproductive. Several studies have demonstrated that it may take as much as twenty-five years to statistically prove that an investment manager has added value. Firing a manager or switching funds after a few years, therefore, borders on craziness. Not only is the record unclear that the incumbent manager has lost his touch, but also no solid judgments can be made about the skills of prospective managers. What then should lead you to change?

First, you may want to move your money if a major change in the fund's organization or a turnover among its key professionals has transpired. In particular, a change in the fund's portfolio manager is a red flag. Second, a change in the fund's investment philosophy is grounds for divorce. Remember, you selected a particular fund chiefly because you were comfortable with the organization, the portfolio manager, and his investment philosophy. If any of these factors change, a careful reassessment of your decision is in order. Third, you should keep an eye on the size of the fund. If its assets grow beyond the size guidelines discussed in Chapter 10, that is good reason to believe that its future performance will be adversely impacted. Finally, a period of five to ten years of underperformance versus similar funds normally is long enough to justify a fund switch. But don't pull the trigger quickly. Unless one of these fundamental changes has occurred, stick with your program, because any changes you make are unlikely to add much value and may end up costing you money.

I promised that the annual review would be short and painless. Long-term investors find that since little or nothing changes from year to year, an originally well-conceived program requires only minimal annual maintenance. I hope that you will heed my advice to focus on the long run and avoid the lure of bobbing and weaving. Compound interest works! You win in this business by consistently earning reasonable returns and avoiding disasters. Don't worry about what the next guy is doing; it has no bearing on the success of your program. If your returns, at times, seem embarrassingly low compared with those of your friends, the odds are that others are either lying or poised for disaster. Have sympathy for them! Remember, the tortoise beats the hare in the investment world.

»»   Graduation Day   «««

You have now completed the five-step course in investing. You should be in a position to formulate and implement a successful investment program. The approach I have described will meet the needs of all but the most adventurous investors. While it may not be sexy, it works! Still, some investors are interested in a little extra pizzazz. To meet their needs, the next chapter describes a few bells and whistles that offer the opportunity for higher returns, albeit with some added risk and complexity.

»»——————— Key Points to Remember ———————«««

- It is essential to review your investment program annually and to make any changes dictated by changes in your personal circumstances.
- If nothing has changed, you need only rebalance your portfolio to the target weightings.
- Avoid the temptation to time markets—even the pros can't do it successfully.
- Don't switch funds after a short period of poor returns.

CHAPTER 14

BELLS AND WHISTLES

To achieve satisfactory results is easier than most people realize; to achieve superior results is harder than
it looks.
—Benjamin Graham,
The Intelligent Investor, 1973

》》 《《

The five-step investment program was designed to be simple
and manageable while also being diversified and sophisticated.
I believe most investors will find that one of the seven portfolios
can accomplish their objectives. My own money is invested according to the structure recommended for risk level three. But I
can also think of at least two reasons to consider a more complex
approach to investing.

First, target returns in the 8–12% range may not be sufficient
to meet your financial goals. Even if returns of this magnitude
are financially acceptable, I can understand that they may not
be emotionally rewarding given the level of hype on Wall Street.
As I mentioned in the first chapter, many investors fall into the
trap of believing "everyone else is getting rich, so why shouldn't
I?" Second, my approach to investing is fairly passive. Once
you set up your program, only a modest amount of effort or
involvement is required. Many Type-A individuals will find this
lack of activity maddening and will want to be more actively
involved.

Because some readers undoubtedly have those inclinations,

this chapter discusses several advanced approaches to investing. While these approaches offer the possibility of enhanced returns, they entail additional complexity and, in some cases, risk. Therefore, you should carefully analyze the tradeoffs involved before taking the plunge.

» **Multiple Strategies** «

Chapter 9 suggested that most approaches to stock selection are variants of either the growth or value investment philosophies. You should recall that neither orientation is inherently superior to the other; investment managers have used both successfully. Moreover, these two kinds of strategies come into and go out of favor regularly, and it is not at all unusual for one to prevail for a few years in a row. Therefore, I recommended that you include both growth and value approaches in your portfolio as a way to protect it from a period of adverse performance and to enhance the stability of returns. Specifically, I recommended the value strategy for the large capitalization sector and the growth approach for the small capitalization portion. Depending upon the asset mix chosen, I also suggested that you invest in international equities through whichever approach will create an overall balance between growth and value for all three stock segments.

The first enhancement to the basic program involves the use of multiple strategies in each of the portfolio sectors. For example, you would select both a growth and value mutual fund for the large capitalization sector of your portfolio and divide the allocation to that portion equally between those two funds. Similarly, you would pick growth and value funds for both the small capitalization and international stock segments and, once again, divide your money equally within each segment. As you know, the bond portion of your portfolio represents a fairly passive hedge against deflation and is invested solely in U.S. government securities. Diversification within this category is therefore not a critical matter, but the use of two bond funds can't hurt. Finally, the lack of sufficient diversification in most Real Estate Investment Trusts led to the recommendation in Chapter 12 that at least two REITs be included in your portfolio. Bringing this all together, the multiple strategy portfolio would consist of ten different funds, two in each of the five asset categories. To help us visualize this structure, Table 14.1 illustrates the multiple strategy version of portfolio four. You will recognize the weightings in the total column as being the proper asset mix for that portfolio.

This approach has obvious pluses and minuses compared with the basic program. First, the pluses: Because this structure is a great deal more diversified than the simple portfolio, it adds both stability and predictability. Thus, while its overall return probably won't be higher than the basic portfolio's, the decrease in volatility should result ultimately in a larger portfolio. My version of the fable of the tortoise and the hare in Chapter 1 is apropos here: A more stable portfolio will have a greater future value than a more volatile one with the same average return.

The primary drawbacks of this approach are related to complexity. First, this portfolio structure requires that you select ten

»» Table 14.1   Multiple Strategy Portfolio (% of Portfolio) ««

Category	Strategy 1		Strategy 2		Total
	Investment	%	Investment	%	%
Large capitalization stocks	Growth fund	17.5	Value fund	17.5	35.0
Non-U.S. stocks	Growth fund	7.5	Value fund	7.5	15.0
Small capitalization stocks	Growth fund	5.0	Value fund	5.0	10.0
Bonds	Fund #1	12.5	Fund #2	12.5	25.0
Real estate	REIT #1	7.5	REIT #2	7.5	15.0
Total		50.0%		50.0%	100.0%

different mutual funds. This task alone certainly will take a greater commitment of time and energy on your part. Similarly, you will have to stay on top of tax information for each fund, and your annual review will be more complicated because of the need to evaluate the performance of each of the ten funds. Likewise, the process of rebalancing will be twice as hard because you must return each of the ten weightings to its target level. Finally, the funds' minimum required investments and sales charges may render this approach uneconomic for very small investors who have limited capital.

But if you are willing and able to deal with these issues, you can enjoy a portfolio that is similar in structure to America's largest pension plans. Multibillion-dollar plans frequently invest in as many as ten different asset classes and employ up to five managers for each class. So these large funds commonly have fifty, or even a hundred, different managers. If each manager is able to exceed the market index for his particular asset class, then the entire fund "beats the market" without ever exposing it to a great deal of risk. Even though your multiple strategy portfolio will be far less complex, the same principle applies. A portfolio consisting of ten different funds should be relatively stable, and if you are either careful or lucky in your selections, you may earn a superior combined return.

While this first approach involves additional complexity, it actually reduces the risk in your portfolio. Unfortunately, the remaining bells and whistles clearly involve some added risks, although you may decide that any given one is justified by its prospect of earning more return.

>>>   **Market Timing Revisited**   <<<

I have argued that once the investor has selected a recommended portfolio mix, he should stick with it through thick and thin and avoid the temptation to time markets. Undoubtedly, the lure of the great potential that timing has to offer will get the best of a few of my readers. If you feel compelled to give it a shot, you may want to consider a disciplined approach called Tactical Asset Allocation.

The main problem with most approaches to market timing is that human emotions tend to get in the way of good judgments and compelling data. As every market bottom and top approaches, the evidence clearly indicates that the market is either undervalued or overvalued, respectively. Unfortunately, most of us tend to ignore this telling information—usually because our emotions are overwhelmed by the prevailing sense of doom or optimism. It is only in retrospect that we realize that the obvious data clearly reflected the impending bottom or top of the market. But that evidence *was* there all the time. Therefore, an ideal approach to market timing would be based on objective, observable data that are not subject to interpretation and rationalization. Further, making changes in the portfolio in response to these data would be fairly mechanical. In other words, the best opportunity for success at market timing would involve as few human foibles as possible. Tactical Asset Allocation is a computerized approach for shifting assets between over- and undervalued markets based solely on objective information.

In Chapter 3, I discussed the linkages between various markets and asserted that stocks, bonds, and other assets eventually return to their "normal" relationships when they get out of kilter with one another. Why do they do this? Capital markets in the United States are dominated by a host of large pension funds. These funds do not have to worry about taxes and are indifferent as to whether returns come from current income, such as dividends and interest, or from capital gains. Pension funds, therefore, have no inherent bias toward either stocks or bonds; they simply move money in the direction of the investment sector that offers the highest rate of return for the risk involved. In other words, different types of investments cannot get too far out of whack with one another, because these funds recognize the market discrepancy and act accordingly. This tendency of financial markets to "return to normal" is the rational basis of Tactical Asset Allocation. By measuring the current relationship between assets and comparing it with long-term averages, Tactical Asset

Allocation determines whether any asset is over -or undervalued versus other assets and, if so, adjusts the portfolio mix accordingly. The more overvalued an asset becomes, the less it is held in the portfolio.

To make this objective approach to market timing still clearer, let's consider a simple example. Most investors are aware that the price-earnings ratio (P/E) is one measure of whether stocks are cheap or expensive. During the postwar era, the P/E on stocks comprising the S&P 500 has averaged about 14. If that P/E is currently 10, it indicates that stocks are cheap relative to their own history, but it does not tell you whether stocks are cheap or expensive as compared to bonds or other assets. Before we can make these judgments, we must evaluate the "earnings yield" of stocks. The reciprocal of a stock's P/E is called the "earnings yield" and is expressed as a percentage. Thus, a P/E of 14 translates into an earnings yield of 7.14% (1 divided by 14). This earnings yield on stocks can then be compared with the interest rate paid on bonds and the difference represents a risk premium—that is, a reward paid to the equity investor for assuming greater risk. Let's assume that bond yields have averaged a little over 5% during the postwar era. That yield level indicates that a 2% risk premium has been the norm (7.14% less 5%). When the spread is much greater than 2%, therefore, stocks are providing an unusually large premium, which means they are cheap. Conversely, a premium that is much less than 2% indicates that stocks are expensive and that bonds are more attractive. Using these relationships, we can develop an automated formula with which to change a portfolio's mix between stocks and bonds at propitious times.

Let's assume that your target asset mix is 60% stocks and 40% bonds and, further, that you will allow your actual stock weighting to fluctuate between 40% and 80%. When the risk premium is close to the normal level, let's say a spread between 1.75% and 2.25%, your portfolio will be invested at the 60%/40% target. If the risk premium then widened to 2.75%, your equity exposure will be increased to 65%. A further increase in the premium to 3.25% will result in an equity weighting of

70%. The process will continue in increments until a premium of 4.25% results in a maximum equity exposure of 80%. This process also works exactly the same way in reverse: as the risk premium narrows, equity exposure is reduced. All of these decisions are mechanical and based on objective data.

You should not attempt to create your own Tactical Asset Allocation model based on the foregoing example, because it represents an oversimplification of a fairly complex process. The computerized programs generally use a variety of additional timing indicators, including various measures of relative valuation, technical data, and current economic information. You cannot hope to maintain this much information. Moreover, you will be limited to a simple Tactical Asset Allocation model that compares stocks with either bonds or money market investments. More complicated versions analyze stocks versus bonds versus real estate versus non-U.S. stocks versus cash. Indeed, the newest generation of these models compare up to three different asset types in each of a dozen different markets around the world. Obviously, these programs depend on some heavy-duty computer power and, in reality, are only available to the largest funds. But an easy way for you to take advantage of this tool is through mutual funds. A number of mutual fund groups offer asset allocation funds. Some represent seat-of-the-pants market timing, while others are based on the kind of elaborate computer models described. Examples of the funds using these techniques are:

Oppenheimer Asset Allocation Fund
Shearson Strategic Investors
Paine Webber Asset Allocation Fund
Vanguard Asset Allocation Fund

Tactical Asset Allocation programs tend to add value to a portfolio over time, but they involve some unique factors that you need to understand before taking the plunge. The chief problem is that they tend to be wrong for long periods of time. I have mentioned that different types of investments ultimately move back to normal when they get out of whack with other alternatives. But the process often takes a while. When stocks

become overvalued, for instance, they do not immediately return
to fair levels. Instead, stocks become progressively more overvalued until the bubble finally bursts. As stocks become overvalued,
Tactical Asset Allocation models will normally begin to reduce
your exposure to them. If the market continues to rise, you may
find that you own no stocks at all. What happens if the market
goes even further? Obviously, you will miss out on some additional potential appreciation. You might respond that this is not
the end of the world, because you will also miss the collapse
when it occurs. That is correct if you stick with your strategy,
but many people throw in the towel at just the wrong time.

In 1987, stocks began to appear overvalued in January, and
most of the tactical allocation models reduced equity exposure
to minimum levels. Yet the market continued to rise for almost
seven more months, and participants in these programs had
dismal performances as compared with the market. Unfortunately, many of these investors withdrew in August and reinvested their money in stocks—just in time to catch the market
crash. Ironically, had they stuck it out for the entire year, their
returns would have been excellent. This memorable example
illustrates that you must be extremely patient and willing to
suffer through a long period of poor performance to make this
approach pay off. While most of us believe we have the discipline
and patience required, it remains awfully tempting to "bail out"
of a market timing program at just the wrong time.

One way to avoid this problem is to place only a small portion
of your overall portfolio in a timing program. If Tactical Asset
Allocation earns good returns, your portfolio will benefit to some
extent, and a sustained period of poor results shouldn't kill you.
In Table 14.2, therefore, I depict portfolio four with the addition
of an asset allocation mutual fund that represents 20% of the mix.

In this structure, 25% of the fund will always be invested in
large capitalization stocks and 15% in bonds. The 20% of the
portfolio invested in the asset allocation fund will move between
stocks and bonds depending upon market relationships. If that
fund were entirely invested in stocks, then your overall equity
weighting would be 70%. At the other extreme, only 50% of

»   **Table 14.2   Basic Portfolio with Market-Timing**   **«**
Enhancement
(% of Portfolio)

Large capitalization equity fund	25
Asset allocation fund	20
Bond fund	15
Non-U.S. stocks	15
Small capitalization stocks	10
Real estate	15
Total	100

your portfolio would be in stocks if the asset allocation fund were entirely invested in bonds. In short, this structure offers you the chance of superior returns from market timing while it protects you from an all-or-nothing decision. An opportunistic investor can add substantial value in ways other than market timing. If you are such an investor, I want you to be able to take advantage of your skill without jeopardizing your entire program if you make a bad call. The approach described next ought to accomplish this objective.

»   **The Core-Satellite Approach**   **«**

The core-satellite approach is a structure in which the bulk of your money is invested in one of the asset mixes presented in Chapter 7, and the remainder is considered "play" money that you can use to move into and out of more specialized strategies that seem particularly timely. In other words, you have a "core" portfolio with one or more satellite strategies. This approach should appeal to those who have opinions regarding certain types of investments, but do not have the time to manage the entire fund.

If you employ this approach, I recommend that you allocate 80% of your portfolio to the core assets and 20% to the specialized strategies. While quite arbitrary, this division should allow you to benefit from good investment selection, while also pro-

»» Table 14.3   Core-Satellite Portfolio (% of Portfolio) ««

Large capitalization U.S. stocks	28
Non-U.S. stocks	12
Small capitalization stocks	8
Bonds	20
Real estate	12
Total core portfolio	80
Satellite strategies	20
Total portfolio	100

tecting you from a disaster. To help you visualize this structure, I have once again altered portfolio four to include this enhancement, as shown in Table 14.3.

Thus, 80% of your money is still committed to a diversified portfolio with asset weightings in proportion to those recommended for risk level four in Chapter 7. The other 20% can be invested in more concentrated and risky strategies. Now, what should you do with your play money? In simple terms, you may opt for one of two broad approaches to investing this money. First, you can place the 20% in a brokerage account with which to buy and sell securities directly. As you know, I do not believe many amateur investors should pick their own investments, but this approach represents a good compromise for those who have the yen.

An alternate approach calls for you to place major strategic bets with your satellite dollars while allowing the pros to handle the nitty gritty details of picking the potential winners. In other words, rather than picking individual securities, you can identify *types* of investments that should perform unusually well and commit your funds to vehicles that specialize in them. For example, you might purchase shares in a Health Care Sector Fund if you become convinced that drug and hospital supply stocks are particularly attractive. This approach is sensible because it allows you to capitalize on market insights without requiring a great deal of hands-on responsibility.

The remainder of this chapter describes opportunistic investment strategies, some of which are rather conventional, others
fairly unique. In no case, however, is my objective to tell you
what to invest in *now*. Rather, I hope to stimulate your thinking
about the full range of potential investments.

»   **Doubling Up**   «

The most straightforward way to make a strategic bet is to
increase the weighting in one of the categories already in your
portfolio. For example, suppose your target asset mix includes a
15% weighting in non-U.S. stocks. If you became convinced that
this category now represents the most exciting place to invest,
you could allocate all of your play money to it, which would
raise the weighting to 35%. Once the trend in foreign stocks had
run its course, you would return their weighting to 15% and
look for the next opportunity in another asset category. This
approach has a lot of appeal because you are already familiar
with your investment categories and you have a carefully selected
vehicle in which you are already invested. If you can spot these
major trends successfully, the impact on the performance of your
fund will be significant. Why don't we consider two such bets
that may be of interest?

I have previously mentioned that small capitalization stocks
underperformed the larger variety from the middle of 1983
through 1990. With few exceptions, this was a discouraging
period for small stock investors. Many experts began to question
whether this category would ever again generate superior performance as it had in the past. As it turns out, a seven-year period
of poor performance is not at all unusual. Since 1926, small
stocks have experienced five sustained periods of poor relative
performance, but each of these episodes was followed by a sustained period of good results. In other words, history is now on
the side of these stocks.

Valuation also favors small capitalization stocks. A widely
used proxy for this group is the T. Rowe Price New Horizons
Fund, which has invested in emerging companies for about thirty

years. At the end of 1990, the P/E of that fund was slightly lower than that of the Standard & Poor's 500. In other words, stocks of smaller, more dynamic companies were cheaper than stocks of larger, more mature competitors. In the history of the New Horizons Fund, this level of relative valuation has been reached only four other times. Analysis of performance over the five-year periods subsequent to these low points bears intriguing revelations. On average, the fund outperformed the S&P 500 by 116.8%. Simply stated, small stocks in prior periods have represented tremendous values at P/E levels comparable to the one that prevailed late in 1990. Will it happen again this time? Who knows! But small stocks began 1991 with a bang, and many investors are once again talking about the virtues of this sector of the market. If you believe we began another five-year or seven-year cycle late in 1990, you might consider allocating some of your play money to your mutual fund devoted to small capitalization stocks.

A similar concept involves your weighting in real estate. As mentioned in Chapter 12, most real estate investors are shell shocked and a host of major players have disappeared from the scene altogether. The conventional wisdom is that the problems in this market will be around for years to come and that future returns will never rebound to former levels. Obviously, I do not know whether we have reached the bottom in the real estate market, and I certainly would not hazard a guess as to the shape of the recovery. But I do know that this scenario is familiar. At every market bottom, a large number of "beaten" investors throw in the towel, and some advisers inevitably craft persuasive arguments that "things have changed" and that returns are permanently impaired. Given the prevailing sense of doom, it is hard to imagine that real estate investing now has much downside risk.

This scenario makes real estate conceptually interesting, and REITs represent an awfully cheap way to get in the real estate game. Many REITs are selling at discounts of 25% to their appraised values; plus, these current values have been marked down from much higher levels. Moreover, lots of REITs have dividend yields of over 9% as compared with U.S. government bond yields of a little over 8% and stock yields under 4%. All things considered, REITs seem to be an inexpensive way to invest in an out-of-favor category. While it may take a little courage to go against the flow, that's how fortunes are made.

The last "doubling up" strategy does not involve a bet on an asset type, but it does entail an extra weighting in one of the investment philosophies represented in your portfolio. If you chose not to index the equity segment of your fund, you were supposed to establish a balance between the growth and value philosophies. Specifically, I recommended that you invest the large capitalization stock portion in a value fund, the small capitalization sector in a growth fund, and use the international stock category to establish the proper balance of the two philosophies. As you know, the growth and value philosophies alternate periodically in terms of which provides the highest rate of return, and it is not unusual for either one to dominate for two or three consecutive years. If you can recognize that a shift is taking place, you may be able to capitalize on it by repositioning some of your funds. The most conservative approach is simply for you to move dollars from a growth fund to a value fund or vice versa, which keeps your overall stock weighting constant. In a more aggressive version, you would allocate some of your play money to either a growth or value fund and, consequently, raise your overall equity weighting.

The key question is how you recognize a change in trend before everyone else. Needless to say, this is an uphill battle, because many investors are trying to make the same calls and a great deal of emotion is involved. But here are a couple of clues. First, information on price earnings ratios and other measures of valuation are readily available, which should give you a sense of whether growth or value stocks are cheaper. Second, many publications list the best performing stocks during the past quarter. By keeping track of whether growth or value stocks are faring well, you may be able to sense a change in the market's emphasis. Finally, growth stocks often do particularly well when investors expect a slow-growth economic environment or a reces-

sion. In such a climate, the financial strength, industry leadership, and consistent earnings of growth companies are highly
valued.

All of the strategies discussed thus far are fairly conventional
and involve investments with which you are familiar. Why don't
we now turn to a few more esoteric concepts? While these strategies may be unfamiliar, each is readily available to small investors through specialized mutual funds.

»   Distressed Securities   «

Excesses in any market create great opportunities for daring
investors. The primary excess of the 1980s was the leveraged
buyout movement and the related growth in the junk-bond market. A leveraged buyout is simply a purchase of a company
using borrowed money. From 1986 through 1989, roughly $175
billion worth of these deals were completed, and many of the
later transactions were structured with extreme levels of debt.
As I mentioned in Chapters 11 and 12, the use of debt magnifies
returns on both the up and down side, and extreme leverage can
lead to bankruptcy. Predictably, the number of corporate bonds
in default increased by approximately 100% in 1990 as compared with the prior year. Such defaults are likely to remain at
a high level for several more years. Frequently, the underlying
business of a company in default is fine; the problem results
simply from too much debt. Restructuring the company often
allows it to emerge from bankruptcy with its business intact and
a much more viable capital structure.

Why is there an opportunity to make money in bankruptcies?
Most investors are scared to death of owning securities of a
company in trouble. Many institutions are allowed to own only
"high grade" investments. Therefore, many bondholders dump
their securities at the first hint of financial distress. The rampant
sell-off frequently results in bond prices that are substantially
lower than the liquidation value of the distressed company. By
purchasing bonds at twenty or thirty cents on the dollar and
waiting out a reorganization of the company, investors have

earned returns of 50% or even 100% per year. But this bet is a *highly risky* business that requires great expertise in credit analysis and a thorough understanding of bankruptcy law. Obviously, it makes absolutely no sense to play in this arena yourself. But you do have two reasonable ways to get into this unusual game.

First, you can buy shares in a junk-bond mutual fund. For the most part, these securities have no place in your portfolio, but a panic such as the one that occurred in 1990 can lead to such high yields as compared with high-quality issues that a temporary investment may be worth a shot. My preferred way of investing in bankruptcies, however, is to buy shares in a mutual fund that specializes in this strategy. Three funds that employ it to some extent are the Fidelity Capital and Income Fund, the Merrill Lynch Phoenix Fund, and Mutual Shares. One word of caution: This strategy is not for the faint of heart. If you intend to play, make sure you have patience and the ability to survive a great deal of volatility. Moreover, you must be mindful that opportunities of this type do not last forever. The value of distressed securities is roughly ten times the funds held by specialists in bankruptcy investing. But investors are increasingly catching on. In all probability, more money will find its way into this category, and it will be time for you to move on to the next one.

»   Energy   «

During the early 1980s, the price of oil and gas dropped significantly and had a devastating effect on the energy industry and the Southwestern real estate market. The low price of oil and gas brought drilling activity to a virtual standstill at the same time that strong economic growth was increasing our energy consumption. This combination increased U.S. dependence on imported oil and reduced the oversupply of natural gas that has plagued domestic producers for years. All of these factors lead some experts to the conclusion that energy prices should increase over time and that natural gas, in particular, will experience rapid price escalation because it is underpriced versus oil. Since energy is so crucial to our economy, rising oil and gas prices effectively translate into rising inflation and interest rates. Historically, the stocks of energy companies have performed strongly during periods of rising energy prices, but importantly, they have also tended to generate positive returns in declining stock markets. As you may recall, Iraq's invasion of Kuwait in August 1990 rattled all of the world's financial markets and resulted in an immediate upward spike in the price of oil. During the quarter ending September 30, 1990, the Standard & Poor's 500 Index declined 13.7%, as almost every sector of the market declined significantly. The lone exception was the energy sector, which yielded a positive return of 5%.

The bottom line is that energy stocks can serve as a hedge against both inflation and the uncertainty of politics in the Middle East. There are two different strategies that you can follow to participate in this group. First, you can make the assumption that, inevitably, the United States will experience another "oil shock" as it did in 1973 and 1979. In this case, you would permanently allocate a portion of your play money to this sector. Alternatively, you can make periodic forays into energy stocks based on current oil prices, economic trends, and global politics—that is, time the market for favorable periods. In either case, the easiest way to invest is through an energy-securities mutual fund, such as the Fidelity Select-Energy Fund or Vanguard Specialized Energy Fund.

»»   Emerging Markets   ««

In all likelihood, the most significant investment trend of the early 1990s will be further diversification by U.S. investors into global markets. As I pointed out in Chapter 7, the typical pension fund has a weighting in non-U.S. investments of less than 10%, whereas an allocation of as much as 60% could be theoretically justified. My best guess is that most funds will move to a portfolio weighting of 15% or 20% for foreign securities during the next few years. The bulk of this money will be invested in the largest and most familiar markets around the world, including those in

Western Europe, Australia, and several in the Far East. These capital flows are likely to make the larger world markets much more competitive, and as that happens, it will be increasingly difficult to earn superior returns.

One way to achieve international diversification while avoiding the herd is to invest in the so-called emerging markets. Because these stock markets tend to be much smaller and less competitive, they should offer substantial return potential. In addition, many of these emerging markets are located in countries that have tremendous potential for economic growth. Needless to say, it is virtually impossible for you to invest directly in these markets, but there is an assortment of closed-end mutual funds that you can buy through any stockbroker. Good examples are the Brazil Fund, India Growth Fund, Indonesia Fund, and the Malaysia Fund. Among the best performing markets recently are those in several Latin American countries; many offer closed-end funds that are available to American investors. A list of closed-end mutual funds is included in the *Wall Street Journal* every Monday. You will note that many funds offer the added advantage of selling at a discount to their net asset values.

» Closed-End Funds «

More generally, the purchase of closed-end funds at a discount offers the potential for superior returns. Just to refresh your memory, a closed-end fund has a fixed number of shares outstanding that are traded on one of the stock exchanges or in the over-the-counter market. Since the price of these shares is influenced by a variety of factors, it often varies significantly from the value of the securities held in the fund's portfolio. In October 1987, for instance, several well-managed funds sold at discounts of 15–20% due to the prevailing sense of doom. Conversely, the Germany Fund sold at a large premium early in 1990 because of the euphoria that accompanied the reunification of the German Republic.

How do you take advantage of these periodic aberrations in the market? An interesting strategy is to put together a portfolio of funds selling at large discounts. But making this work is more complicated than simply purchasing those discounted by the greatest percentage. First, you should do your homework on each prospective fund to make sure that it is well managed. Second, you should consider the level of discount at which the fund has traded in the past. That information is available in several of the reference sources listed in Chapter 10. The ideal strategy is to assemble a portfolio of several well-managed funds that are currently trading at the low end (greatest discount) of their historical range. In all likelihood, the discount will narrow over time, and that will give your return a boost. In addition, you may be lucky enough to get in the way of a "raider." Some savvy investors acquire major positions in funds trading at big discounts and then attempt to force them to convert to the open-end structure. When these efforts are successful, the discount disappears because open-end funds are redeemable daily at the net asset value.

»   Picking Satellite Strategies   «

I have discussed several strategies that are candidates for the "opportunistic" section of your portfolio. By definition, opportunistic strategies come and go, which means that mine will soon become dated. Their inclusion here is not to suggest that they will always be timely, but rather to illustrate some ways of thinking about unique investments. All of these strategies have one element in common: They are out of the mainstream. Whether they are simply unpopular in today's markets or require unique skills, these strategies place one on the fringe of the investment world.

The best opportunity for you to earn extraordinary returns is to invest in unpopular or difficult areas. In his book *The Templeton Touch*, William Proctor discusses noted investor John Templeton and distills the twenty-two guiding principles that have contributed to his success. Three of those tenets are particularly relevant to this chapter:

- It is impossible to produce a superior performance unless you do something different from the majority.
- If a particular industry or type of security becomes popular with investors, that popularity will always prove temporary and, when lost, won't return for many years.
- If you buy the same securities as other people, you will have the same results as other people.

So, try to figure out where the crowd is going and then look for unique areas that Wall Street has missed.

» Bells and Whistles Revisited «

Each of the higher risk strategies covered in this chapter offers a potential enhancement to your basic program. All are widely practiced by sophisticated investors. I do not believe that any of them are necessary to achieve the objectives of most investors, but they represent a sound means of increasing the sophistication and, hopefully, the return on a portfolio. Unfortunately, these strategies also add complexity to your program. To employ any one of them, you must be willing to commit to a higher level of interest and involvement. If you are ready to invest this added time and energy, the inclusion of one or more of these strategies will yield a portfolio that is as diversified and advanced as just about any in the United States.

» Key Points to Remember «

- The use of two funds in each asset category will add to diversification and stability, albeit with added complexity.
- Aggressive strategies should be limited to about 20% of your portfolio.
- The best way to earn unusually high returns is to invest in unpopular securities.

CHAPTER 15

OFF TO THE RACES

But the bravest are surely those who have the clearest vision of what is before them, glory and risk alike, and yet not withstanding go out to meet it.

—Thucydides

»» ««

As a result of twenty years of hard work and a strong commitment to saving, you have amassed a nest egg that should serve as the foundation of a comfortable retirement. This nest egg represents your life savings, virtually everything you have in the world. All that remains is for you to invest this sum intelligently for the next fifteen years, and you will be able to live the comfortable life that you have worked so hard to achieve. Yet you have a nagging concern about the way you are handling your investments. A portion of your assets is invested in municipal bonds with the remainder allocated to a small number of stocks. While this mix has no particular rhyme or reason, you believe it is a relatively cautious structure. On the other hand, you have an occasional nightmare in which your portfolio gets clobbered in another October 1987–type massacre. When your broker calls to recommend a stock, you have no real basis for evaluating whether it makes sense in your account. Similarly, you are exposed to a steady stream of potential investments in limited partnerships, specialized mutual funds, and insurance products—each of which seems to promise outstanding results. While you think your investments have performed reasonably well, you constantly hear about the extraordinary returns that your peers seem to be earning. Maybe you aren't doing so well after all. Finally, the conflicting opinions of all the experts leave you in a state of confusion. Should you buy or sell? Is the economy in an uptrend or headed for a recession? What types of investments are right for you?

This scenario is uncomfortably familiar to many small investors. In fact, I meet very few investors who genuinely feel they are doing a first-class job of managing their assets. More often, they feel a lack of direction, an inability to control their own destiny, and a great deal of suspicion that they are being taken advantage of in investment dealings. All of the advice they receive seems only to further confuse matters, not make their job easier. Perhaps even more disconcerting is the fact that many large pools of capital suffer from the same deficiencies in organization and discipline. It is not at all unusual for substantial funds to be managed without written objectives, guidelines, or standards. And many individuals serving in fiduciary capacities have no understanding of the implications of the decisions they make.

>>>   **You Can Take Charge**   <<<

After reading this book, you know that there is another way. You are now in a position to create and implement an organized investment program that will meet your goals. The approach I have recommended to you is the antithesis of the scenario just described. It is disciplined, logical, and feasible; moreover, it is designed to ensure that *you* are in control. If you follow this approach, you should enjoy competitive rates of return, and your portfolio should be diversified enough to prevent a disaster. Most important, you built in the ability to adjust your program over the course of your life as circumstances change. This approach to investing may be a bit tame and boring for adventurous investors, but I am willing to bet that the tortoise will outperform the hare over the long haul.

Many investors are frustrated and unsuccessful because they have no sense of direction. Very few have developed a set of investment objectives, and even fewer fully understand the relationship between risk and return. Lacking these fundamentals, most investors do not (and cannot) objectively assess investment results, and most also tend to assume either too much or too little risk. In contrast, through my approach, your overall portfolio has a specific rate of return objective, and you have developed a strong indication that your target is realistic. Moreover, after carefully evaluating your emotional and financial circumstances, you have selected the risk:return combination that represents the best compromise in light of your needs.

Even those investors who have clear thoughts about risk and return often have a difficult time translating their goals into an appropriate investment strategy. How in the world does one select among the dozens of investment alternatives that are widely available? Once you have chosen several for your portfolio, how do you decide what percentage of your funds to allocate to them? I have solved both of these problems for you. I carefully selected a total of six different asset classes and recommended that most portfolios contain between three and five of them. By combining these asset classes in the correct proportions, I created seven portfolio structures that should be relatively stable and, more important, should survive even adverse market environments.

It is all well and good to talk about the structure of a portfolio, but someone must actually select individual investments. Because the stock market is quite efficient, it is very difficult for even professionals to "beat the market." Since your odds would be still lower, I recommended that your portfolio's equity portion be held in index funds in order to ensure marketlike returns. Since most investors want to attempt to beat the market indices, however, I also provided you with detailed information on the selection of mutual funds as well as a framework for managing your own securities investments. Regardless of which approach you choose, your understanding of this material will make you a more informed and knowledgeable investor.

Finally, even a well-conceived portfolio requires a little annual maintenance. Your review should consist of a reassessment of your investment objectives and a brief analysis of your returns during the last year. In most cases, nothing significant will have changed from the previous year; thus, you need only rebalance your portfolio to the target weightings. But if your circumstances have changed, you will have the expertise to modify the structure of your program with confidence.

At this point, I hope my approach to investing seems both familiar and simple. There is no magic involved! What is required is a little bit of expertise and a modest amount of time and energy. I have supplied the necessary expertise. It is up to you to implement and maintain your program.

» Principles to Remember «

Underlying this approach to investing are ten fundamental principles that are based on my own experience in the investment world as well as the teachings of Wall Street's best thinkers. I have discussed each of these precepts once or more in the course of this book. A quick review here will help you tie it all together.

First, there are no guarantees, free rides, or sure things. Returns of 8–12% are realistic. Anyone who promises performance greatly in excess of this range should be viewed with great suspicion. In the frothy environment of the 1980s, returns of 8–12% seem fairly pedestrian, but it is a serious mistake to extrapolate that exceptional performance into the future. Rather, you should base your investment plan on realistic goals and hope for a pleasant surprise.

Second, it is not necessary to earn extraordinary rates of return in order to accumulate a sizable net worth. Compound interest is such a powerful force that even moderate rates of return should allow most investors to achieve reasonable goals. At a 10% annual return, for instance, a couple who each contribute $2,000 to an IRA during a thirty-five-year working career will retire with a portfolio valued at $1,084,000. And that sum is almost eight times the amount of money the couple will actually pay in. Therefore, the focus of every investment program should be on earning reasonable, consistent rates of return while avoiding losses.

Third, to avoid losses, you must deal with the issue of risk. Every investment entails risk of one kind or another. Hence, you should be very skeptical of any product that has the word *guaranteed* in its marketing pitch. In particular, you should steer clear of investments that offer high returns with little risk. In the real world, there is always a tradeoff between risk and return; you should never expect to get one without the other. Happily, risk is controllable through asset allocation and the careful selection of investments that do not move in tandem. But risk will never disappear entirely. The key is to structure your program in such a way that you understand the risks involved and can have enough faith in your program to ride out the tough times without making an irrational and costly decision.

Fourth, though you undoubtedly got this message, diversification is absolutely critical. The single most common mistake that novice investors make is to place all of their eggs in one basket. Your portfolio should be diversified by asset type, and in each category, you should invest in a large number of specific securities. Moreover, you should employ several investment advisers or mutual fund sponsors to further spread your risk. I cannot guarantee that your investment program will meet its objectives, but I can assure you that diversification will reduce the risk in your portfolio and increase the odds of a satisfactory outcome.

Fifth, the investment business is fiercely competitive and is populated by bright and extremely motivated individuals. These professionals are abundantly armed with computer power, data bases, research departments, resident economists, and a gaggle of consultants. Yet despite all of these resources, few are able to beat a simple strategy of buying and holding the securities that comprise the market. In fact, after deducting transaction costs and fees, the average professional has significantly underperformed the market. If the pros can't win, you really don't have much of a chance. Therefore, most investors should opt for index funds because their returns always roughly equal the market's return. If you hope to beat the market, either you or your adviser must have an edge on the competition. Remember, your competitors are a sophisticated group, so it will be difficult to gain any edge for long.

You may have noticed that very little of this book has been devoted to taxes. This was not an oversight. My sixth principle holds that your financial welfare is best served by constructing an investment program that is based on economic principles and not on tax avoidance. You can take a few steps to minimize your tax liability, such as placing the bond and real estate portions of your fund in a retirement vehicle. Both of these categories generate a high level of current income that will not be taxed in an IRA or Keough account until withdrawals begin at retirement. But these simple steps do not in any way influence the basic structure of your portfolio. Indeed, my advice that you invest solely in U.S. government bonds will, in all likelihood, actually raise your tax liability. While municipal bonds generate more after-tax income for many investors, I have made the judgment that the risk of their default is sufficient to warrant a small insurance premium that tax payments represent. Taxes are simply a cost of doing business. The bottom line is that the safety of your portfolio is paramount.

My seventh basic rule is that your investment program should be fundamentally the same whether you have $50,000, $500,000, or $5 million to invest. The asset mixes and investment vehicles recommended in this book were carefully selected to ensure that they are available to even the smallest investor. While most large funds use other types of investments, I am not sure they really end up with portfolios that are any more attractive than those described herein. In fact, the $600 million fund for which I am responsible has risk and return characteristics quite similar to portfolio four, which is used as a model throughout this work.

The eighth fundamental tenet is that every investor is his or her own worst enemy. No one is immune from swings in emotion, manias, and the herd mentality. Your vulnerability to these sirens has nothing to do with intelligence, education, or experience. Wall Street professionals who have been through any number of market cycles are just as susceptible to greed and fear as everyone else. The safest course is simply to accept that your judgment can be clouded by emotion and to structure your program accordingly. In specific terms, you should review your investment program on the same dates each year and make any needed changes only at that time; this practice should remove the temptation to react to recent market swings. Moreover, I argued against trying to time markets but suggested a computerized approach for those who feel compelled to give it a shot. Both of these recommendations are designed to minimize the impact of your emotions on your returns.

The ninth commandment is "thou shalt minimize costs." None of us have any control over the markets; indeed, the gross returns we earn are largely dictated to us. But we can control the cost of investing that determines our net return. I recommended that you avoid load mutual funds unless you have compelling information to suggest that a given fund's performance is sufficiently above average to overcome the sales charge. Similarly, you should carefully evaluate annual expense ratios when analyzing both mutual funds and REITs. In all cases, it makes sense to begin with the assumption that the lowest-cost funds are the most attractive. If you choose to manage your own account, it is important to choose a broker who will meet your needs at the lowest possible cost.

The tenth and final basic principle is that most activity in this business is both expensive and counterproductive. The primary beneficiary of a high level of trading will be your broker. It is unlikely to enhance the returns on your portfolio. Similarly, most decisions to switch funds or investment managers are ill-advised. In all likelihood, you will abandon a fund at just the wrong time, and its replacement will have just completed a string of good years, which almost ensures that your new fund is poised for a fall. The message is that by leaving your program alone, you will come out ahead in the long run. Set up your portfolio very carefully, review it annually, and make any changes that are dictated by significant changes in your circumstances. Otherwise, stick with the plan, don't panic, and your money will work for you.

»   Present at the Creation   «

Late in the thirteenth century, Alfonso the Wise said, "Had I been present at the creation, I would have given some useful hints for the better ordering of the universe." You *are* present at the creation of your investment universe, and you know everything required to enjoy a better order.

Appendix 1 Future Value of a Single Sum of $1.00

n	1½%	2½%	4%	4½%	5%	5½%	6%	6½%
1	1.015000	1.025000	1.040000	1.045000	1.050000	1.055000	1.060000	1.065000
2	1.030225	1.050625	1.081600	1.092025	1.102500	1.113025	1.123600	1.134225
3	1.045678	1.076891	1.124864	1.141166	1.157625	1.174241	1.191016	1.207950
4	1.061364	1.103813	1.169859	1.192519	1.215506	1.238825	1.262477	1.286466
5	1.077284	1.131408	1.216653	1.246182	1.276282	1.306960	1.338226	1.370087
6	1.093443	1.159693	1.265319	1.302260	1.340096	1.378843	1.418519	1.459142
7	1.109845	1.188686	1.315932	1.360862	1.407100	1.454679	1.503630	1.553987
8	1.126493	1.218403	1.368569	1.422101	1.477455	1.534687	1.593848	1.654996
9	1.143390	1.248863	1.423312	1.486095	1.551328	1.619094	1.689479	1.762570
10	1.160541	1.280085	1.480244	1.552969	1.628895	1.708144	1.790848	1.877137
11	1.177949	1.312087	1.539454	1.622853	1.710339	1.802092	1.898299	1.999151
12	1.195618	1.344889	1.601032	1.695881	1.795856	1.901207	2.012196	2.129096
13	1.213552	1.378511	1.665074	1.772196	1.885649	2.005774	2.132928	2.267487
14	1.231756	1.412974	1.731676	1.851945	1.979932	2.116091	2.260904	2.414874
15	1.250232	1.448298	1.800944	1.935282	2.078928	2.232476	2.396558	2.571841
16	1.268986	1.484506	1.872981	2.022370	2.182875	2.355263	2.540352	2.739011
17	1.288020	1.521618	1.947900	2.113377	2.292018	2.484802	2.692773	2.917046
18	1.307341	1.559659	2.025817	2.208479	2.406619	2.621466	2.854339	3.106654

19	1.326951	1.598650	2.106849	2.307860	2.526950	2.765647	3.025600	3.308587
20	1.346855	1.638616	2.191123	2.411714	2.653298	2.917757	3.207135	3.523645
21	1.367058	1.679582	2.278768	2.520241	2.785963	3.078234	3.399564	3.752682
22	1.387564	1.721571	2.369919	2.633652	2.925261	3.247537	3.603537	3.996606
23	1.408377	1.764611	2.464716	2.752166	3.071524	3.426152	3.819750	4.256386
24	1.429503	1.808726	2.563304	2.876014	3.225100	3.614590	4.048935	4.533051
25	1.450945	1.853944	2.665836	3.005434	3.386355	3.813392	4.291871	4.827699
26	1.472710	1.900293	2.772470	3.140679	3.555673	4.023129	4.549383	5.141500
27	1.494800	1.947800	2.883369	3.282010	3.733456	4.244401	4.822346	5.475697
28	1.517222	1.996495	2.998703	3.429700	3.920129	4.477843	5.111687	5.831617
29	1.539981	2.046407	3.118651	3.584036	4.116136	4.724124	5.418388	6.210672
30	1.563080	2.097568	3.243398	3.745318	4.321942	4.983951	5.743491	6.614366
31	1.586526	2.150007	3.373133	3.913857	4.538039	5.258069	6.088101	7.044300
32	1.610324	2.203757	3.508059	4.089981	4.764941	5.547262	6.453387	7.502179
33	1.634479	2.258851	3.648381	4.274030	5.003189	5.852362	6.840590	7.989821
34	1.658996	2.315322	3.794316	4.466362	5.253348	6.174242	7.251025	8.509159
35	1.683881	2.373205	3.946089	4.667348	5.516015	6.513825	7.686087	9.062255
36	1.709140	2.432535	4.103933	4.877378	5.791816	6.872085	8.147252	9.651301
37	1.734777	2.493349	4.268090	5.096860	6.081407	7.250050	8.636087	10.278636
38	1.760798	2.555682	4.438813	5.326219	6.385477	7.648803	9.154252	10.946747
39	1.787210	2.619574	4.616366	5.565899	6.704751	8.069487	9.703507	11.658286
40	1.814018	2.685064	4.801021	5.816365	7.039989	8.513309	10.285718	12.416075

Appendix 1 (continued) Future Value of a Single Sum of $1.00

n	7%	8%	9%	10%	12%	14%	16%	20%
1	1.070000	1.080000	1.090000	1.100000	1.120000	1.140000	1.160000	1.200000
2	1.144900	1.166400	1.188100	1.210000	1.254400	1.299600	1.345600	1.440000
3	1.225043	1.259712	1.295029	1.331000	1.404928	1.481544	1.560896	1.728000
4	1.310796	1.360489	1.411582	1.464100	1.573519	1.688960	1.810639	2.073600
5	1.402552	1.469328	1.538624	1.610510	1.762342	1.925415	2.100342	2.488320
6	1.500730	1.586874	1.677100	1.771561	1.973823	2.194973	2.436396	2.985984
7	1.605781	1.713824	1.828039	1.948717	2.210681	2.502269	2.826220	3.583181
8	1.718186	1.850930	1.992563	2.143589	2.475963	2.852586	3.278415	4.299817
9	1.838459	1.999005	2.171893	2.357948	2.773079	3.251949	3.802961	5.159780
10	1.967151	2.158925	2.367364	2.593742	3.105848	3.707221	4.411435	6.191736
11	2.104852	2.331639	2.580426	2.853117	3.478550	4.226232	5.117265	7.430084
12	2.252192	2.518170	2.812665	3.138428	3.895976	4.817905	5.936027	8.916100
13	2.409845	2.719624	3.065805	3.452271	4.363493	5.492411	6.885791	10.699321
14	2.578534	2.937194	3.341727	3.797498	4.887112	6.261349	7.987518	12.839185
15	2.759032	3.172169	3.642482	4.177248	5.473566	7.137938	9.265521	15.407022
16	2.952164	3.425943	3.970306	4.594973	6.130394	8.137249	10.748004	18.488426
17	3.158815	3.700018	4.327633	5.054470	6.866041	9.276464	12.467685	22.186111
18	3.379932	3.996019	4.717120	5.559917	7.689966	10.575169	14.462514	26.623333

19	3.616528	4.315701	5.141661	6.115909	8.612762	12.055693	16.776517	31.948000
20	3.869684	4.660957	5.604411	6.727500	9.646293	13.743490	19.460759	38.337600
21	4.140562	5.033834	6.108808	7.400250	10.803848	15.667578	22.574481	46.005120
22	4.430402	5.436540	6.658600	8.140275	12.100310	17.861039	26.186398	55.206144
23	4.740530	5.871464	7.257874	8.954302	13.552347	20.361585	30.376222	66.247373
24	5.072367	6.341181	7.911083	9.849733	15.178629	23.212207	35.236417	79.496847
25	5.427433	6.848475	8.623081	10.834706	17.000064	26.461916	40.874244	95.396217
26	5.807353	7.396353	9.399158	11.918177	19.040072	30.166584	47.414123	114.475460
27	6.213868	7.988061	10.245082	13.109994	21.324881	34.389906	55.000382	137.370552
28	6.648838	8.627106	11.167140	14.420994	23.883866	39.204493	63.800444	164.844662
29	7.114257	9.317275	12.172182	15.863093	26.749930	44.693122	74.008515	197.813595
30	7.612255	10.062657	13.267678	17.449402	29.959922	50.950159	85.849877	237.376314
31	8.145113	10.867669	14.461770	19.194342	33.555113	58.083181	99.585857	284.851577
32	8.715271	11.737083	15.763329	21.113777	37.581726	66.214826	115.519594	341.821892
33	9.325340	12.676050	17.182028	23.225154	42.091533	75.484902	134.002729	410.186270
34	9.978114	13.690134	18.728411	25.547670	47.142517	86.052788	155.443166	492.223524
35	10.676581	14.785344	20.413968	28.102437	52.799620	98.100178	180.314073	590.668229
36	11.423942	15.968172	22.251225	30.912681	59.135574	111.834203	209.164324	708.801875
37	12.223618	17.245626	24.253835	34.003949	66.231843	127.490992	242.630616	850.562250
38	13.079271	18.625276	26.436680	37.404343	74.179664	145.339731	281.451515	1020.674700
39	13.994820	20.115298	28.815982	41.144778	83.081224	165.687293	326.483757	1224.809640
40	14.974458	21.724521	31.409420	45.259256	93.050970	188.883514	378.721158	1469.771568

»» Appendix 2   Probability of Achieving Certain Annual ««
Return Targets Over a Five-Year Period

	Risk Level						
Target	1	2	3	4	5	6	7
14%	40	36	29	25	17	7	3
13%	46	42	36	31	24	12	6
12%	52	48	43	34	31	19	10
11%	58	54	50	47	40	29	18
10%	63	61	57	55	49	39	27
9%	69	67	64	63	58	51	40
8%	74	72	71	70	67	63	53

Source: William T. Spitz Estimates

Index

ABOUT THE AUTHOR

William T. Spitz is the treasurer of Vanderbilt University and adjunct professor in its Owen School of Management. As treasurer, he is responsible for the management of approximately $1 billion in stock, bond, venture capital, real estate, and oil and gas investments. He serves as a director of The Common Fund, Endowment Advisors, Inc., and The Bradford Funds. These investment organizations have combined assets in excess of $13 billion. Prior to his current position, Bill spent 11 years in the investment management business in New York serving as an analyst, portfolio manager, and chief investment officer. He is a chartered financial analyst and holds an MBA degree from the University of Chicago. Bill lives with his wife and three daughters in Nashville, TN.